WRITING THE BODIES OF CHRIST
THE CHURCH FROM CARLYLE TO DERRIDA

For Jean Genet, celebrated thief and homosexual, 'the church [is] a box of surprises'. The first surprise is that, as 'the body of Christ', it is exposed to all the perils and paradoxes of being a body in space and time.

Starting with Thomas Carlyle's claim that 'Books ... are the ... Church' and ending with Derrida's remark that 'we have [still] not left the Church', these exciting new essays offer radically different accounts of churches, both literal and metaphorical, in writing that ranges from Kierkegaard to Kristeva, Engels to Eliot, and Darwin to Feinberg. Here we encounter the church of history and literature, a quirky kaleidoscopic church that is, by turns, revolutionary, totalitarian, blind, panoptic, criminal, philosophic, telephonic, queer, and even sub-atomic. The result is a book that might just alter the way that readers and writers imagine, experience, and even are the church.

to the church invisible

'Now ye are the body of Christ'
1 Corinthians 12:27

Writing the Bodies of Christ
The Church from Carlyle to Derrida

Edited by
JOHN SCHAD
Loughborough University

LONDON AND NEW YORK

First published 2001 by Ashgate Publishing

Reissued 2018 by Routledge
2 Park Square, Milton Park, Abingdon, Oxon OX14 4RN
711 Third Avenue, New York, NY 10017, USA

Routledge is an imprint of the Taylor & Francis Group, an informa business

Copyright © John Schad 2001

The Editor has asserted his right under the Copyright, Designs and Patents Act 1988 to be identified as the Editor of the Work.

All rights reserved. No part of this book may be reprinted or reproduced or utilised in any form or by any electronic, mechanical, or other means, now known or hereafter invented, including photocopying and recording, or in any information storage or retrieval system, without permission in writing from the publishers.

Notice:
Product or corporate names may be trademarks or registered trademarks, and are used only for identification and explanation without intent to infringe.

Publisher's Note
The publisher has gone to great lengths to ensure the quality of this reprint but points out that some imperfections in the original copies may be apparent.

Disclaimer
The publisher has made every effort to trace copyright holders and welcomes correspondence from those they have been unable to contact.

A Library of Congress record exists under LC control number: 2001022192

Typeset by Bournemouth Colour Press, Parkstone.

ISBN 13: 978-1-138-73299-5 (hbk)
ISBN 13: 978-1-138-73296-4 (pbk)
ISBN 13: 978-1-315-18790-7 (ebk)

> Pamphlets, Poems, Books, these are the real, working, effective Church of a modern country.
> Thomas Carlyle

> ... that articulate body of signs we call the church.
> Terry Eagleton

> We have not left the Church.
> Jacques Derrida

Contents

List of Plates ix
Notes on Contributors xi
Acknowledgements xiii

'These are My Bodies': An Introduction　　1
　John Schad

Part I The Church Militant

Chapter 1　Communing with the Church: Revelation and Revolution in Engels' 'On the History of Early Christianity' (1894–95)　　11
　Willy Maley

Chapter 2　The Writings in the Church: T.S. Eliot, Ecclesiastes and the *Four Quartets*　　25
　Terence R. Wright

Chapter 3　Joycing Derrida, Churching Derrida: *Glas, église* and *Ulysses*　　41
　John Schad

Part II The Church (In)visible

Chapter 4　The Matter of Faith: Incarnation and Incorporation in Tennyson's *In Memoriam*　　59
　Julian Wolfreys

Chapter 5　'A City Without a Church': *The Origin of Species*, the Tree of Life and the Apocalypse　　75
　Kevin Mills

Chapter 6　Candlesticks in the Miasmal Mist: The Church and T.S. Eliot　　89
　Martin Warner

Chapter 7　Christ's Breaking of the 'Great Chain of Being'　　105
　Slavoj Zizek

Part III The Church Subjective

Chapter 8   Christendom and the Police: Kierkegaard Inside the Panopticon   113
              Jeremy Tambling

Chapter 9   Christ's Queer Wound, or Divine Humiliation Among the
              Unchurched   127
              Kathryn Bond Stockton

Chapter 10   *Histoires de l'Église*: The Body of Christ in the Thought of
              Julia Kristeva   145
              Luke Ferretter

Chapter 11   The Private Parts of Jesus Christ   159
              Nicholas Royle

Church After Church: In Conclusion   177
   John Schad

Index   179

List of Plates

1. Lauretti Tommaso, *Triumph of Christianity, or the Exaltation of the Faith*. By kind permission of the Vatican Museum.   2
2. Leonardo da Vinci, *Madonna Litta*. By kind permission of The State Hermitage Museum, St Petersburg.   164

Notes on Contributors

Kathryn Bond Stockton is Associate Professor of English at the University of Utah. She is the author of *God Between their Lips: Desire Between Women in Irigaray, Brontë, and Eliot* (Stanford University Press) and has published articles in *boundary 2*, *Novel* and *Cultural Critique*. She is currently working on another book for Stanford University Press entitled *Heaven's Bottom: Essays on Debasement in 'Black' and 'Queer' Fictions 1956–96*.

Luke Ferretter is a British Academy Junior Research Fellow at Wolfson College, Cambridge. He is the author of 'The Trace of the Trinity: Christ and Difference in St. Augustine's Theory of Language' which recently appeared in *Literature and Theology*, and is currently working on 'Catholicism and Phenomenology in France'.

Willy Maley is Professor of Renaissance Studies at the University of Glasgow. He is the author of *A Spenser Chronology* (Macmillan) and *Salvaging Spenser: Colonialism, Culture and Identity* (Macmillan), and co-editor of *Representing Ireland* (Cambridge University Press), *A View of the Present State of Ireland* (Blackwell) and *Postcolonial Criticism* (Longman). He has also written on Derrida, Eagleton, Fanon, Foucault, Gates, hooks, Lloyd, JanMohamed, and Lyotard.

Kevin Mills is Lecturer in English at the University of Portsmouth. He is the author of *Justifying Language: Paul and Contemporary Literary Theory* (Macmillan), 'Love Paul: Closing the letter' in de Graef (ed.), *Sense and Transcendence* (Leuven University Press), and various essays in *Textual Practice*, *Literature and Theology*, and *Prose Studies*.

Nicholas Royle is Professor of English at the University of Sussex. He is the author of *Telepathy and Literature* (Blackwell), *After Derrida* (Manchester University Press) and *E. M. Forster* (Nothcote House), and co-author (with Andrew Bennett) of *Elizabeth Bowen and the Dissolution of the Novel* (Macmillan) and *An Introduction to Literature, Criticism and Theory* (Harvester).

John Schad is Reader in Victorian Studies at Loughborough University. He is the author of *The Reader in the Dickensian Mirrors* (Macmillan) and *Victorians in Theory: from Derrida to Browning* (Manchester University Press), and editor of *Dickens Refigured* (Manchester University Press) and Thomas Hardy's *A Laodicean* (Penguin). He is currently completing a book called *Christian Unreason – from Darwin to Joyce*.

Jeremy Tambling is Professor of Comparative Literature at the University of Hong Kong. He is the author of *Confession* (Manchester University Press), *Dickens, Violence and the Modern State* (Macmillan) and *Opera and the Culture of Fascism* (Oxford University Press), and editor of Charles Dickens' *David Copperfield* (Penguin).

Martin Warner is Senior Lecturer in Philosophy, and was founding Programme Director of the Centre for Research in Philosophy and Literature, at the University of Warwick. He is the author of *Philosophical Finesse* (Oxford University Press) and *A Philosophical Study of T.S. Eliot's 'Four Quartets'* (Mellen), editor of *The Bible as Rhetoric* (Routledge) and *Religion and Philosophy* (Cambridge University Press), and co-editor of *Terrorism, Protest and Power* (Elgar), *Addressing Frank Kermode* (Macmillan) and *The Language of the Cave* (Academic Printing and Publishing).

Julian Wolfreys is Associate Professor of English at the University of Florida. He is the author of numerous books including *Readings: the Act of Close Reading in Literary Theory* (Edinburgh University Press), *Writing London: The Trace of the Urban Text from Blake to Dickens* (Macmillan), and *Deconstruction: Derrida* (Macmillan). He is currently editing the *Edinburgh Encyclopaedia of Literary Criticism and Theory* (Edinburgh University Press).

Terence R. Wright is Professor of English at the University of Newcastle-upon-Tyne, where he is also the co-director of the MA in Religion and Literature. He is the author of *The Religion of Humanity* (Oxford University Press), *Theology and Literature* (Blackwell), *Thomas Hardy and the Erotic* (Macmillan), and *D.H. Lawrence and the Bible* (Cambridge University Press). He is one of the European editors of the journal *Literature and Theology*.

Slavoj Zizek is Senior Researcher at the Department of Philosophy, University of Ljubljana, Slovenia, and until recently, Co-ordinator of a research project at Kulturwissenschaftliches Insitut, Essen. He is the author of many books, his most recent being *The Fragile Absolute: Why is the Christian Legacy worth Fighting For?* (Verso) and *Did Somebody Say Totalitarianism? Five Essays on the Misuse of a Notion* (Verso). Blackwell recently published *The Zizek Reader*.

Acknowledgements

I should like to thank Sarah Lloyd for ensuring this book came to publication, and my fellow contributors for entrusting their work to me. I hope I have not let anyone down.

An alternative version of Kathryn Bond Stockton's essay appeared in *Aesthetic Subjects*, ed. Pamela Matthews and David McWhirter (University of Minnesota Press, 2001).

Finally, I am very grateful to Faber and Faber for permission to reproduce extracts from various poems by T.S. Eliot.

John Schad
Loughborough

'These Are My Bodies':
An Introduction

John Schad

In Lauretti Tommaso's sixteenth-century painting, the *Triumph of Christianity, or the Exaltation of the Faith* (Plate 1), the focal point is a crucifix raised on a plinth at the foot of which lies a shattered statue of Hermes, the classical god. To view the painting from our own century, an age marked by the *defeat* of Christianity, is a strange experience; for it is to see not one body of Christ but two, to see the shattered body as suggestive of the Christ who is broken and smashed by modernity. To see more than one body of Christ is by no means a new illusion, or trick, it has been going on ever since Christ said of the bread, '*this* is my body' (Matt. 26:26); ever since, indeed, he said 'I was an hungred, and ye gave me meat ... naked, and ye clothed me ... in prison, and ye came unto me' (Matt. 25:35–6). Christ's bodies include those of the hungry, the naked and the imprisoned. And then, of course, there is the church, that collective body of Christ: writing to the Christians of Corinth St. Paul famously declares, 'Now ye are the body of Christ' (1 Cor. 12:27).

It is this Pauline, ecclesial body of Christ that provides the focus for our volume of essays. It is not, of course, possible to separate completely one body of Christ from another, and the essays do not make the attempt. When it comes to the body of Christ the volume will always see double at least, if only because the church is itself a multiple or fragmented body; when T.S.Eliot asks 'Is one church all we can build?'[1] the answer is obviously 'no', we clearly can build many churches. For Eliot, and some of the volume's contributors, this might just be cause for celebration or hope, but for others it is not. Indeed, for many, one church is more than enough; however attractive the person of Christ might be, the church remains unlovely – as Nietzsche declares, 'The church is the barbarization of Christianity.'[2] For many, the barbarization lies simply in the fact the church is an institution, an institution often founded on wealth, power, privilege and even violence. The dark, institutional history of the church is a running theme, a running sore, throughout this volume; in that sense the essays respond to Michel Foucault's insistence that we should be mindful of the institutions that surreptitiously inform our discourse and culture.

There is, though, another aspect to the linguistic, or semiotic life of the church; and here the volume returns to Terry Eagelton's *The Body as Language*, a book written in his early Catholic phase which speaks of 'that articulate body of signs we call the church'.[3] These signs are the very stuff of this volume, dealing as it does with the myriad ways in which the church is named, spoken and, above all, written

Plate 1 Lauretti Tommaso, *Triumph of Christianity, or the Exaltation of the Faith*

in the age of secularization. In this sense, the contributors are simply exploring the relationship between the church and modern writing, and to do so we take as our starting point the mid-nineteenth century since by then writing actually *is* the church – or at least that is the astonishing claim made by Thomas Carlyle in 1844:

> Pamphlets, Poems, Books, these are the real working effective Church of a modern country.[4]

Our volume starts, then, at the point at which the church begins to disappear, to vanish into print, into writing. The church survives in a modern country but (only) as text; *ecclesia*, if you will, becomes *écriture* – the sheltered life of the church is exposed to the strange, dangerous and multidimensional space of writing.

By the same token, though, the securely secular world of modern literature proves to be haunted by the arcane ways of the church; what Henry James calls 'the house of fiction'[5] is doubled by the house of God, the peculiar institution of literature is made forever in the after-image of the church. This, in a sense, is Eagleton's point when he argues that the rise of English Literature as an academic discipline in the late nineteenth century is a direct response to the demise of the church.[6] If so, have those of us who belong to that discipline ever left the church? Indeed, is it possible to do so? This, in part, is the force of Derrida's claim that 'We have not left the church.'[7] It is because of this remark that Derrida is made the endpoint of this volume.

Derrida does not, of course, lend himself to end-points, or limits, but neither does the church, or at least not the church as envisaged in several of the essays here. For whilst some contributors read the writing of the church from inside the church and some from outside, others occupy a liminal space which is neither or both, which blurs the limit of the church. I should here stress that these are very diverse essays, diverse in both content and style; if the volume is itself a church it is a broad one.

Just one small indicator of this breadth is the way that, when referring to the church in general, some contributors choose 'Church' and others 'church'. In this respect, as editor, I have not felt it right to enforce a standard practice. I have, though, very tentatively gathered the essays into three thematic clusters: namely, the church militant, the church (in)visible, and the church subjective. Reflecting the book's historical range, each cluster is organised chronologically, beginning with an essay on nineteenth-century writing and ending with an essay on either Derrida or, if you will, the 'Derridean' era or moment. What follows is a brief guide to each of these clusters.

The Church Militant

> The Church ... [is] said to be 'waging the war of faith' against 'the world, the flesh and the devil.' It is therefore militant, or in warfare.
> *Brewer's Dictionary of Phrase and Fable*

The church is indeed to be found 'in warfare', warfare of many kinds – the church is militant in more senses than one. For Willy Maley, in his essay on Friedrich Engels, the church might just be found in class war, might just be militant in a political sense. Observing that Engels' comparison between the early church and modern socialism appears as part of a study of the Book of Revelation written very near the end of his life, Maley argues that Engels' church militant is marked by a profound sense of an ending. In this sense it anticipates Derrida's apocalyptic meditation on the militancy of spirit in *Specters of Marx*; whilst, though Engels finally seeks to explain away the radical church, Derrida senses that such radicalism is part of a continuing apocalypse, an ending that is itself without ending.

Equally without ending, argues Terence Wright, is the Jewish writing, or 'Writings' that so characterize the Christian formalism of Eliot's *Four Quartets* – this is the paradox at the centre of Wright's essay. Eliot, he argues, not only imagines the church to be a perfected whole built of the fragments of the Jewish Temple but develops a version of literary tradition that, in its claim to encompass the 'European Mind', is made in the image of a pseudo-universal church. In its intolerance of difference, this literary church parallels something of the anti-Semitism to be found in the contemporaneous killing of six million Jews. There is, it seems, murder in the cathedral of the twentieth century. This conceit also runs through John Schad's essay on the warring churches of Joyce's *Ulysses* and Derrida's *Glas*. In each case the church, argues Schad, is implicated in not only the Holocaust but, strangely, Hiroshima; both Joyce and Derrida return us to what Nietzsche calls 'Christian dynamite', a dynamite that relates to what Schad calls the '*Jewish* dynamite' of nuclear fission. As, though, both Joyce and Derrida attempt to gather up the scattered fragments of the exploding church, the church militant is dramatically reconfigured, its swords turned into ploughshares.

The Church (In)visible

> **Church Visible (The)**. All ostensible Christians; all who profess to be Christians. (see CHURCH INVISIBLE.)
> *Brewer's Dictionary of Phrase and Fable*

As both visible and invisible, seen and unseen, the church leads, in relation to the eye, a curiously double life, or even death. The first essay to explore this life-cum-death is by Julian Wolfreys who locates in '*In Memoriam*' what he calls 'the ghostly effects of the incarnation', a doctrine that Tennyson wrests from the metaphysical grasp of the church. In so doing, Tennyson encounters 'Christ incorporate', a Christ who is at once both corporate and, indeed, incorporate; Tennyson describes an incarnation of faith, 'a materiality without matter', without even visibility. Faith and blindness, it seems, do go together, though not as 'blind faith' but rather the faith to which the official, visible church is blind. Blindness, or what Kevin Mills calls 'the tragedy of the human eye', is central to his account of both the church and Darwin's theory of evolution. Rereading *The Origin of Species* alongside the Book of Revelation, Mills sees the church visible rapidly becoming invisible as it disappears into the city; Mills has in mind both the industrialized city of the nineteenth century and the metaphorical city that he locates in the apocalyptic rhetoric of *The Origin*. As St John on the New Jerusalem, so Darwin on the city, or *polis* of nature: 'I saw no Temple there'; in both cases there is no church to be seen.

For T.S. Eliot, though, the church visible is all too visible; so argues Martin Warner in his essay on Eliot and the ecclesiology of his day. Continuing with Revelation – in particular the 'seven candlesticks' by which its seven churches are imaged – Warner argues that 'the scandal of the Church' is all too visible in the very different light of the Cross. This terrible and paradoxical light is, indeed, reflected in 'the incandescent terror' seen above wartime London by the fire-watching Eliot; it is in this deadly light that Warner finally rereads the 'secluded chapel' at the end of 'Little Gidding'. This, of course, is the chapel where 'the light fails', and in the final essay Slavoj Zizek proposes that the failing of the light, the light of transcendence, is the precondition of every chapel, every church. Reading the Cross, via Hegel, as the end or disappearance of the transcendent God, Zizek argues that the God who remains is no more (and, indeed, no less) than the community of believers. For Zizek, this community is the Spirit who Christ said could only come once *he* (Christ) had gone (John 16:7) ; the human body of Christ that is the church cannot, therefore, coexist with the transcendent body of Christ that is God – the two bodies of Christ cannot coexist, cannot be seen together.

The Church Subjective

'i am a little church'
e e cummings[8]

As the house of God or house of prayer, a church entails, or represents an obviously impossible space; since neither God nor prayer can be housed, a church is an inside-out house describing an inside-out subjectivity, a self that is not in itself. This theme is first explored by Jeremy Tambling who argues that, for Søren Kierkegaard, the state church, or what he calls Christendom, entails the subjectivity of subjection, of being subject to the church and the state it serves. Such a church, argues Tambling, reproduces the surveillance strategies of Foucault's panopticon society, a society which individualizes in order to control – the intensely private Kierkegaard is its secret agent. Tambling's Kierkegaard is, though, a double agent in that, as a theological flâneur, he not only polices but loves the crowd; in the crowd he finds a church made in the image of the criminal and the reckless, or absurd, subjectivity of the criminal. An outlawed church is also on the mind of Kathryn Bond Stockton in her essay on novels by Rayclyffe Hall, Leslie Feinberg and Jean Genet. Beginning with St. Paul's the church-as-body-of-Christ and, in particular, 'those members we think to be less honourable', Stockton locates in the gay and lesbian communities of her texts a less honourable and even shameful church, a church outside the church. The humiliation of this church is answered not only by the shame and wounds of the crucified Christ but, still more strangely, the queer life of clothes: for

Stockton, to dress is to be called out of oneself into an embrace that might just constitute 'a strange cloth church'.

This ecclesial embrace outside or beyond oneself, at the outer or stranger limits of ourselves, also concerns Luke Ferretter in his essay on Julia Kristeva. Defining Christ as the 'absolute subject' of the church, Kristeva interprets the crucifixion in terms of the melancholic 'abjection' of the ruptured human subject. In becoming a subject of the church, the believer thus reenacts an abjection s/he has already experienced; in so doing s/he joins, argues Ferretter, a community made of those who are, twice over, strangers to themselves. Or should that be 'secret to themselves'? That is just one question thrown up by Nicholas Royle's essay on the private parts of Jesus Christ. Looking closely at Leonardo da Vinci's 'Madonna Litta' alongside the private, 'Christian' parts of Jacques Derrida, Royle sees a private, even secretive Jesus, a Jesus as secret as dreams. Royle ends his essay by writing a church made in the impossible image of such secrecy; this secret sect is, for Royle, an 'unidentifiable church'.

Often unidentifiable, often invisible, the churches that crowd this volume relate to each other in ways that are themselves hard to identify, hard to see. The same may be said of the essays, each of which connect, or speak to the others in ways that are sometimes obscured by the clusters into which they are organized. These connections and conversations are, in the end, for the reader to uncover; but he or she may be helped in this by the following guide, or map:

- *For the uncanny, spectral aspects of the church as the haunted house of God*, see Wolfreys on the ghost-like church in *In Memoriam*, Schad on Joyce's church of the dead, and Royle on Derrida's spectral Jesus.

- *For the place of the laughter in the church*, see Schad on Joyce's 'Joking Jesus' and Tambling on the Kierkegaardian absurd.

- *For the relationship between church and State*, see Tambling on Kierkegaard's Danish Church, and Ferretter on Kristeva and the fourth-century Church of imperial Rome.

- *For the (im)possibility of recovering the ancient idea of 'Mother Church'*, see both Ferretter and Royle on the body of Christ in relation to Mary, 'mother of the church'.

- *For the (im)possibility of the church as a collective, corporate body*, see both Tambling and Stockton on the church-of-the-self, and both Zizek and Ferretter on the community of faith, the church-of-the-many.

- *For the relationship between the church and capitalism*, see Schad on the Judaeo-Christian idea of Jubilee and Zizek on the economy of salvation.

- *For the church and the sense of an Ending*, see Maley, Mills and Warner on the apocalyptic churches of Engels, Darwin and Eliot, respectively.

- *For the church as a place of burial and mourning*, see Wolfreys on *In Memoriam*, and Tambling and Ferretter on the churchy melancholia of Kierkegaard and Kristeva, respectively.

– *For a church that might stand outside of the values of the West*, see Maley on the eastwardness of the communist 'church', Schad on the 'Black' churches of Derrida and Joyce, and Ferretter on the east-European Orthodoxy of Kristeva.

Notes

1. *The Complete Poems and Plays of T.S. Eliot* (London: Faber and Faber), p. 166.
2. Friedrich Nietzsche, *Will to Power*, tr. W. Kaufmann (New York: Vintage, 1968), p. 125.
3. Terry Eagleton, *The Body as Language: Outline of a 'New Left' Theology* (London: Sheed and Ward, 1970), pp. 11–12.
4. *Thomas Carlyle: Selected Writings*, ed. A. Shelston (Harmondswoth: Penguin, 1971), pp. 42–3.
5. Henry James, Preface to *The Portrait of a Lady* (Harmondsworth: Penguin, 1966), p. ix.
6. Terry Eagleton, *Literary Theory: An Introduction* (Oxford: Blackwell, 1983), pp. 22–3.
7. Jacques Derrida, *Spurs: Nietzsche's Styles* (Chicago: University of Chicago Press, 1979), pp. 90–91, translation modified.
8. e e cummings, *Complete Poems 1904–1962*, ed. G.J. Firmage (New York: Liveright, 1991), p. 749.

I

THE CHURCH MILITANT

New churches, new economies.
Elizabeth Barrett Browning, *Aurora Leigh*

... placing danger signs by the church.
Marianne Moore, 'The Steeple Jack'

The church is present in ... the oppressed and exploited.
Terry Eagleton, *The Body as Language*

Derrida's work is 'protestant' in its battle against any *katholikós* ... Derrida doth protest – religiously – and asks the same of his followers.
Alice Jardine, *Gynesis*

With regard to political struggles ... where the Church was, there the Army should arrive.
Slavoj Zizek, 'St Paul; Or, the Christian Uncoupling'

Chapter 1

Communing with the Church: Revelation and Revolution in Engels' 'On the History of Early Christianity' (1894–95)

Willy Maley

For Germany, the *criticism of religion* is in the main almost complete, and criticism of religion is the premise of all criticism.
    Marx, *Toward the Critique of Hegel's Philosophy of Right*

Feuerbach ... does not see that the 'religious sentiment' is itself a *social product*, and that the abstract individual whom he analyses belongs in reality to a particular form of society.
    Marx, *Theses on Feuerbach*, VII

Religious distress is at the same time the expression of real distress and the protest against real distress. Religion is the sigh of the oppressed creature, the heart of a heartless world, just as it is the spirit of an unspiritual situation. It is the opium of the people.
    Marx, *Toward the Critique of Hegel's Philosophy of Right*

In *Literary Theory: An Introduction*, Terry Eagleton remarked: 'If one were asked to provide a single explanation for the growth of English studies in the later nineteenth century, one could do worse than reply: "the failure of religion".'[1] Not surprisingly, the 'rise of English' story told by Eagleton leads, a century later, to 'the end of English', or 'the crisis of English', a crisis of faith, and funding. More recently, Fredric Jameson observed in response to Derrida's *Specters of Marx* that 'religion is once again very much on the agenda of any serious attempt to come to terms with the specificity of our own time.'[2] The implications for Marxism of this (re)turn to the church are grave indeed. It is after all Derrida's contention in *Specters of Marx* that 'Religion ... was never one ideology among others for Marx.'[3] The problem for Marxists is that the church is to some extent, if not unfamiliar territory, then at least an unwelcome guest. Wasn't it done and dusted, relegated, the account settled long ago? How can the church be other than a dead letter where Marxism is concerned? Did Marx and Engels not dispense with the subject in those two early co-authored works, *The Holy Family* (1845) and *The German Ideology* (1846)? Marx, famously, had compared the church and socialism thus:

> The social principles of Christianity declare all the vile acts of the oppressors against the oppressed to be either a just punishment for original sin and other sins, or trials which the Lord, in his infinite wisdom, ordains for the redeemed.
> The social principles of Christianity preach cowardice, self-contempt, abasement, submissiveness and humbleness, in short, all the qualities of the rabble, and the proletariat, which will not permit itself to be treated as rabble, needs its courage, its self-confidence, its pride and its sense of independence even more than its bread.
> The social principles of Christianity are sneaking and hypocritical, and the proletariat is revolutionary.
> So much for the social principles of Christianity.[4]

And so much, or so it seemed, for the comparison between socialism and religion. Teodor Oizerman, citing this passage, concludes that 'the struggle against religion constituted one of the most important aspects in the development of the Marxist world view. Whatever the problems they tackled', Marx and Engels 'always substantiated scientific, proletarian atheism'.[5]

What is the political constituency of the church? Does it represent the interests of a particular class, party or political grouping? Has it always served the rulers rather than the ruled? In this essay, drawing on the work of Marx, Engels, Lenin and Derrida, I shall argue that the church remains relevant as a vital source of liberation theology and a lasting site of social dissent. If the British Marxist tradition, especially on the literary critical, cultural and historical side, has never, unlike its French counterpart, been especially assiduous about reading the primary texts of Marx and Engels, then going back to the so-called 'originals' is not the solution. The truth must lie somewhere in between reading as gospel and not reading at all. Writing in 1893, Engels remarked: 'The different Russian émigré groups interpret passages from the writings and correspondence of Marx in the most contradictory ways, exactly as though they were texts from the classics or from the New Testament.'[6]

At almost exactly the same time as he was writing this letter, in the last years of his life, and the last years of the century, Engels himself was turning to Scripture as a way of interpreting Marx. It's an ironic turn for Engels, since fifty years earlier the Revelation of John had been parodied – by Marx – in the conclusion to *The Holy Family*, in the form of a 'Critical Last Judgement'.[7] Marx and Engels can be seen to lean on the church even as they seek to mark out a critical distance from it. Given his belated return to Revelation in his most mature work, and in a far less satirical mode, the established view of Engels' celebrated 'advance to atheism' appears less compelling.[8]

On the back of a recent essay entitled 'Spectres of Engels', in which I argued that Marx's other half had already anticipated – but by no means answered or exorcised – the questions of spectrality and spiritualism with which Derrida was preoccupied,

I want to do something much more modest.[9] In that essay I examined a neglected text by Engels, a chapter from *Dialectics of Nature* on 'Natural Science in the Spirit World', dating from 1878, but dealing with the mediumistic craze and obsession with spirit photography of the 1840s.[10]

So, *Nightmare on Engels Street*, Part 2. In this companion piece, I want to unearth another example of late Engels, the very latest, one of the last, in fact, of those ephemera written in the wake of Marx's death and in expectation of his own, a text entitled 'On the History of Early Christianity', published in 1894–95.[11] There's nothing more predictable than the prophetic moment, that last instance that comes along in every career, every life, when you get a glimpse into a future of which you are unlikely to form a part, but may in some way have brought about.

'On the History of Early Christianity' sees Engels take Revelation very seriously indeed. One commentator has said this essay of Engels is of special interest for its 'explicit recognition of the religious character of the communist movement', and its 'endorsement of Renan's words: "If I wanted to give you an idea of the early Christian communities I would tell you to look at a local section of the International Workingmen's Association"' (p. 209). Unlike 'Natural Science in the Spirit World' (1878), which performs an exorcism on the text of spiritualism, Engels is more intent upon reconciliation than refutation in his last testament on the church. In the earlier essay, Engels had begun with a definition of dialectics 'that has found its way into popular consciousness ... expressed in the old saying that extremes meet', and in so doing he had mocked those philosophers and scientists who turn to Christ in the twilight of their lives, specifically the tendency of empiricists to endorse the wildest imaginings:

> In accordance with this we should hardly err in looking for the most extreme degree of fantasy, credulity and superstition, not in that trend of natural science which, like the German philosophy of nature, tries to force the objective world into the framework of its subjective thought, but rather in the opposite trend, which, exalting mere experience, treats thought with sovereign disdain and really has gone to the furthest extreme in emptiness of thought. This school prevails in England. Its father, the much-lauded Francis Bacon, already advanced the demand that his new empirical, inductive method should be pursued to attain, above all, by its means: longer life, rejuvenation – to a certain extent, alteration of stature and features, transformation of one body into another, the production of new species, power over the air and the production of storms. He complains that such investigations have been abandoned, and in his natural history he gives definite recipes for making gold and performing various miracles. Similarly Isaac Newton in his old age greatly busied himself with expounding the Revelation of St. John. (p. 68)

Bacon's advocacy of alchemy and miracles aside, much of what he dreamed of, and Engels dismisses as 'the most extreme degree of fantasy, credulity and superstition', namely 'longer life, rejuvenation – to a certain extent, alteration of stature and features, transformation of one body into another, the production of new species, power over the air and the production of storms', is now common currency. Yesterday's fantasy is today's reality. It was not only Isaac Newton who, in his old age, or adage, greatly busied himself with expounding an interpretation of the Revelation of St John. In his last year on earth, Engels lives up to his name and rushes in where he had hitherto feared to tread. In 'On the Early History of

Christianity', he advances a reading of John from an historical materialist perspective. This short text, overlooked both by Marxists and theologians, as well as by critics of the period, is a classic instance of late Victorian *fin de siècle* unease. It is also one place in the Marxist corpus where the connection between the church and the commune is made most explicit, for Engels reads John as an allegory of political struggle. Engels begins at the beginning:

> The history of early Christianity has notable points of resemblance with the modern working-class movement. Like the latter, Christianity was originally a movement of oppressed people: it first appeared as the religion of slaves and emancipated slaves, of poor people deprived of all rights, of peoples subjugated or dispersed by Rome. Both Christianity and the workers' socialism preach forthcoming salvation from bondage and misery; Christianity places this salvation in a life beyond, after death, in heaven; socialism places it in this world, in a transformation of society. Both are persecuted and baited, their adherents are despised and made the object of exclusive laws, the former as enemies of the human race, the latter as enemies of the state, enemies of religion, the family, social order. And in spite of all persecution, nay, even spurred on by it, they forge victoriously, irresistibly ahead. Three hundred years after its appearance Christianity was the recognised state religion in the Roman world empire, and in barely sixty years socialism has won itself a position which makes its victory absolutely certain. (p. 209)

To the question 'Why didn't socialism follow the overthrow of the Roman Empire in the West?', Engels replies:

> ... this 'socialism' did in fact, as far as it was possible at the time, exist and even become dominant – in Christianity. Only this Christianity, as was bound to be the case in the historic conditions, did not want to accomplish the social transformation in this world, but beyond it, in heaven, in eternal life after death, in the impending 'millennium'. (p. 210)

Engels develops the analogy between the early church and the rise of a radicalised working class in terms of the tendency of both bodies to attract a range of dissenting voices from the culture at large:

> And just as those who have nothing to look forward to from the official world or have come to the end of their tether with it – opponents of inoculation, supporters of abstemiousness, vegetarians, anti-vivisectionists, nature healers, free-community preachers whose communities have fallen to pieces, authors of new theories on the origin of the universe, unsuccessful or unfortunate inventors, victims of real or imaginary injustice who are termed 'good-for-nothing pettifoggers' by the bureaucracy, honest fools and dishonest swindlers – all throng to the working-class parties in all countries – so it was with the first Christians. All the elements which had been set free, i.e., at a loose end, by the dissolution of the old world came one after the other into the orbit of Christianity as the only element that resisted that process of dissolution – for the very reason that it was the necessary product of that process – and that it therefore persisted and grew while the other elements were but ephemeral flies. There was no fanaticism, no foolishness, no scheming that did not flock to the young Christian communities and did not at least for a time and in isolated places find attentive ears and willing believers. (pp. 214–15)

Engels's invocation of this rainbow coalition of non-stakeholders, from New Age travellers to tee-totallers, rings a bell today, though our attitude to this anonymous International – or postmodern community – may have changed. We are now inclined to be much more tolerant of what Cornel West calls 'dissensus'.[12]

Engels considers Revelation to be 'a far more important source from which to define what early Christianity really was than all the rest of the New Testament, which, in its present form, is of a far later date' (p. 217). This raises the question of the relative status of early versus late texts in determining authority.[13] In fact, what Engels does is to argue that censorship and secrecy covered an essentially secular struggle with a transcendental veil. In its origins, the church afforded a means by which an oppressed group could forge resistance to some dominating force. As far as Engels is concerned, from the perspective of historical materialism, the elucidation of the Revelation of John puts paid to apocalyptic discourse as a whole. That genre has been demystified for once and for all, shown to be intimately bound up with a specific political and social project. However, Engels, in calling for an end to calls for an end, recalls (us to) Jacques Derrida, who has spoken of this apocalyptic impulse to oppose apocalypse in apocalyptic terms.[14] The idea that you become (like) the thing to which you are ostensibly opposed is a critical tenet of deconstruction. Engels's shift from scourge of the church to herald of its contribution to proto-communist struggle is instructive in this regard.

In his closing passage, Engels observes that this religion of the East could only take hold in the West. One might say the reverse of communism – that a religion of the end could only take hold in the beginning. One thinks here immediately of the subsequent shift in Marx's theory of revolution, from the early assertion that it would occur first in advanced capitalist countries, to the later emphasis on the colonial margins as the exemplary sites of change, a view articulated most famously in Lenin's juxtaposition, in his 'Prediction on the Revolutionary Storms in the East', of 'backward Europe and advanced Asia'.[15] Communism, like the church itself, is East-facing.

Lenin, despite his charged advocacy of anti-ecclesiastical propaganda and the fact that he sees the church as serving the interests of the ruling class, remains caught up in an emancipatory discourse that looks to the East for fulfilment, and anticipates a classless society and the withering away of the state in the language of apocalypse. In an essay entitled 'Classes and Parties in their Attitude to Religion and the Church', he speaks of a 'battle cry' that will be taken up by 'millions of proletarians, who will spread it among the masses and who will know how to translate it into revolutionary action when the time comes'.[16] Marx's parody of a Critical Last Judgement is here offered with a straight face, again one that looks to the East for redemption.

There has always been a special relationship between the university and the church, partly because of the substitution story, as told by Eagleton and others, that is, the tale of how modern literary culture supplanted religion, as the authority of the Word passed from pulpit to lectern. There is a classical Marxist version of this. Engels alluded to universities as 'Protestant monasteries', and Lenin endorsed Joseph Dietzgen's view that our modern philosophers are 'graduated flunkeys of clericalism'.[17] Lenin ridiculed those proto-liberation theologians who sought to oppose the state by strengthening the church, but were in fact strengthening the state. 'Police religion', Lenin wrote, 'is no longer adequate for befuddling the masses: give us a more cultivated, more up-to-date, more skilful religion, one that will be effective in a self-governing parish – that is what capital is demanding of the autocracy'.[18] The corporate university of the twenty-first century is, as it were, the new *right* church.

By following the flights of Engels in this crucial essay, one can also trace a revealing elaboration of the relationship between scientific socialism and its utopian version.[19] Despite his claims that science and socialism are overtaking – and taking over from – the church, here is Engels, literally on his last legs, intent on preserving the legacy of Marx, and equally intent on interpreting the Word of God, which may come down to the same thing. Engels' essay offers a compelling instance of what Derrida calls in *Specters of Marx* a messianism without a Messiah, as well as an intriguing case of an attempt to put an end to the end, since Engels is trying to get to the radicalism at the root of John's Apocalypse by reading it as a political allegory of revolution.

In the beginning was Apocalypse. Or was it the end? We Marxists and militant materialists might think we have successfully stepped outside the church, but is such a step possible? We might know the nature of the beast, but do we know its name, and is its number up? Amid the current furore around 'the end of Marxism' and 'the death of communism', this belated and untimely text by Engels reminds us that the church is pressing and pertinent right up to the end, an old ghost that rises up again at Engels' last hour. Derrida's interest in apocalypse and the spirit of emancipation are thus perfectly in keeping with the late, the latest, the last and most mature manifestations of Marxist thought.

Moving onto the main body of his essay – a reading of the Revelation of John, the first 'Dear John' letter in history – Engels declares:

> ... we have in the New Testament a single book the time of writing of which can be defined within a few months, which must have been written between June 67 and January or April 68: a book, consequently, which belongs to the very beginning of the Christian era and reflects with the most naive fidelity and in the corresponding idiomatic language the ideas of the beginning of that era. This book, therefore, in my opinion, is a far more important source from which to define what early Christianity really was than all the rest of the New Testament, which, in its present form, is of a far later date. This book is the so-called Revelation of John. And as this, apparently the most obscure book in the whole Bible, is moreover today, thanks to German criticism, the most comprehensible and the clearest, I shall give my readers an account of it. (p. 217)

Engels acknowledges that the Revelation of John was one of fifteen contemporary apocalypses, but the rest are doubtful in terms of dating and authorship: 'If ... John's Revelation were really the work of its alleged author it would be the only exception among all apocalyptic literature' (p. 219). Engels emphasizes the text's urgency of tone, and writes:

> We therefore see that the Christianity of that time, which was still unaware of itself, was as different as heaven from earth from the later dogmatically fixed universal religion of the Nicene Council; one cannot be recognised in the other. *Here we have neither the dogma nor the morals of later Christianity, but instead a feeling that one is struggling against the whole world and that the struggle will be a victorious one, an eagerness for*

the struggle and a certainty of victory which are totally lacking in Christians of today and which are to be found in our time only at the other pole of society, among the socialists. (p. 221: emphasis added)

Engels, reading John, next addresses himself to the visions of Apocalypse, which John culled from earlier models, 'so that he not only shows great poverty of mind, but even himself proves that he never experienced even in his imagination the alleged ecstasies and visions which he describes' (226–7).

Engels, with the help of some recent German criticism of the Bible, including the work of Ewald, Lücke, and Benary, popularized by Renan, reads John in terms of allegory, censorship and subversion. In this reading, the 'beast is Roman world domination, represented by seven Caesars in succession', namely Augustus, Tiberius, Caligula, Claudius, Nero, Galba and Otho. Engels dates the Revelation of John to the reign of Galba, on the eve of the revolt that overthrew him, or to the first three months of the next emperor. Galba ruled from 9 June 68 to 15 January 69 AD. John may have written up to 15 April 69 AD. Having rounded up his unusual suspects – the Kaiser's seven – Engels goes on to explain the number of the beast:

> But who is the eighth who was, and is not? That we learn from the number 666.
> Among the Semites – Chaldeans and Jews – there was at the time a kind of magic based on the double meaning of letters. As about three hundred years before our era Hebrew letters were also used as symbols for numbers: a=1, b=2, g=3, d=4, etc. The cabala diviners added up the value of each letter of a name and sought from the sum to prophesy the future of the one who bore the name, e.g., by forming words or combinations of equal value. Secret words and the like were also expressed in this language of numbers. This art was given the Greek name *gematriah*, geometry; the Chaldeans, who pursued this as a business and were called *mathematici* by Tacitus, were later expelled from Rome under Claudius and again under Vitellius, presumably for 'serious disorders.' (p. 230)

Engels, having cracked the code, proceeds to decipher the meaning of 666:

> It was by means of this mathematics that our number 666 appeared. It is a disguise for the name of one of the first five Caesars. But besides the number 666, Irenaeus, at the end of the second century, knew another reading – 616, which, at all events, appeared at a time when the number puzzle was still widely known. The proof of the solution will be if it holds good for both numbers. (p. 230)

Ferdinand Benary of Berlin is credited with the solution that Engels now offers:

> The name is Nero. The number is based on ... Neron Kesar, the Hebrew spelling of the Greek Nerôn Kaisar, Emperor Nero, authenticated by means of the Talmud and Palmyrian inscriptions. This inscription was found on coins of Nero's time minted in the eastern half of the empire. And so - n *(nun)* = 50; r*(resh)* = 200; v *(vau)* for o = 6; n *(nun)* = 50; k*(kaph)* = 100; s *(samech)* = 60; r *(resh)* = 200. Total 666. If we take as a basis the Latin spelling *Nero Caesar* the second *nun* = 50 disappears and we get 666-50= 616, which is Irenaeus's reading. (p. 230)

But Nero, Engels admits, was dead at the time of John's writing, so how could he be the threatening beast? Engels has all the angles covered. As he explains, with the patience of a saint:

> ... at the very time at which the Revelation must have been written there appeared a false Nero, who settled with a fairly considerable number of supporters not far from Patmos and Asia Minor on the island of Kytnos in the Aegean Sea (now called Thermia), until he was killed while Otho still reigned. What was there to be astonished at in the fact that among the Christians, against whom Nero had begun the first great persecution, the view spread that he would return as the Antichrist and that his return and the intensified attempt at a bloody suppression of the new sect that it would involve would be the sign and prelude of the return of Christ, of the great victorious struggle against the powers of hell, of the thousand-year kingdom 'shortly' to be established, the confident expectation of which inspired the martyrs to go joyfully to death? (p. 231)

Engels maintains that the historical identity of the Beast was common knowledge at the time, but as John's text was caught up in apocalyptic discourse it lost its referent, or, as Engels puts it, its 'trace':

> Christian and Christian-influenced literature in the first two centuries gives sufficient indication that the secret of the number 666 was then known to many. Irenaeus no longer knew it, but, on the other hand, he and many others up to the end of the century also knew that the returning Nero was meant by the Beast of the Apocalypse. This trace is then lost, and the work which interests us is fantastically interpreted by religious-minded future-tellers; I myself as a child knew old people who, following the example of old Johann Albrecht Bengel, expected the end of the world and the last judgment in the year 1836. The prophecy was fulfilled, and to the very year. The victim of the last judgment, however, was not the sinful world, but the pious interpreters of the Revelation themselves. For in 1836, F. Benary provided the key to the number 666 and thus put a torturous end to all the prophetical calculations, that new *gematriah*. (p. 231)

This attempt by Engels to close the door on the earliest of apocalyptic writings begs the question of, in Derrida's words, 'how to distinguish between the analysis that denounces magic and the counter-magic that it still risks being?'[20] Of this apocalyptic impulse to oppose apocalypse, Derrida has said:

> So we, *Aufklärer* of modern times, we continue to denounce the imposter apostles, the 'so-called envoys' not sent by anyone, the liars and unfaithful ones, the turgidity and the pomposity of all those charged with a historic mission of whom nothing has been requested and who have been charged with nothing. Shall we thus continue in the best apocalyptic tradition to denounce false apocalypses?[21]

What's the difference between Engels' last word on John as a call to arms, from the standpoint of historical materialism, and the Marxist demand for social justice, which borrows from the same apocalyptic discourse on the end? The emancipatory desire that Engels admires in the early church yet wants in some ways to explain, decipher, fix, historicize and be done with, is precisely what Derrida wishes to hold on to, what he believes survives in Marx, and in Marxism.[22]

Engels' essay is a classic example of apocalyptic anxiety, a late longing for life beyond death, in Engels' case life beyond the death of Marx and his own impending demise. It makes explicit and reinvigorates the tired analogy between Christianity and communism. Engels' praise of the militancy made manifest in John accords with his own profession of faith in a socialist future to come:

> The faith of these early militant communities is quite different from that of the later victorious Church: side by side with the sacrifice of the Lamb the imminent return of Christ and the thousand-year kingdom which is shortly to dawn form its essential content, this faith survives only through active propaganda, unrelenting struggle against the internal and external enemy, the proud profession of the revolutionary standpoint before the heathen judges, and martyrdom, confident in victory. (p. 233)

What Engels likes about this original and authentic apocalyptic discourse is the fact that it can be shown to be rooted in a desire for political revolt. This is a model of the church that comes close enough to the Marxist project for Engels to take comfort from it in the last year of his life. It is, after all, in the last years – of life, or of the century, or of a millennium – that one seeks reassurance in the sense of an ending, the solace of a conclusion. In Engels' reading of John, the early church is a proto-communist movement. It carries within it the seed of socialist struggle:

> The core of the universal religion is there, but it includes, without any discrimination, the thousand possibilities of development which became realities in the countless subsequent sects. And the reason why this oldest writing of the time when Christianity was coming into being is especially valuable for us is that it shows, without any dilution, what Judaism, strongly influenced by Alexandria, contributed to Christianity. (p. 234)

Clearly, 'the proud profession of the revolutionary standpoint' is something that Engels values:

> All that comes later is Western, Greco-Roman addition. It was only by the intermediary of the monotheistic Jewish religion that the cultured monotheism of later Greek vulgar philosophy could clothe itself in the religious form in which alone it could grip the masses. But once this intermediary was found it could become a universal religion only in the Greco-Roman world, and that by further development in and merging with the thought material that world had achieved. (pp. 234–5)

In closing, Engels observes that this religion of the East could only take hold in the West. One might say the reverse of communism – that a religion of the West could only take hold in the East. An Occident of history, perhaps? Or of geography?

There was a shift of perspective in Marxist thought on religion between the sceptical standpoint of the 1840s as expressed in texts like *The Holy Family* and *The German Ideology*, and the 1890s, by which time Engels is taking the longer view and adopting a less polemical, more penitent tone. Writing in and of the earlier period it's clear that Engels saw religion, whether dominant or dissenting, as a displacement and distraction. Half a century later, religion is painted in a much more positive light, as an early expression of class struggle. There's an analogy to be drawn here with Toni Morrison's idea of occulted traditions, and of the spirit as a site of resistance:

> [in *Song of Solomon*] I could blend the acceptance of the supernatural and a profound rootedness in the real world at the same time with neither taking precedence over the other. It is indicative of the cosmology, the way in which Black people looked at the world. We are very practical people, very down-to-earth, even shrewd people. But within that practicality we also accepted what I suppose could be called superstition and magic, which is another way of knowing things. But to blend those two worlds together at the same time was enhancing, not limiting. And some of those things were 'discredited knowledge' that Black people had; discredited only because Black people were discredited therefore what they *knew* was 'discredited'. And also because the press toward upward social mobility would mean to get as far away from that kind of knowledge as possible. That kind of knowledge has a very strong place in my work.[23]

It is paradoxical that Morrison sees the relinquishing of the supernatural as linked with social mobility, where Engels identifies the class struggle and the censorship it endures as the cause of a turning towards spirit. Morrison's claim for the charged political nature of occulted communities and other ways of knowing can instructively be read in the light of Engels' gloss on John.

Interviewed in Edinburgh in 1980, Derrida spoke of the relationship between deconstruction and an 'open Marxism' – which he admitted was a tautology – an 'open Marxism' which he defined as one that did not shun developments or problematics 'which appear to have come from outside'.[24] In *Specters of Marx*, Derrida identified the demand for justice as that in Marx which must be salvaged, 'a certain experience of the emancipatory promise'.[25] 'On the History of Early Christianity' is testimony to the continuing relevance within the Marxist corpus of exactly those themes that Derrida identifies as key in *Specters of Marx*. Of all the ends predicted, proposed, pontificated upon, 'the end of Christianity', says Derrida, 'was the most serious naïveté.'[26] Engels' text is a tale of militancy, prophecy and revivalism without end.

Despite the best efforts of Engels to distinguish between the real Nero and the false Nero, and to get his name and (toll free) number so that he could be bagged and tagged in the event of an emergency, the name of Nero lives on as an example of authoritarian government to which all revolutionaries must stand opposed. The *Oxford English Dictionary* defines 'Neronian' as referring not only to the life and times of Nero, but to any 'cruel, licentious, tyrannical' form of rule. As a new century dawns, the ends of Marxism are once more entangled with those of the church. Amid the clamour on the end of history and politics, we continue to labour under a Nero for the Nineties – otherwise known as NATO, which, in my best American accent, I pronounce 'Nero'.[27] Apocalypse now for anyone opposed to Western hegemony, from Nero to Nato, with its phantoms and mirages, its hawks and harriers, its stealths and spectres and sorties. Derrida has spoken eloquently on the lasting temptation of voice and vision in apocalyptic discourse:

> I tell you this in truth; this is not only the end of this here but also and first of that there, the end of history, the end of the class struggle, the end of philosophy, the death of God,

the end of religions, the end of Christianity and morals (that ... was the most serious naïveté), the end of the subject, the end of man, the end of the West, the end of Oedipus, the end of the earth, *Apocalypse Now*, I tell you, in the cataclysm, the fire, the blood, the fundamental earthquake, the napalm descending from the sky by helicopters, like prostitutes, and also the end of literature, the end of painting, art as a thing of the past, the end of psychoanalysis, the end of the university, the end of phallocentrism and phallogocentrism, and I don't know what else? And whoever would come to refine, to say the finally final ... namely the end of the end, the end of ends, that the end has always already begun, that we must still distinguish between closure and end, that person would, whether wanting to or not, participate in the concert. For it is also the end of metalanguage on the subject of eschatological language. With the result that we can wonder if eschatology is a tone, or even the voice itself.[28]

It is getting late, and yet it is still early. What's left for Marxists to do, but to maintain 'the proud profession of the revolutionary standpoint', and pray for a Second Coming?[29]

Notes

A version of this essay was read at the Deconstruction Reading Politics Conference at Staffordshire University on 28 July 1999. I wish to thank Martin McQuillan, the organizer, for inviting me to speak on that occasion.

1. Terry Eagleton, *Literary Theory: An Introduction* (Oxford: Blackwell, 1983), p. 22. Eagleton's insistence on the religious origins of literary studies has an autobiographical element to it, in so far as his own intellectual trajectory passed through a radical Christian period. Specifically, Eagleton assumed the editorship of *Slant*, a journal founded in 1964 with the aim of reconciling socialism and Catholicism, funded on a (left-)wing and a prayer. For an example of a more conservative contemporary Catholic approach to socialism, see John Meagher, *Marxism, Death and Fear* and *Marxism rooted in Prussianism* (both Dublin: Catholic Truth Society of Ireland, 1948). On this episode in Eagleton's theoretical formation, see Adrian Cunningham, 'The December Group: Terry Eagleton and the New Left Church', in Stephen Regan (ed.),'Barbarian at the Gate: Essays for Terry Eagleton', *The Year's Work in Critical and Cultural Theory*, 1 (1991) (Blackwell: Oxford, 1994), pp. 210–15. Eagleton's work in this early stage of his development includes *The New Left Church* (London and Melbourne: Sheed & Ward, 1966), and, as editor, *Directions: Pointers for the Post-Conciliar Church* (London and Sydney: Sheed & Ward, 1968).
2. Fredric Jameson, 'Marx's Purloined Letter', *New Left Review* 209 (1995), p. 98.
3. Jacques Derrida, *Specters of Marx: The State of the Debt, the Work of Mourning, and the New International*, trans. Peggy Kamuf (London: Routledge, 1994), p. 42.
4. Karl Marx, 'The Communism of the *Rheinischer Beobachter*', cited in T.I. Oizerman, *The Making of Marxist Philosophy*, trans. Yuri Sdobnikov (Moscow: Progress Publishers, 1981), p. 428.
5. Oizerman, p. 428. In my University Library, at Glasgow, there is a collection of writings by Marx and Engels, *On Religion* (Moscow: Progress Publishers, 1957), catalogued under 'Religion – Controversial literature'. Apparently someone still believes that religion is a live issue.
6. Engels to Gurvitsch, 27 May 1893, cited in Michael Evans, *Karl Marx* (London: Allen & Unwin, 1975), p. 52.

7   See Karl Marx and Friedrich Engels, *The Holy Family*, (Moscow: Progress Publishers, 1980), pp. 260–61. The 1890s witnessed, on the one hand, an increasing marginalisation of the church, and, on the other, a revival of a politically radical church in Britain. Engels recognized the radical potential of the church only belatedly. Neither Engels nor Marx, in their early engagement with religion, concerned themselves, for example, with the 'Chartist chapels' that arose in the 1830s and 1840s. See Harold Faulkner, *Chartism and the Churches: A Study in Democracy* (London: Cass, 1970). I am grateful to John Schad for directing my attention to this. Engels, ironically, identified the Church as a key element in the reaction against Chartism in his essay 'On Historical Materialism', which formed the core of the Introduction to the 1892 English edition of *Socialism: Utopian and Scientific*. According to Engels, what 'the English middle class ... had learned, during the Chartist years' was precisely the value of religion as a means of social control: 'Now ... the people must be kept in order by moral means, and the first and foremost of all moral means of action upon the masses is and remains – religion. Hence the parsons' majorities on the school boards, hence the increasing self-taxation of the bourgeoisie for the support of all sorts of revivalism, from ritualism to the Salvation Army.' See Friedrich Engels, 'On Historical Materialism', in Lewis S. Feuer (ed.), *Marx and Engels: Basic Writings on Politics and Philosophy* (Fontana: Glasgow, 1976), p. 106.

8   See T.I. Oizerman, 'Engels's Advance to Atheism. Formation of His Revolutionary-Democratic Views', in *The Making of Marxist Philosophy*, pp. 73–80. For some efforts to reconcile or reckon with Marxism and religion, see Herve Leclerc, *Marxism and the Church of Rome* (London: Institute for the Study of Conflict, 1974); Delos B. McKown, *The Classical Marxist Critiques of Religion: Marx, Engels, Lenin, Kautsky* (The Hague: Nijhoff, 1975); David McLellan, *Marxism and Religion: A Description and Assessment of the Marxist Critique of Christianity* (Basingstoke: Macmillan, 1987); Karl Marx and Friedrich Engels, *On Religion* (Moscow: Progress Publishers, 1957); John Meagher, *Missionary Marxism* (Dublin: Catholic Truth Society of Ireland, 1948); Suke Wolton (ed.), *Marxism, Mysticism and Modern Theory* (Basingstoke: Macmillan,1996). For Derrida's most recent engagement with the subject, see Jacques Derrida, 'Faith and Knowledge: the Two Sources of "Religion" at the Limits of Reason Alone,' in Jacques Derrida and Gianni Vattimo (eds), *Religion*, trans. David Webb and others (Stanford: Stanford University Press, 1998) pp. 1–78.

9   Willy Maley, 'Spectres of Engels', in Peter Buse and Andrew Stott (eds), *Ghosts: Deconstruction, Psychoanalysis, History* (London: Macmillan, 1999), pp. 23–49.

10 Friedrich Engels, 'Natural Science in the Spirit World', in *Dialectics of Nature* (Moscow: Progress Publishers, 1954), pp. 68–82.

11 Friedrich Engels, 'On the History of Early Christianity', in Feuer (ed.), *Marx and Engels: Basic Writings on Politics and Philosophy*, pp. 209–35. All subsequent references to this work will be given by page number in the text.

12 Cornel West, 'Minority discourse and the pitfalls of canon formation', in Jessica Munns and Gita Rajan (eds) *A Cultural Studies Reader* (Harlow, Essex, and New York: Longman, 1995), p. 416.

13 According to Geoff Bennington: 'In general, there is no simple division of Derrida's texts into "early" and "late"' – see Geoff Bennington, 'Demanding History', in *Legislations: The Politics of Deconstruction* (London: Verso, 1994), p. 98, n. 9. The same could be said of the Marxist corpus, and I am aware that there is a problem with granting special status to this example of 'late Engels'.

14 See for example, Jacques Derrida, 'On a Newly Arisen Apocalyptic Tone in Philosophy', trans. John P. Leavey, Jr, in Peter Fenves (ed.), *Raising the Tone of Philosophy: Late Essays by Immanuel Kant, Transformative Critique by Jacques Derrida* (Baltimore and London: Johns Hopkins University Press, 1993), pp.117–71; pp. 158–59.

15 V.I. Lenin, 'Backward Europe and Advanced Asia', in *Lenin's Prediction on the Revolutionary Storms in the East* (Peking: Foreign Languages Press, 1970), pp. 7–9.
16 Lenin, 'Classes and Parties in their Attitude to Religion and the Church', in *On Religion*, p. 38.
17 Lenin, 'On the Significance of Militant Materialism', in *On Religion*, p. 68.
18 Lenin, 'Classes and Parties,' in *On Religion*, p. 34.
19 On the curious reversibility of facticity and fantasy see, for example, Zhang Longxi, 'Marxism: from Scientific to Utopian', in Bernd Magnus and Stephen Cullenberg (eds), *Whither Marxism?: Global Crises in International Perspective* (London: Routledge, 1995), pp. 65–77.
20 Derrida, *Specters*, pp.46–7.
21 Jacques Derrida, 'On a Newly Arisen Apocalyptic Tone in Philosophy', tr. John P. Leavey, Jr, in Peter Fenves (ed.), *Raising the Tone of Philosophy: Late Essays by Immanuel Kant, Transformative Critique by Jacques Derrida* (Baltimore and London: Johns Hopkins University Press, 1993), pp. 117–71, 158–9. See also Jacques Derrida, 'No Apocalypse, Not Now (full speed ahead, seven missiles, seven missives)', tr. Catherine Porter and Philip Lewis, *Diacritics* 14:2 (1984), pp. 20–31; Jacques Derrida, 'How to Avoid Speaking: Denials', tr. Ken Frieden, in Sanford Budick and Wolfgang Iser (eds), *Languages of the Unsayable: The Play of Negativity in Literature and Literary Theory* (New York: Columbia University Press, 1989), pp. 3–70.
22 It is also what critics like Cornel West identify as a vibrant spirit of popular resistance and a lasting demand for political freedom. See Cornel West, *Keeping the Faith: Philosophy and Race in America* (New York and London: Routledge, 1993), and *Prophesy Deliverance!: An Afro-American Revolutionary Christianity* (Philadelphia: Mentor, 1982).
23 Toni Morrison, 'Rootedness: the ancestor as foundation', in Dennis Walder (ed.), *Literature in the Modern World: Critical Essays and Documents* (Oxford: Oxford University Press, 1990), p. 330.
24 Cited in Antony Easthope, *British Post-Structuralism: Since 1968* (London and New York: Routledge, 1988), pp. 239–40.
25 Derrida, *Spectres*, p. 59.
26 Derrida, 'Of an Apocalyptic Tone', p. 145.
27 While I was writing this paper, during the bombing of Belgrade – or was it Baghdad? – an American general interviewed on a news bulletin alluded to 'the aims of Nero'.
28 Derrida, 'Of an Apocalyptic Tone', pp. 145–6.
29 In this regard, it is worth noting that the Second International was founded in 1889 and that one of Engels' final public engagements was his presence at its 1893 Zurich conference, the year before he wrote 'On the History of Early Christianity'. Second Comings were clearly on his mind.

Chapter 2

The Writings in the Church: T.S. Eliot, Ecclesiastes and the *Four Quartets*

Terence R. Wright

The Bible, as many critics have remarked,[1] 'echoes and re-echoes in Eliot's poetry', sometimes through direct quotation, sometimes indirectly, through a single word or phrase, often 'through the device of rhythm'. The biblical citations in the *Four Quartets*, however, are not always easily identifiable because 'whole congeries of sources', layer upon layer of allusions to a wide range of texts, are often mingled together almost inseparably.[2] Unlike *The Waste Land*, a positive Babel of different languages, which stand out as separate fragments in a world irreducible to a single meaning, quotations in the *Four Quartets* are often unmarked, woven into a 'tonal and stylistic homogeneity', the musical metaphor of the poem's title reinforcing the attempt to create harmony from diverse elements.[3] Each quartet, of course, focuses upon one of the four elements seen by Heraclitus to comprise the unity of the world. Just as the Church, according to St Paul, has 'diversities of gifts, but the same Spirit' (1 Cor. 12:4), its several parts comprising a single body, so Eliot in the *Four Quartets* can be seen quite literally to *write* the Church, employing 'the discursive practices of the English Church', in particular the Book of Common Prayer and the Jacobean Bible, 'whose rhythms, tonalities and ... phrases' are evident throughout.[4] In the final words of the poem, the pentecostal

> ... tongues of flame are in-folded
> Into the crowned knot of fire
> And the fire and the rose are one.[5]

The 'scattered leaves of the universe' which Dante 'saw ingathered, bound by love in one mass', to quote an earlier translation by Eliot of a line from the *Paradiso*,[6] are thus fused together, forged (whether by divine heat or literary artifice) into unity.

Such literary craft, of course, such complex intertextual writing, does not come easily. This final quartet, for example, went through eighteen drafts. As Lyndall Gordon explains in her recent biography, *T.S. Eliot: An Imperfect Life*, the original plan was to celebrate the state of grace and the divine fire of inspiration more positively.[7] But Eliot made the final ending more tentative, adding the voices of two English mystics, Dame Julian and the anonymous author of *The Cloud of Unknowing*, and presenting the quest as one of 'exploration' towards an end not yet achieved: 'All shall be well and/ All manner of things shall be well' *but not yet*. I stress the muted nature of this ending because my main concern in this essay is to consider one of the problems in Eliot's writing of the Church, his appropriation of voices which may resist being 'in-folded', brought into the Church's fold (or pen), voices which include those of the Hebrew Bible, especially the Writings.

The Writings, in Hebrew *Kethubim*, in Greek *Hagiographa*, are the third group of texts in the Hebrew Canon, regarded within Judaism as lesser in importance than the Law and the Prophets. They include the Psalms and what has become known as Wisdom literature, of which the best-known examples are the Book of Job, Proverbs and Ecclesiastes. Ecclesiastes, of course, is a Greek word with a decidedly ecclesiastical ring, employed by the Septuagint for the Jewish word Qoheleth, which is normally taken to be a participle of the verb *qahal*, to assemble, referring to the Preacher's function to address the assembly. But it could also be that the title reflects the book's assemblage or gathering together of wisdom sayings. The opening verse of Ecclesiastes, "The words of the Preacher, the son of David, king in Jerusalem', has led the book to be attributed to Solomon himself, who famously chose wisdom when asked what gift he would like (1 Kings 9), but it is now commonly accepted that it is a product of the school of Solomon, a professional class of wise men and scribes operating in the later centuries of the Second Temple.[8] Eliot too in the *Four Quartets*, like Dante, that earlier collector of 'the scattered leaves of the universe', gathers together the sayings of numerous earlier writers, one of whom is Qoheleth, whose voice can be heard particularly in the first two quartets. As Solomon finds a place among the twelve spirits of the wise surrounding Beatrice in Dante's *Paradiso* Canto X, so Eliot includes Ecclesiastes in his own vision of the universal Church, which also has a place for pre-Socratic Greek wisdom, represented by Heraclitus, and that classic of Hindu religious writing, the Baghavad Gita.

Such inclusiveness, however, is not without its problems. The Christian appropriation of the Hebrew Bible as the Old Testament, completed and fulfilled by the New, has been a continual source of tension ever since the two communities separated. Even the order of the books is significantly altered in the Christian Old Testament, the Poetical Books coming after the Pentateuch and the Histories but before the Prophets, whom we are invited to read as harbingers of Christ. Christian liturgy further encourages such a typological reading of the Hebrew Bible by juxtaposing passages of the Old and the New Testaments. For 'Temple' read 'Church' (as in George Herbert's collection of poems increasingly admired by Eliot).[9] This has led Jewish critics such as Harold Bloom to complain repeatedly of the replacement of words by the Word, of a book by a man, of writing by real presence, while Jacques Derrida associates belief in Christ as Logos or Word with a more widespread denial of the freedom and flexibility of words, of writing. Orthodox Christian theology, he claims, involves 'the humbling of writing beneath a speech dreaming its plenitude', its subordination to the 'full presence' of the incarnate Word, literally the last word, the finalization of meaning, making all further interpretation redundant.[10] Such logocentrism, traced by Derrida throughout Western thought, involves a denial or suppression of writing, of the complex textuality which produces literature.

Eliot, perhaps the best-known Christian writer of the twentieth century, provides an interesting test for these theories. Maud Ellmann explicitly links his 'distrust of

Jews' with his 'distrust of writing', his resentment at the nomadic wandering, the refusal to 'stay in place' of both word and Jew.[11] Eliot's own comments on the Bible are often uncompromisingly Christian, unambiguously logocentric. His introduction to a book entitled *Revelation* takes it 'for granted that Christian revelation is the only full revelation; and that the fullness of Christian revelation resides in the essential fact of Incarnation, in relation to which all Christian revelation is to be understood'.[12] His recently published correspondence with the Jewish cultural critic, Horace Kallen, whose work on Job he admired, also acknowledges that, however much he defends the Jewish religion and wants it to survive in the modern world *as a religion* and not simply as a cultural tradition, he harbours a 'millennial' desire that all should become Christian.[13]

Before I examine Eliot's 'baptising' of the Writings, however, in particular his assimilation of Ecclesiastes into the *Four Quartets*, I need to acknowledge first the notorious anti-Semitism of some of his earlier work. I will also consider how he understood 'writing', the development of his concept of literary tradition, along with his use of the Hebrew Bible in his own earlier work. My main point is that his later work, in particular the *Four Quartets*, displays an ongoing tension in the poem between the Christian claim to 'Truth' and the recognition that this remains never fully understood. It also demonstrates an openness to the insights of other religious traditions, especially that from which Christianity was born and to which it is both historically and theologically bound. No Christian, the later Eliot acknowledges, should speak disrespectfully of Judaism, a point on which he was critical of Simone Weil, who by 'denying the divine mission of Israel' rejected 'the foundation of the Christian Church'.[14] The *Four Quartets*, I will argue, write the Church in ways which, while reading the Hebrew Bible, in particular the Book of Ecclesiastes, through Christian eyes, fully acknowledge the Jewish contribution to the Church's self-understanding, its textuality in Derrida's sense. The *Four Quartets* in this respect re-enacts the history of the Church, re-presenting its construction out of Jewish fragments.

First, however, I need to deal with the issue of anti-Semitism, which 'is *not* a marginal issue in Eliot's work (revealed only in unfortunate asides, and discernible only to the paranoia of Jewish critics)'.[15] James Wood argues that it exists on two levels: one relatively superficial, 'the fashionable contempt of his age', and the other more serious, 'dogmatic Christianity's anti-Semitism'.[16] The roots of this serious anti-Semitism, it is now accepted, go back as far as the New Testament itself, where Christ is portrayed openly challenging the Law and scandalizing the orthodox by his claims to divinity. Matthew, in particular, has the Jews accept the blame for his crucifixion: 'his blood be on us, and on our children' (Matt. 27:25). Although the Jesus of the gospels is, at least, clearly a Jew, readable within the Jewish tradition as prophet, sage, rabbi or Messiah, by the fourth century the Jesus of the creeds appears to have become fully Hellenized, the second person of the Trinity.[17] The Jewish and Hellenic strands of the early Church are not, of course, so easy to separate. It is possible to argue that the Jewish wisdom tradition, itself increasingly recognized as 'an intercultural and interethnic' phenomenon,[18] merges with the Platonic celebration of the Logos in such texts as the opening chapter of St. John's Gospel and Paul's celebration of Christ as 'the wisdom of God' (1 Cor. 1:24).

Within Western culture, the two strands are woven inextricably together, so that in Joyce's words, 'Jewgreek is greekjew.'[19] Such textual intertwining, unfortunately, has not prevented two millennia of conflict between Christians and Jews, culminating, of course, in the years which saw the completion of the *Four Quartets*, 1935–42.

Most of the anti-Semitism to be found in Eliot's work, it could be claimed, is of the relatively superficial kind. Poems of 1920 such as 'Gerontion', with its unpleasant persona full of contempt for his landlord, 'the Jew' who 'squats on the window sill,

> Spawned in some estaminet of Antwerp,
> Blistered in Brussels, patched and peeled in London (37),

belong to this category, as does Bleistein in 'Burbank with a Baedeker' and 'Rachel nee Rabinovitch', who 'Tears at the grapes with murderous paws' in 'Sweeney Among the Nightingales' (56–7). Both of Eliot's recent biographers, Peter Ackroyd and Lyndall Gordon, acknowledge an unpleasant combination of anti-Semitism and misogyny not only in these personae but in the insecure personality of their creator.[20] Ethnically a WASP, descended from a long line of New England Puritans whose hegemony over American culture was being challenged not least by Jewish intellectuals, he defended himself by stinging. These early poems, as Anthony Julius persuasively argues, repel Jewish readers, giving them no option but to read them adversarially.[21] But they should be recognized, however unfortunately, as typical of the 1920s. In Orwell's words, 'who didn't say such things at that time?'[22] Peter Ackroyd quotes Leonard Woolf, himself a Jew, classifying Eliot as 'slightly anti-semitic in the sort of vague way which is not uncommon'[23] while Hermione Lee finds even worse examples in Virginia Woolf herself and in others of their circle.[24] This is not, of course, to justify these poems but to place them in context.

Eliot's prose of the 1920s and even of the 1930s contains similarly indefensible material. Moreover, as editor of the *Criterion*, he allowed one contributor in 1924 to announce, 'no Jew can be a great artist'[25] and another (overzealously identified by Julius as Eliot himself) to complain of the 'sensationalism' of a book published in 1936 recounting the persecution of the Jews in Nazi Germany.[26] The following year a commentary undoubtedly by Eliot criticized Oxford University for refusing to participate in the bicentenary of the University of Göttingen in protest against its dismissal of Jewish academics. Perhaps the most notorious instance is the sentence in *After Strange Gods* – a series of lectures given in 1933 – in which, praising the advantages of a 'homogeneous' population for the cultivation of a united religious tradition, Eliot claims that 'reasons of race and religion combine to make any large number of free-thinking Jews undesirable.'[27] Eliot himself never allowed these lectures to be republished, telling Helen Gardner that they were the product of a sick mind. His main target, of course, are freethinkers of all kinds – in Ezekiel's words, 'foolish prophets, that follow their own spirit' (Ezek. 13:3).[28] What Eliot is principally deploring is the erosion of a sense of tradition among Jews themselves, whose religion is in danger of being undermined from within.[29]

Eliot's position, it should also be noticed, did gradually mellow. By 1941, he was finally warning readers of the *Christian News-Letter* of the dangers of anti-

Semitism.³⁰ In 1962, he added a footnote to his 1948 *Notes Towards the Definition of Culture* recommending as 'highly desirable that there should be close culture-contact between devout and practising Christians and devout and practising Jews' since too much cross-cultural contact tended to be between freethinkers on both sides.³¹ In 1954, Eliot warned Ezra Pound, who regarded the Hebrew scriptures as 'the record of a barbarian tribe',³² that he would tolerate no more insults 'to his religion which included the Jewish religion'.³³ The claim to 'include' Judaism within Christianity, however, is part of the problem. Certainly, in the legal terms pursued with 'polemical relentlessness' by Julius,³⁴ Eliot is guilty of anti-Semitism both 'superficial' and serious. But on one point Julius is wrong: Jews do not 'leave Eliot's poetry' with 'A Song for Simeon', that poem of 1928 in which the devout Jew who has waited for the Messiah all his life, happily resigns himself to death, having no more to offer (71). Before, though, exploring the ecclesiastical inclusion of Qoheleth in the *Four Quartets* I want to consider that word 'writing' in relation to Eliot's understanding of literary and religious tradition.

When Eliot writes about literary tradition, most famously in his 1919 essay 'Tradition and the Individual Talent', he often makes it sound uncomfortably like the Church. The individual poet, he insists, should feel compelled by 'the historical sense' to

> write not merely with his own generation in his bones , but with a feeling that the whole of the literature of Europe from Homer ... has a simultaneous existence and composes a simultaneous order.³⁵

The 'mind of Europe' of which Eliot writes resembles Newman's rather than Bossuet's model of the Church in that it is not *semper eadem* – always the same, but perpetually changing, adjusting to accommodate the new work of art. For Eliot, there is perfect 'conformity between the old and the new' and 'this change is a development which abandons nothing.'³⁶ In a less well-known review published in *The Egoist* in the same year, however, Eliot recognises that this 'development' is not always without friction on the part of the individual, whose recognition of debt to a precursor can give rise to 'hatred'.³⁷ An essay on Philip Massinger the following year distinguished between the way 'immature poets imitate' while 'mature poets steal'. Good poets alter their precursors, welding their 'theft into a whole of feeling which is unique, utterly different from that from which it was torn'.³⁸ This model certainly fits the Church's appropriation of the Old Testament.

In 1932, however, in the august setting of King's Chapel, Boston's first Anglican church, in an as yet unpublished address on 'The Bible as Scripture and as Literature', Eliot was altogether more cautious about literary and religious theft. 'You cannot effectively "borrow" an image,' he insists, 'unless you borrow also, or have spontaneously, something like the feeling which prompted the original image.' He proceeds to question whether 'Henry James was justified in naming a novel *The Golden Bowl*' without adequately representing the original text of Ecclesiastes.³⁹ Poets, he repeatedly insists, cannot avoid their relation to earlier writers, although he told a Dublin audience in 1936 that a poet 'should submit himself to as many influences as possible, to escape from any one influence'.⁴⁰ He praises Blake for his 'immense power of assimilation',⁴¹ Herbert for absorbing both the Bible and the liturgy of the Church so thoroughly,[42] and Dante for being 'the most *universal* of poets in the modern languages', a quality he attributes to the Italian of his day being 'the product of universal Latin',[43] the language of the universal Church. He disapproves, by contrast, of Donne's more esoteric interests in the Kabbalah and in Maimonides.[44] Jewish writing (apart from the Hebrew Bible) appears to have remained marginal to Eliot's notion of the European mind, which was in other respects reasonably open.

Eliot's idea of the 'European Mind' is perhaps best represented by *The Criterion*, the magazine he founded in 1922 around what he wanted to be 'as homogeneous a group as possible'. Looking back in its final issue in 1939 at the seventeen previous volumes, Eliot writes proudly of the range of first-rate European writers who had contributed to it before lamenting that the 'European Mind' subsequently 'disappeared from view'.[45] One of the writers to appear in *The Criterion*, translated by Eliot himself, was Charles Maurras, founder of the Action Française, itself violently pro-clerical, anti-republican, anti-Semitic, and launched out of anger at the outcome of the Dreyfus affair. When Maurras collaborated with Petain in 1940, Eliot explained to readers of the *Christian News-Letter* that he had shown 'a dangerous intolerance' towards Jews, Protestants and Freemasons but he continued to regard him in Dantesque terms as 'une sorte de Virgile qui nous conduisait aux portes du temple'.[46] The temple here is a Roman rather than Jewish anticipation of the Church, reflecting the authoritarian model which lies behind Eliot's idea of a culturally homogeneous tradition as it appeared both in *After Strange Gods* of 1934 and *The Idea of a Christian Society* of 1939.

Eliot continued even after the war to talk about 'The Unity of European Culture' in three broadcast talks on German radio in 1946, happily discussing 'the common tradition of Christianity which has made Europe what it is'[47] with not even a hint that it had recently been shorn of six million Jews. An article in the *Sewanee Review* on 'The Man of Letters and the Future of Europe' refers to the sources of European culture in Greece and Rome before adding, 'I should say Israel also, but that I wish to confine myself, so far as that is possible, to the cultural, rather than the religious aspect.'[48] As in his refusal to accept the Bible as 'literature' in the 1935 essay on 'Religion and Literature' which fulminates against 'men of letters' who 'talk of the Bible as a "monument of English prose" ... a monument over the grave of Christianity',[49] Eliot seems intent on regarding the Hebrew Bible as a religious rather than a cultural product, as if the two could be separated, as if the Bible were not a form of literature, of writing.

Eliot's fascination with the Bible, however, is evident from his earliest poetry. His recently published Harvard poems tend to employ it mock-heroically, contrasting the futility of the present with the grandeur of the past. For example, 'Oh little voices of the throats of men', written in 1914, deplores not only their 'little voices' and 'twisted little hands' but their 'Impatient tireless undirected feet/So confident on wrinkled ways of wrong',[50] an ironic echo of the Book of Proverbs 16:9: 'A man's heart deviseth his way; but the Lord directeth his steps.' The poem ends with its persona surrounded by shadows and voices of which it is said, 'You had not known whether they laughed or wept',[51] again an ironic contrast with Ecclesiastes 3:4, which recognises that there is 'A time to weep and a time to laugh'.

The same passage in Ecclesiastes, prominent in 'East Coker', is reconceived, as Ricks points out, in 'The Love Song of J. Alfred Prufrock', who is similarly haunted by the pettiness of his own life:

> There will be time, there will be time
> To prepare a face to meet the faces that you meet;
> There will be time to murder and create,
> And time for all the works and days of hands
> That lift and drop a question on your plate

The words of Ecclesiastes modulate into those of a popular song: 'Time for you and time for me', as Prufrock contemplates 'a hundred indecisions' before 'the taking of a toast and tea' (14). The problem with Prufrock, as with so many of Eliot's personae in his early poetry, is that they share the scepticism of Qoheleth about the meaning of the everyday cycle of life but have none of his faith in God.

'Gerontion' too, like Ecclesiastes 12, presents an old man in a decaying house (here, as in Ecclesiastes, a metaphor for death), lacking all hope and convinced (like Qoheleth) that history only 'Guides us by vanities' (38): 'Vanity of vanities, saith the preacher; all is vanity' (Ecc. 12:8). 'A Cooking Egg', also of 1920, parodies Psalm 23, with its catalogue of the things Pipit lists that she 'shall not want' in heaven (44), while *The Waste Land* provides 'a heap of broken images' (30) mainly from the prophets Ezekiel, Jeremiah and Isaiah, although the cricket and perhaps some of the dust can be traced to Ecclesiastes.[52] The point, however, is not to pinpoint every single allusion, which can end simply in pedantry, but to recognise the sheer density of biblical allusion even in Eliot's early poetry. In *The Waste Land*, of course, these prophetic voices are mingled with those of other religious and literary traditions, most famously the Upanishads, while the final section of the poem, with its well-known references to the Garden of Gethsemane, clearly (if tentatively) suggests that the Hebrew prophets find their fulfilment, the answer to their spiritual thirst, in Christ.

It is only after his public avowal of Christianity in 1927, with poems such as 'Journey of the Magi and 'A Song for Simeon', that Eliot's writing becomes explicitly 'Christian'. 'Ash Wednesday', as a number of critics have recognized, employs the readings and the psalms appointed for that festival, especially Psalm 51 and Isaiah 58.[53] The grasshopper of Ecclesiastes 12 makes another appearance, while the voices of the Hebrew prophets are again mixed with more secular poetic echoes: Dante, Cavalcanti, Shakespeare and so on. But the poem clearly advertises itself as Christian. The two 'Coriolan' poems of 1931–32, as Eliot told his theological friend P.E. More, were also written 'under the inspiration of, chiefly, Isaiah and Ezekiel'.[54] 'Choruses from "The Rock"', written in 1934 for a pageant to raise money for the rebuilding of London's churches, continually build on the typological reading of the Jewish Temple as the precursor of the Christian Church, Isaiah's rock clearly identified with Peter. However much he poses as a prophet, even adopting the alias of Nehemiah to talk about the Temple,[55] it is clear that 'The Pope of Russell Square', as Mary Trevelyan called him, is really discussing the Church.

A recognition of the many references to the Hebrew Bible in Eliot's poetry prior to *Four Quartets* should predispose a reader of this poem to hear similar echoes there (although surprisingly few have). Northrop Frye claims that the cycle as a whole reflects the structure of the Christian Bible, which also

> ... begins with the story of a man in a garden. Man then falls into a wilderness or waste land, and into a still deeper chaos symbolised by a flood. At the end of time he is restored to his garden, and to the tree and water of life that he lost with it. But by that time the garden has become a city as well, a fiery city glowing with gold and precious stones, so that the tree of life (symbolised in Dante by a rose) is a tree in which 'the fire and the rose are one'.[56]

Frye's summary of the Bible rather overemphasizes the beginning and the end, paying no attention at all to the quest for wisdom which occupies much of the middle of the story. It is also important to acknowledge that the poem, as Dante would have insisted, must be read on a literal as well as an allegorical level. The garden it begins with is not just symbolic of Eden but is the real garden at Burnt Norton, visited in 1934 by Eliot with Emily Hale, where he had a mystical experience and pondered their possible future. The fire and city it talks of is not only the celestial city, the New Jerusalem, but also the London of the Blitz where Eliot acted as an air-raid warden. Each quartet is anchored in a real place and his own personal experience.

It is also important to recognize that the Bible provides only one of many levels of discourse in this polyphonous text. David Moody has identified many of the other writers who comprise the 'compound ghost' encountered in 'Little Gidding'.[57] Writing is clearly presented in this section of the poem as 'an encounter with a ghostly multiple precursor', an 'historical echolalia through multiple, proliferating and ultimately indeterminate echoes of past writing'.[58] Helen Gardner similarly lists some of the supposed sources of the rose garden in 'Burnt Norton', which include not only the Garden of Eden and the Song of Solomon but Lewis Carroll, Rudyard Kipling and Elizabeth Barrett Browning.[59] Staffan Bergsten suggests even more possible allusions.[60]

Nevertheless, the Bible is a dominant element in the poem. Lyndall Gordon even claims that Eliot, like 'any number of Americans' is consciously writing 'a form of scripture'. He not only draws on its cadences, 'its rhythmic cumulation, its riddling, oracular language' but also its repetition and 'alternation of prosaic and poetic'.[61] Take, for example, the opening lines of the whole poem, originally written for the second priest in *Murder in the Cathedral*[62]:

> Time present and time past
> Are both perhaps present in time and future
> And time future contained in time past.

These lines, as Raymond Preston has remarked, can be read as 'a meditation on the words of Ecclesiastes 3:15:[63] 'That which hath been is now; and that which is to be hath already been; and God requireth that which is past.' Both the sense and the rhythms of Ecclesiastes are echoed by Eliot. Again, we need to recognize other allusions, most importantly Augustine's meditations on time in Book XI of *The Confessions*, 'that all which is both past and future is created and doth flow out from that which is always present'.[64] The lines which follow in the poem,

> What might have been and what has been
> Point to one end, which is always present.
> Footfalls echo in the memory ...

also recalls Augustine's image of words as the traces of things, the 'footsteps ... imprinted in our minds'.[65] Meister Eckhart too writes of God making 'the world and all things in this present Now'[66] while Hegel claims of the Spirit that 'with it there is no past, no future, but an essential *now*.'[67] Ecclesiastes, in other words, is only the beginning of a long process of meditation culminating in these opening lines of the *Four Quartets*.

Eliot himself recognizes the long history of these words, which 'echo/ Thus, in your mind' before asking, like Qoheleth, 'to what purpose' they do so, 'Disturbing the dust on a bowl of rose-leaves'(171). All three images here – dust, roses and bowl – are to be found in Ecclesiastes while Qoheleth also asks, 'What profit hath a man of all his labour' (Eccles. 1:3), 'what profit hath he that hath laboured for the wind?' (5:16). In the Royal Experiment of chapters 2–3, in which 'Solomon' relates his attempts to unlock the secret of happiness, he too, like the persona of 'Burnt Norton', tries laughter and mirth (2:2), and builds a garden which includes 'pools of water' before concluding that all 'is vanity and vexation of spirit' (2:26). Similarly, at the end of 'Burnt Norton', after 'the hidden laughter / Of children in the foliage' and the moment of illumination, the final lines echo the conclusion of the Preacher: 'Ridiculous the waste sad time/ Stretching before and after' (176). Again, we should recognize that the Preacher's refrain ('vanity of vanities; all is vanity') is overlaid here with other voices, in particular that of Kierkegaard pondering 'the mystic's lament over the dull moments' which succeed 'the luminous moment'.[68] But the refrain and the scepticism it embodies, I would argue, stem from Ecclesiastes.

The gloomy ending of Ecclesiastes Chapter 2, of course, gives way to a more positive appreciation of what von Rad calls 'The Doctrine of the Proper Time',[69] encapsulated in the famous opening verses of Chapter 3, which celebrates the fact that there is 'a season, and a time to every purpose under the heaven' (Eccles. 3:1). The end of this chapter, it should be noted, returns to a more melancholy meditation on the similarities between the life of men and beasts:

> For that which befalleth the sons of men befalleth beasts; even one thing befalleth them: as the one dieth, so dieth the other; yea, they have all one breath; so that a man hath no preeminence above a beast: for all is vanity. All go unto one place; all are of the dust, and all turn to dust again. (19–20)

Similarly, in clear imitation of Ecclesiastes, 'East Coker' begins by dwelling on death and decay as part of a natural cycle to which men must acquiesce: 'Houses live and die: there is a time for building/And a time for living and generation ...' (177). The phrase 'Houses rise and fall' in the second line of the poem is linked by Peter Milward with the wording of Simeon's blessing of Mary and Joseph: 'Behold, this child is set for the fall and rising again of many in Israel' (Luke 2:24). So when Eliot proceeds to contemplate their crumbling, extension, restoration or replacement, 'Old stone to new building', it is clearly possible to read this as yet another claim for the Church to have superseded the Temple although the implication is that this process of renewal and reinterpretation must continue.[70]

The poem at this point makes a chronological detour to Tudor England. Eliot had traced his ancestry back to the noble Eliots of fifteenth-century Devon, identifying in particular with Sir Thomas Elyot, author of *The Book of the Governor*, which supplies the particular form of the dancing and embracing of Ecclesiastes: 'The association of man and woman / In daunsinge, signifying matrimonie'. But 'East Coker' 'soon returns to the 'mirth' and 'laughter' and 'seasons' of Ecclesiastes along with the melancholy end to which they lead:

> The time of the coupling of man and woman
> And that of beasts. Feet rising and falling.
> Eating and drinking. Dung and death. (178)

Qoheleth comes to the conclusion that, because of this, 'man hath no better thing under the sun, than to eat, and to drink, and to be merry' (Ecc. 8:15), a judgement challenged by Jesus in Luke 12:19–20. Eliot too proceeds to challenge 'the wisdom of age' in the second section of 'East Coker':

> Had they deceived us,
> Or deceived themselves, the quiet-voiced elders ...
> The wisdom only the knowledge of dead secrets
> Useless in the darkness into which they peered
> Or from which they turned their eyes. (179)

Ecclesiastes repeatedly contrasts 'wisdom' and 'folly', claiming that 'wisdom excelleth folly, as far as light excelleth darkness', only to see that the wise man dies as the fool and that 'there is no remembrance of the wise more than of the fool.' Qoheleth comes, as a consequence, to hate life: 'for all is vanity and vexation of spirit'(2:13–17). Eliot in 'East Coker' appears to be rejecting this 'wisdom': 'Do not let me hear / Of the wisdom of old men,' he insists, 'but rather of their folly ... The only wisdom we can hope to acquire / Is the wisdom of humility; humility is endless' (179), endless in both senses: it lasts for ever and it is not overcome by death.

It is the fourth section of 'East Coker' that introduces Christ, the 'wounded surgeon' whose sacrificial death redeems the world, to be celebrated in the 'dripping blood' and 'bloody flesh' of the eucharist (181–2), although the final section again acknowledges the wisdom of the doctrine of the proper time: 'There is a time for the evening under starlight / A time for the evening under lamplight'. 'East Coker', which began with the claim, 'In my beginning is my end', concludes with the motto that Mary Queen of Scots had embroidered on her chair of state, 'In my end is my beginning'.[71] Ecclesiastes had taught, 'It is better to go to the house of mourning, than to go to the house of feasting: for that is the end of all men ... Better is the end of a thing than the beginning' (Eccles. 7:2, 8). The difference between Mary Queen of Scots and Ecclesiastes, it is implied, is that as a good Catholic she believes that death is quite literally the beginning, the entrance into new life, whereas Ecclesiastes cannot see beyond the grave. The conclusion of his book is sensible enough, within its own limitations: we all die and return to the dust; all, therefore, is vanity and the best we can do is live a righteous life: 'Fear God, and keep his commandments' (Eccles. 12:7–8, 13). A Christian, however, Eliot suggests, has the hope of eternal life through the resurrection of Christ and the sacraments of the Church.

'East Coker', in other words, can be read at one level as a dialogue between Jewish and Christian texts, Qoheleth and the Church. The third quartet, 'The Dry Salvages', continues this dialogue, although it is less explicit, less obviously echoing the biblical text. The opening chapter of Ecclesiastes, however, does contain a poem on the cycle of life which feeds both into the way the *Four Quartets* meditates upon Heraclitus's four elements (air, earth, water and fire) and into the melancholy sestina of 'The Dry Salvages'. Ecclesiastes dwells on the passing of generations in comparison with the endless cycle of the elements, the earth, which 'abideth for ever', the sun and the wind, which always return, and the recycling of water: 'All the rivers run into the sea; yet the sea is not full' (1:4–7). If 'Burnt Norton' had been about air and 'East Coker' about earth (to which all return), then 'The Dry Salvages' is clearly about water, in particular the rivers and the sea: 'The river is within us, the sea is all about us' (184).

As in Ecclesiastes, the second section of 'The Dry Salvages', a sestina, sees no point in the natural cycle of the seasons:

Where is there an end of it, the soundless wailing,
The silent withering of autumn flowers ...
There is no end but addition: the trailing
Consequence of further days and hours.

There is no end, and no point, the sestina concludes, without the Annunciation (the revelation to Mary that she carries the long-awaited Messiah). After the third section's exploration of the Hindu tradition, what Krishna has to say about the moment of death and 'the equal mind', the fourth section of 'The Dry Salvages' is a hymn to Our Lady, 'Figlia del tuo figlio / Queen of Heaven'. For it is to her that the good news of the Incarnation, the 'point of intersection of the timeless / With time', is first announced. 'Here the past and future / Are conquered, and reconciled', the 'answers' given to the questions and doubts raised by Ecclesiastes.

'Little Gidding' might appear to celebrate those 'answers' unambiguously, the ruins of the Anglican community founded by Nicholas Ferrar and destroyed by Cromwell having been the focus for Eliot's own pilgrimage there in 1936. Again, however, there appears to be a dialogue taking place in the text between Jewish wisdom, represented by Ecclesiastes, and Christian faith. The second section of the poem moves from the dust which marks 'the place where a story ended' through 'Dead water' to purging and redeeming fire. It is, though, in the second stanza that the most obvious echoes of Ecclesiastes occur, stressing the 'vanity' of all earthly labour:

The parched eviscerate soil
Gapes at the vanity of toil,
Laughs without mirth.
This is the death of earth. (193)

The compound ghost of this section also pours scorn upon the 'gifts reserved for age' in the manner of Ecclesiastes 12, with body and soul beginning 'to fall asunder' and 'the conscious impotence of rage / At human folly' (194). It takes the Pentecostal fire celebrated in the fourth section of 'Little Gidding' to reach what the final section sees as 'The end ... where we start from' (197). The cycle ends with the lines already quoted in which all tongues are 'in-folded/Into the crowned knot of fire' (198).

So what are we to make, finally, of this attempt to 'in-fold' Ecclesiastes, to bring Solomon into the Christian fold via the 'universal' language of Dante and the Church? Eliot, Julius could argue, clearly presents the Jewish wisdom of Ecclesiastes as ultimately superseded by the explicitly Christian theological concepts of the Annunciation and the Incarnation. The language of 'Little Gidding', as David Moody observes, is noticeably latinate, full of words like 'sempiternal' in the second line, while 'Pentecostal', of Greek origin, encapsulates a history in itself: the transformation of the Jewish Harvest Festival into a Christian occasion 'not in the scheme of generation'. Eliot contrasts 'time's covenant' (that of the Old Testament) with the 'eternal covenant' (that of the New).[72] The *Four Quartets*, in this respect, cannot escape the charge of Christian triumphalism, of that serious anti-Semitism involved in Christianity's first breaking with its Jewish roots.

It is possible to suggest, however, that in writing the Church in the *Four Quartets*, Eliot does not ignore the complexity either of writing or of the Writings, whose role in the construction of the Church he clearly acknowledges. There is a whole strand of the poem, one of the themes recapitulated in each quartet, which focuses on the relationship between words and the Word. Language, Eliot recognizes, is historical ('Words move, music moves? Only in time'). Words have a history, a past and a future, requiring Christians to accept that they think in terms derived from Jewish ways of thought. The Church is built on and with the ruined fragments of the Temple. The *Four Quartets*, therefore, even while claiming to go beyond the Hebrew Bible, are never disrespectful, never irreverent. The complex layers of writing, from the Heraclitean epigraph and the language of Ecclesiastes through subsequent layers of Christian meditation upon them, represent an accumulation of textual commentary whose historicity and whose writing (in Derrida's sense) is fully acknowledged. The *Four Quartets*, in other words, represents (re-presents and re-enacts) that complex historical and linguistic phenomenon, with all its tension but also all its richness, which we call the Judaeo-Christian tradition.

Notes

1. More often as a generalization than in sustained commentary. Two articles explore the biblical allusions in Eliot's poetry in some detail: Florence Jones, 'T.S. Eliot Among the Prophets', *American Literature* 38 (1966), pp. 285–302 and Cornelia Cook, 'The Hidden Apocalypse: T.S. Eliot's Early Work', *Literature and Theology* 10 (1996), pp. 68–80.
2. Leonard Unger, *T.S. Eliot: Moments and Patterns* (Minneapolis, University of Minnesota Press, [1956] 1967), pp. 118, 142.
3. John Paul Riquelme, *Harmony of Dissonances: T.S. Eliot, Romanticism, and Imagination* (Baltimore and London: Johns Hopkins University Press, 1991), pp. 2–3.

4   John Xiros Cooper, *T.S. Eliot and the Ideology of the 'Four Quartets'* (Cambridge: Cambridge University Press, 1995), p. 26.
5   T.S. Eliot, *The Complete Poems and Plays* (London: Faber and Faber, 1969), p. 198. All future references to the poems in brackets after quotations are to this edition.
6   T.S. Eliot, *Selected Essays*, 3rd edn (London: Faber and Faber, 1951), p. 228.
7   Lyndall Gordon, *T.S. Eliot: An Imperfect Life* (London: Vintage, 1998), pp. 379–85.
8   Paul J.Achtemeier, ed., *Harper's Bible Dictionary* (San Francisco: Harper and Row, 1985), pp. 1135–7.
9   Eliot's early references to Herbert are less positive than his final assessment in a pamphlet produced for the British Council: 'only gradually, as we familiarize ourselves with the whole work, do we appreciate *The Temple* as a coherent sequence of poems setting down the fluctuation of emotion between despair and bliss, between agitation and serenity, and the discipline of suffering which leads to peace of spirit', *George Herbert* (London: Longman, 1962), p. 25. For a detailed analysis of Herbert's use of the Bible, see Chana Bloch, *Spelling the Word: George Herbert and the Bible* (Berkeley: University of California Press, 1985).
10 Jacques Derrida, *Of Grammatology*, trans. Gayatri Spivak (Baltimore: Johns Hopkins University Press, 1976), p. 71. For a discussion of logocentrism in relation to Eliot, see William V. Spanos, 'Hermeneutics and Memory: Destroying T.S. Eliot's *Four Quartets*', Genre 11 (1978), pp. 523–73.
11 Maud Ellmann, 'The Imaginary Jew: T.S. Eliot and Ezra Pound', in Bryan Cheyette, ed., *Between 'Race' and Culture: Representations of 'the Jew' in English and American Culture* (Stanford: Stanford University Press, 1996), p. 93.
12 Staffan Bergsten, *Time and Eternity: A Study in the Structure and Symbolism of T.S. Eliot's 'Four Quartets'* (New York: Humanities Press, 1973 [1960]), p. 47.
13 Ranen Omer, '"It is I Who Have Been Defending a Religion Called Judaism": The T.S. Eliot and Horace M. Kallen Correspondence', *Texas Studies in Literature and Language* 39 (1997), pp. 321–56, 344.
14 James Wood, *The Broken Estate: Essays on Literature and Belief* (London: Jonathan Cape, 1999), p. 146.
15 Graham Martin, ed., *Eliot in Perspective: A Symposium* (Trowbridge: Humanities Press, 1970), p. 24.
16 Wood, pp. 142–5.
17 'Notes to the New Testament', in Robert Carroll and Stephen Prickett, ed., *The Bible* (Oxford: Oxford University Press), pp. 398–400.
18 Robert L.Wilken, ed., *Aspects of Wisdom in Judaism and Early Christianity* (Notre Dame: University of Notre Dame Press, 1975), p. xvi.
19 See Jacques Derrida, *Writing and Difference*, trans. Alan Bass (Chicago: Chicago University Press, 1978), p. 153.
20 Gordon, *T.S. Eliot: An Imperfect Life*, pp. 104–105; Peter Ackroyd, *T.S. Eliot* (London: Hamish Hamilton, 1984), pp. 303–304.
21 Anthony Julius, *T.S. Eliot, Anti-Semitism and Literary Form* (Cambridge: Cambridge University Press, 1995), p. 2.
22 A. David Moody, *T.S. Eliot: Poet* (Cambridge: Cambridge University Press, 1994) p.376.
23 Ackroyd, *T.S. Eliot*, p.304.
24 Hermione Lee, *Virginia Woolf* (London: Chatto and Windus, 1996) pp.313–14.
25 Gordon, *T.S. Eliot: An Imperfect Life*, p.195
26 Julius, *T.S. Eliot, Anti-Semitism and Literary Form*, pp.167–8.
27 T.S. Eliot, *After Strange Gods: A Primer of Modern Heresy* (London: Faber and Faber, 1934) p.20.

28 Ibid., p.61.
29 Gordon, *T.S. Eliot: An Imperfect Life*, p. 180.
30 Julius, *T.S. Eliot, Anti-Semitism and Literary Form*, p. 171.
31 T.S. Eliot, *Notes Towards the Definition of Culture* (London: Faber and Faber, 1948), p. 70.
32 Gordon, *T.S. Eliot: An Imperfect Life*, p. 103.
33 Ibid., p. 683.
34 Ibid., p. 695.
35 Eliot, *Selected Essays*, p. 14.
36 Ibid., pp. 15–16.
37 Harold Bloom, *The Breaking of the Vessels* (Chicago: Chicago University Press, 1982), p. 19.
38 Eliot, *Selected Essays*, p. 206.
39 Christopher Ricks, ed., *Inventions of the March Hare: Poems 1909–1917 by T.S. Eliot* (London: Faber and Faber, 1996), p. xxiv.
40 Ibid.
41 Eliot, *Selected Essays*, p. 318.
42 Eliot, *George Herbert*, p. 24.
43 Eliot, *Selected Essays*, pp. 238–9.
44 T.S. Eliot, *The Varieties of Metaphysical Poetry*, ed. Ronald Schuchard (London: Faber and Faber, 1993) pp. 70 and 83.
45 John Peter, 'Eliot and the *Criterion*', in Martin, *Eliot in Perspective*, pp. 252–66, p. 260.
46 Roger Kojecky, *T.S. Eliot's Social Criticism* (London: Faber and Faber, 1971), pp. 67, 62.
47 Eliot, *Notes*, p.122.
48 Julius, *T.S. Eliot Anti-Semitism and Literary Form*, pp. 197–8.
49 Eliot, *Selected Essays*, p. 390.
50 Ricks, *Inventions of the March Hare*, p. 75.
51 Ibid., p.76.
52 Unger, *T.S. Eliot: Moments and Patterns*, p. 154. See the articles by Cook and Jones for details of references to the prophets.
53 Grover Smith, *T.S. Eliot's Poetry and Plays* (Chicago: University of Chicago Press, 1974 [1956]) p.139; Eloise Knapp Hay, *T.S. Eliot's Negative Way* (Cambridge, Mass.: Harvard University Press, 1982) p.91.
54 Kojecky, *T.S. Eliot's Social Criticism*, p. 103.
55 Gordon, *T.S. Eliot: An Imperfect Life*, p. 461.
56 Northrop Frye, *T.S. Eliot: An Introduction* (Chicago: University of Chicago Press, 1981 [1963]) p.79.
57 Moody, *T.S. Eliot: Poet*, p. 252.
58 Riquelme, *Harmony of Dissonances*, pp.22 and 83.
59 Helen Gardner, *The Composition of the 'Four Quartets'* (London: Faber and Faber, 1978).
60 Bergsten, *Time and Eternity*, pp. 164–6.
61 Gordon, *T.S. Eliot: An Imperfect Life*, p. 341.
62 Gardner, *The Composition of the Four Quartets*, p. 16.
63 Raymond Preston, *'Four Quartets' Rehearsed: A Commentary on T.S. Eliot's Cycle of Poems* (London: Sheed and Ward, 1946), p. 9.
64 Paul Murray, *T.S. Eliot and Mysticism: The Secret History of 'Four Quartets'* (London: Macmillan, 1991), p. 48.
65 Bergsten, *Time and Eternity*, p. 97.
66 Ibid., p.98.

67 Gordon, *T.S. Eliot: An Imperfect Life*, p. 384.
68 Murray, *T.S. Eliot and Mysticism*, pp.113–14.
69 Gerhard von Rad, *Wisdom in Israel* (London: SCM Press, 1972), p. 138.
70 Peter Milward, *A Commentary on T.S. Eliot's 'Four Quartets'* (Tokyo: Hokuseido Press, 1968), pp. 73–4.
71 Ibid., p. 73.
72 Moody, *T.S. Eliot: Poet*, p. 244.

Chapter 3

Joycing Derrida, Churching Derrida: *Glas, église* and *Ulysses*

John Schad

Before

... a riddling sentence to be woven and woven on the church's looms.
Ulysses

... everything here is woven against a church.
Glas[1]

The riddling sentences of *Glas* and *Ulysses* weave both on and against the church; even when opposing the church these churchy texts could not exist without it. To follow this very particular weaving, my reading will shuttle between *Glas* and *Ulysses*, a movement that is itself churchy, or ecclesial in that the French for 'shuttle', *navette*, is also – as *Glas* reminds us – 'a church term' (208b), meaning 'incense vessel.' But then, so many of the seemingly secular words of *Glas* and *Ulysses* double as church terms; they have, as it were, a buried and distant ecclesial life – such words, to use yet another, 'communicate' from *afar*. For this reason, the church in *Glas* and *Ulysses* must *tele*-communicate[2]; in both, as Derrida observes of Genet's fiction, 'the Gospel [is] ... violently ... fragmented ... as if [it] ... reached us over ... an overloaded telephone exchange' (196b).

In *Ulysses* the church quite literally telecommunicates: the 'archbishop's letter' is 'repeated in the *Telegraph*' (100); Buck Mulligan cries 'Telegram! A papal bull' (163); 'the signal for prayer ... [is] given by megaphone' (253), and 'His grace [the Bishop] phone[s] ... twice [in one] ... morning' (97). In Dublin, a city full of priests, the church never stops ringing: '... a priest round the corner is elevating it. Dringdring! And two streets off another locking it into a pyx. Dringadring! And in a ladychapel another taking housel all to his own cheek. Dringdring!'(33).

It is, of course, the dringdring of the eucharist bell, but Joyce cannot resist reimagining the church as a bizarre network of telephone lines: in *Ulysses* we read not only that 'his grace phoned' but also that, in quite another place and time, 'Buck Mulligan antiphoned' (169). Derrida also antiphones, or rather anti-phones, for just as *Glas* is woven '*against* the church' so it is wired against, or in despite of, the official church; in Genet's 'overloaded telephone exchange' it is only on 'a wire-tap' that Derrida hears, or rather over-hears the church and its gospel – he is listening in from without. This is the church inside-*out*, where tele-communication comes close to ex-communication. In *Glas* we hear not just the passing-bell but 'all the bells of a church' (89b), including both the telephone bell and the 'bell, book and candle' (280) that excommunicates.[3] It is an illicit and excommunicated church that *Glas*, through Genet, seeks to write, or wire-tap.

It is, of course, a dangerous wire to tap – when Derrida reads Genet's 'The Funambulists' the wire in question is a high-wire; here we encounter an 'acrobat ... twenty-five ... feet from the ground ... pray[ing] and cross[ing] himself' (101b). Genet's story shifts, writes Derrida, 'from vigil to wire' and, indeed, back again with the 'saltimbanques who ... danced in front of ... cathedrals' (102b). The Genet quote continues, '"I don't know to what god you will address your feats of dexterity, but you need one"'; the later Derrida *does*, of course, address his feats to a god – most obviously in 'Circumfession': 'I am,' writes Derrida, 'addressing myself here to God.'[4] Addressing God begins, though, in *Glas* where Derrida himself performs in front of cathedrals. In returning Hegelian thought to the 'Christianity of which it is the truth' (95a), Derrida opens up a space for philosophy *before* philosophy, a space he calls 'the parvis' – the enclosed area before a cathedral. *Glas* here locates a church *before* the church, a church before what Derrida calls philosophy's 'church of stone' (72a), Hegel's petrified abstraction of Christianity. Derrida, like the whole theatre of religion – 'advent ... the cross ... [and] resurrection play' – joins the saltimbanques in 'play[ing] on the parvis ...*before* philosophy's erect construction' (96a).

Though this 'church of stone' is built of philosopher's stone, it also invokes the stone that is St Peter: as Derrida reminds us (86a), Jesus declares, 'thou art Peter [meaning 'rock'] and upon this rock I will build my church' (Matt. 16:18).[5] St Peter, indeed, is also invoked by the very word 'parvis,' deriving as it does from *paradisus*, or 'Paradise,' the portico in front of St Peter's Church in Rome. In *Ulysses*, Bloom comes across a book called *Why I left the church of Rome* (148), in *Glas* it sometimes seems as if all roads lead *back* to that church. The word 'parvis' leads to the court where the Pope takes a hammer to the church: in a ceremony performed once every twenty-five years, the Pope (that latter-day Peter) knocks down the walled-up Holy Door.[6] It is an act, or moment that Derrida chances upon when he predicts, of the church of stone, that 'the stone [*pierre*] itself will give rise ... to ... fracture ... [and] ruin' (72a). The ruining of the walled-up door to which *the Pope* gives rise marks the beginning of the Roman Year of Jubilee, a year of remission from the penal consequences of sin named after the Jewish Jubilee, that 50-yearly remission of debts in which, as Derrida observes, not just 'property [but] ... the proper is ... equalized [and] levelled' (52a). For Derrida, the Jewish Jubilee takes a hammer to the very logic of property, the logic of the proper, or self-same.[7]

Twenty-five years on, in 1999, as *Glas* itself enjoys a jubilee,[8] it is time to recognize that Derrida's weaving against Hegel's church of stone mimics the Roman Jubilee in which the Pope hammers against a church *door* of stone. Indeed, in doing so Derrida anticipates the millennial jubilee that is (or was) the international debt-relief campaign, Jubilee 2000. Concerned as it is with 'the space of debt' (243a), *Glas* not only includes the parable of two forgiven debtors (62a) but dreams of ways to 'escape ... the operation of ... debt' (101a) through 'the giving of ... the pure *cadeau* [that] ... does not let itself be thought by ... dialectics' (243a), the dialectics of indebtedness. *Glas* comes even closer to jubilee at the level of pure sound; for whilst '*glas* is first of all [etymologically] ... the signal of a trumpet' (86b),'jubilee' is first of all *yobel* – 'a ram's horn.' The *glas*-trumpet, however, 'is destined to *call* [or] ... gather together ... a *class* of the Roman people' – it serves, that is, the very citizenship, the very *proper*tied class against which the jubilee-trumpet sounds. In this sense, *Glas*'s jubilee is ironized, is itself woven against. Though *Glas* performs upon the parvis before the Hegelian church of stone, it does so under the philosophical sign of the proper: 'this work of mourning is called – *glas*. It is always for/of the proper name' (86b).

In *Glas*, however, the proper name is never simply being mourned; also at work is a jubilee that jubilates at the proper name's passing, a jubilee that celebrates and even hastens the destabilizing of names. In cancelling debt every fifty years, the Jewish Jubilee redefines not only property but the proper name, the name in which property is held – both become provisional, liable to change. As Derrida puts it, 'jubilee ... constitutes ... [both] possession as loan [*en prêt*], and ... the name as [merely] a lent-name [*prête-nom*]' (52a).[9] Indeed, in so doing, jubilee impacts upon the very name of the church – for here *prêt* becomes *prête*, an anagram of 'Peter', the lent-name which both founds the church and signals its end as *perte* ('ruin'), another anagram, or ruin of 'Peter' that appears in the very last line of *Glas*. By so scrambling the church's proper name, jubilee – like Genet – leads the church into 'the occulted tradition of anagrammatizing names', a tradition that Derrida identifies with 'the depths of a crypt' (41b), that dark church beneath a church which, for Derrida, is not only a crypt but cryptic: there are, he writes, 'anagrams ... in ... a crypt'.[10] There is also a thief; for Genet here 'moves [like] ... a thief in the night'; this church beneath a church redistributes property as well as proper names. It is a church made in the im-proper image of jubilee.

Something of this church is also found in *Ulysses*; here the proper name of '*Joyce*' is always already purloined by a church that en*joys* itself, that is beside itself with laughter.[11] For all the novel's funerals and passing-bells here 'joybells ring in ... church' (393) and so, indeed, do 'rams' horns' (397). Hegel's friend Niethammer speaks of '"the comedy of Christianity"' (177a) – it is, for Niethammer, a comedy to be avoided; in *Ulysses*, however, we encounter not just 'the ballad of joking Jesus' (16) but his church – as Joyce observes, 'the ... Church was built on a pun.'[12] And what makes all this joking a jubilee is that it, somehow, witnesses to suffering. When, in November 1906, Joyce is in Rome, an anarchist bomb goes off in St Peter's – in his letter the next day he remarks 'it's a bloody funny church';[13] it is as if the church is most funny when it is also, quite literally, bloody.

This irony is repeated when, in 'Circe', we encounter not Simon *Peter* but Simon *Stephen* – namely 'His Eminence Simon Stephen cardinal Dedalus' (427). Here, at the moment of high parody, is a church founded not on Peter-the-rock but Stephen-the-stoned, Stephen the church's first martyr who was stoned to a bloody death. What Stephen himself calls the 'nightmare' of 'history' (28) is, in the case of the church, so bloody it has to be funny; if it is to be communicated at all it must be as a joke. For Niethammer, of course, this is unthinkable: '"[it is only] weak individuals ... who play the comedy of Christianity with cross, blood ... and self-degradation'" (177a); Derrida, however, is of a different mind – on the very last page of *Glas* we read that

> ... the syllogism of spiritual art (epos, tragedy, comedy) leads aesthetic religion to revealed religion. Through comedy then.

Perhaps Joking Jesus laughs so much he cries – after all, according to revealed religion, that is precisely what he does: as the New Testament reveals, 'Jesus wept' (John 11:35). Joyce's Jesus certainly comes close to crying in the very moment of laughter:

>   She laughed:
> —O wept! ...
>   With sadness. (212)

For 'Jesus wept' read 'O wept!,' for revealed religion read exclamation; here laughter, or comedy leads not toward revealed religion but away from it. This is a Jesus who simultaneously cries and laughs, appears and vanishes – 'O' is no one. But if history is a nightmare, the more hallucinatory is Jesus the more historical he is.

This is certainly the lesson of *Glas* – for when Derrida declares it is 'a time to perfect the resemblance between Dionysus and Christ' (262a) he invokes a Nietzschean Christ, or anti-Christ, a figure that is at once both wildly irrational and violently historical.[14] Such an anti-Christ is glimpsed earlier when Derrida speaks of 'Jesus' pharmacy' (104b) – for Derrida, the word 'pharmacy' famously entails both drug (*pharmakon*) and violence (*pharmakos* meaning 'scapegoat').[15] Shades, of course, of the Marxian line that 'religion is ... the opium of the people'; but whilst Marx presents the church as an hallucinatory escape from history, Derrida knows there is no such escape in Jesus' pharmacy. Indeed, from pharmacy, or chemistry, originates the science behind the most explosive nightmare of history – namely, nuclear fission. The bomb in St Peter's in 1906 is not the only the bomb to go off in the twentieth-century church.

Bomb

> I hear the ruin of all space, shattered glass and toppling masonry. (20)

As the Second Watch in Nighttown declares – even as church bells toll – 'The bomb is here' (385). That bomb is, in one sense, a Fenian bomb; as Fairhall remarks, 'the [1867] Clerkenwell explosion resounds throughout *Ulysses*.'[16] The Fenian bomb particularly resounds in All Hallows; it is there that Bloom recalls 'that fellow that turned queen's evidence on the invincibles' – the Fenian splinter group which carried out the Phoenix Park murders of 1882: 'that fellow used to receive the,

Carey was his name, the communion every morning. This very church' (66). The Clerkenwell bomb resounds in that fellow's very name – one of the bombers was called Ca*s*ey. The fellow Carey was not the only Fenian within Irish Catholicism;[17] in that sense, All Hallows was not the only turn-of-the-century Dublin church in which the Fenian bomb resounded – that is a simple lesson of history. Indeed, as *Glas* demonstrates, one lesson of the dictionary is that a bomb resounds in every church: '*glas* "ringing of all the bells of a church" ... *glas* ... "noise of a bomb"' (89b).

This noise is, perhaps, first heard in church by Nietzsche who in 1888 warns that the doctrine of 'equality of souls' is 'Christian dynamite' capable of 'ignit[ing] a "world conflagration"'.[18] In 1888, of course, no explosive is capable of igniting the world; fifty-seven years before Hiroshima, Nietzsche locates in the church a dynamite that somehow anticipates the far more terrible 'dynamite' of nuclear fission. Joyce, still twenty-three years before Hiroshima, does something similar in *Ulysses* – here the Magnificat becomes 'magnificandjewbang' (88) and Boylan cries 'Godblazegrukbrukarchkhrasht!' (462); in both cases it is as if the church's creed is so outrageous as to somehow split what Molly calls the 'atom of ... expression' (639). Such a splitting, or fission, was already on the way in contemporary physics – in June 1922 Niels Bohr tells Werner Heisenberg that 'electrons ... [are] not ... things.'[19] Joyce himself did not, in a sense, need to be told, did not need to join 'Father Butt in the physics theatre' (548); though *Finnegans Wake* (1939) speaks of 'reading work on German physics',[20] such physics was always already Joycean, or Bloomian. After all, German physics was also known as 'modernist' or 'Jewish' physics[21] – the field was dominated by Jews. There is, it seems, not only Christian dynamite but *Jewish* – as *Ulysses* puts it, 'magnificand*jew*bang'.

Glas puts it differently, but it too comes close to the Judaeo-Christian dynamite at work in a nuclear explosion. The *Sa* of *Glas* – whether read as Hegel's *savoir absolu* or Freud's *ça* (the id) – is explosive. Of Genet we read, 'he is wherever that explodes' – wherever '*ça sa*ute' (207b); here *ça* explodes but so too does the *sa* of *sa*ute. Derrida argues that *savoir absolu* arises from a dialectic driven by the 'metaphor ... of the bomb': the first 'moment' of the dialectic – namely, 'the passage into the absolute opposite' – is compared by Hegel to the point at which 'a bombshell at its zenith effects a jolt' (106-7a). The final 'moment' of Hegel's dialectic, the point at which the opposite reflects the subject, or self, is yet more explosive: 'Hiroshima', argues Mark C.Taylor, 'might be understood' as 'the self affirm[ing] ... itself through ... absolute negation'.[22] As Genet writes, and Derrida cites, '"total presence ... is transformed into a bomb of ... terrific power"' (174a). In this sense, it is always the case that 'the bomb is here' since what is explosive, what can annihilate the other, is the 'is here', the self-present.

But, of course, for Joyce in Rome on 18 November 1906, the bomb in St Peter's is, most crucially, not here but there; as he writes to his brother, 'I had intended going to the morning service (and would consequently have been in the church at the time of the explosion) but that I waited in for a letter from you.'[23] This letter is unusual – as Carla de Petris observes, 'in [the rest of] his [Rome] letters ... the hundreds of churches [Joyce] ... had to pass ... every day are not even mentioned'; for Joyce in Rome, any bomb in the church was, necessarily, there rather than here.

There is, though, a bomb in the church which actually derives its terrific power from what is always already elsewhere; this is the buried theme of Derrida's declaration that 'the institution, the stone of the Church will provoke another fission' (71a). Fission of the nuclear kind is, of course, a chain reaction of splitting upon splitting of atomic nuclei, an almost infinite impossibilizing of the centre of the atom that comes very close to deconstruction's critique of self-presence. Witness Mark Taylor's pointedly Derridean remark that 'atomic fission ... make[s] ... centeredness impossible.'[24]

The trace, or ghost, of nuclear fission may certainly be pursued throughout *Glas*, a text that does itself split and then split again – here (and there), in *Glas*'s own words, 'each textual atom ... bursts' (172b). Paraphrasing Hegel, Derrida writes that 'one divides itself into two, such is the distressing source of philosophy' (95a) – if so, *Glas* represents an almost infinite chain reaction to that philosophical splitting; it is, though, a fission that also comes from the church. For whilst 'the Hegelian reading of Christianity seems,' writes Derrida, 'to describe a reconciliation ... Christianity [in fact] opens a new morseling' (91a). This is most conspicuous in the Eucharist, when the church is quite literally morseling – that is, biting and breaking the body of Christ; it is at this moment that 'divinity stands, very precariously, between swallowing and vomiting ... neither solid nor liquid, neither outside nor in' (71a). Split between two states and two locations, the Eucharistic body of Christ is 'here' in crisis – it gives, in other words, a quite new and explosive sense to that Marxian phrase which appears later in *Glas*: namely, 'the "critical Christ"' (203a). Derrida writes of a 'religion [that] would have a *critical* effect on *Sa*' (221a), but *Glas* has a critical effect on religion, in particular the mass; indeed, in *Glas* – as the nuclear physicists say – the mass goes critical.

It is, though, always already critical in that, as the 'perpetual memorial of Christ's sacrifice', the church's breaking of bread is a perpetual process of dividing, or splitting. In the Dublin of *Ulysses* this is obvious – Stephen imagines himself a priest administering the mass whilst, of course,

> ... at the same instant perhaps a priest round the corner is elevating it.
> Dringdring! And two streets off another locking it into a pyx. Dringadring!
> And in the lady chapel another taking housel all to his own cheek.
> Dringdring! Down, up, forward, back ... Dan Occam thought of that. (33)

In a city full of Catholic churches the Real Presence is never purely and simply present. Jacques Derrida, in a sense, thought of that – it is what he calls, in *Glas*, the '*not yet* of philosophy' (95a), a not yet that echoes the not yet of the mass that is 'a perpetual memorial *until he comes again*'. For Derrida, this Christological not yet is also, however, the not yet of total nuclear war. In 'No Apocalypse: Not Now' (1984), Derrida ends his meditation on the absolute uniqueness of such a war, 'its-being-for-the-first-time-and-perhaps-for-the-last-time', with the Christ of the Apocalypse, with him who declares '"I am the first and the last."'[25] This Apocalyptic Christ is akin to the 'non-event' of nuclear war. Once again, there is a bomb in the church.

It is, perhaps, fear of an actual, anarchist bomb that keeps Joyce passing by the churches of Rome; whatever, in so doing he falls into step with Hegel: '"I never,"' he writes, '"more than pass by churches"'(153a). Genet, however, does do more, he does go in; what Jean Cocteau calls 'the Genet bomb'[26] is habitually drawn to churches, his writing is full of them. This, for Genet, is because 'the church [is] ... a box of surprises'; for Derrida, it is because Genet thought of *that*, of *ça* – 'Genet is wherever *ça* explodes' even, it seems, when *ça* explodes in church.

This is quite literally true of Genet's play *Blacks*; in September 1963 at the height of the Civil Rights movement, one particular American performance replaced Genet's line 'One hundred thousand youngsters who died in the dust' with the words 'Four little girls who died in a Birmingham church' – the girls were Black, they had been killed by a bomb.[27]

Black

> The white stone becomes black. (255a)

Unlike Joyce, Genet – or at least his play – *is* there when the bomb goes off in church. But then 'he is wherever it explodes [because] he no longer inhabits the ... Christian West' (207b); 'it explodes,' implies Derrida, *outside* the Christian West, and so it does in 1963 in the sense that the church in Birmingham is a Black church, its congregation is of African origin. It is, though, still a church – the Genet bomb may go off outside the Christian West but it is not outside the church. The terrible lesson of '63 is that there *is* an explosive church outside the Western church – a black church. This is a lesson that Genet himself needed to learn; for though the play seeks to invert all conventional values by declaring black all that is conventionally white, this does not include the church:

> ... black was the colour of priests ... But everything is changing. Whatever is gentle and kind and good and tender will be black. Milk will be black, sugar, rice, the sky, doves, hope, will be black.[28]

Though the play dreams of a black that has left behind the black of the priests, it is a dream that the bomb of '63 explodes.

Glas does something similar; for here Genet's inverted and absolutely black world *does* entail a black church. Derrida locates Genet, of course, 'in the depths of a crypt' dedicated to 'a nocturnal God'(214a) and thief-in-the-night-Christ. In *Glas*, this crypt operates as the black other of a Hegelian church of stone that proves to be 'white stone' (255a) – quite literally, a 'white mythology':[29] we are reminded that 'missionary reports' inform Hegel's declaration that 'Africa ... "has no history"' (207–9a).

The idea, or conceit of a black counter-church is also a Joycean one. Joyce delighted in the fact that in Rome the leader of the Jesuits, that 'church' within the Church, was known as the 'Black Pope'.[30] In *Ulysses*, there is talk of 'the ... African heresiarch' (17), 'Black candles' are lit for a black, or 'reversed ... mass' (489), and Bloom goes 'through a form of clandestine marriage ... in the shadow of the Black church' (438). This church is black because made of black Dublin rock,[31] but Joyce's black church is made also of Black African souls: 'Father Conmee thought of ... the

African mission and of the millions of black and brown ... souls' (183); in *Ulysses*, the black church is not only a trope, not only a metaphoric dark continent, it is also and at the same time a historical reality. The same may be said of Genet's *Blacks* as performed in America in September 1963 when the terrible reality of the Black church in Birmingham, Alabama is that the church is not just Black but blackened, bombed, burnt – 'four little girls killed in a church'.

According to Derrida, Black children are still being killed within the church, or at least under the sign of the church and its code of sacrifice; in *The Gift of Death* the story of Abraham and Isaac prompts Derrida to return to the theme of jubilee with the terrible declaration that 'because of ... external debt ... [our] "society" *puts to* death ... millions of children ... in [an] ... incalculable sacrifice.'[32] We think, of course, that child-sacrifice could not happen today – as Derrida puts it, 'we can hardly imagine a father taking his son to be sacrificed on the top of ... Montmartre.' Perhaps not; but the irony of Derrida's remark is that the city fathers of Paris *did* imagine building Sacré Coeur on the top of Montmartre to commemorate the many sons that were sacrificed in the Franco-Prussian War of 1871. Built of white stone, Sacré Coeur is quite literally a white church, but it soon grows symbolically white – a white church for white Isaacs, white Christs – as Derrida reminds us of how easily we forget the millions of Black children whom debt also kills in the Christ-like image of Isaac, the sacrificed son.

Black Christs are, likewise, on the mind, or conscience of Joyce; witness Bloom's reading of the newspaper: '*Black Beast Burned in Omaha, Ga. ...* a Sambo strung up in a tree with ... a bonfire under him. Gob, they ought to ... crucify him to make sure' (269). Later, Molly exclaims, 'Jesusjack, that child is a black' (611), but here Jesusjack is himself a Black – indeed, he is, quite terribly, *black*ened. If Genet is wherever *ça* explodes, Joyce is, in this case, where both Ga explodes and *Sa*-mbo burns – namely, *Ga*lile*a*, the next state along from Birmingham, Alabama. It is as if all roads lead to a Black and blackened church or Christ in the Deep South; that, it seems, is where both Freud's *ça* and Hegel's *Sa* wind up. This is, of course, a variation on the familiar theme of contemporary America as the dead-end of psychoanalysis and the end, or telos, of Hegelian history;[33] in Genet and Joyce the blackened church is witness to the fact that the *Sa/ça* in America is violently white. So too is the *Sa/ça* in Dublin, the blackened Christ of Ga reappearing as Bloom, in Nighttown – here Bloom stands dressed in 'a seamless garment marked I.H.S.' with a 'bag of gunpowder round his neck' whilst figures 'in black ... kneel down and pray ... [until he] becomes ... carbonized ... black in the face' (406–7).

Again, Jesusjack is a Black. So too was that Jewishjack, Jacques Derrida – as a child in Algeria, Derrida was, in his own words, 'a little black and very Arab Jew'.[34] Indeed, just like Bloom's crucified Sambo, the Derrida of *Glas* finds himself in Ga – not the Ga that is Georgia but the Ga that is Galilee: in the Genet column 'we are', writes Derrida, 'in Galilee' (106a). To be more specific, 'we are in Galilee between 1810 and 1910', the long nineteenth century of European colonialism – the text at this point cuts to '"Frenchmen bombarding Algiers in 1830"'. We are not, however, stuck in a nineteenth-century, Eurocentric Galilee; for in *Glas* we encounter not so much the Victorians' famously 'pale Galilean' but the spectre of a dark Galilean.[35] 'Could it be that you are from Galilee too?' (197b), the question is first put to Jesus but it rebounds upon *Glas'* Algerian author – *Glas* is published, of course, by Éditions Galilée. Alluding to this, Geoffrey Hartman declares that '*Glas* is of the House of Galilee.' What we must add is that, in *Glas*, Galilee is identified with bombarded Algiers as closely as *Glas'* Galilean author is identified with a galerien, or galley-slave: 'the author,' writes Derrida, 'rows with the application of a ... galerien' (69–70b). *Glas's* Galilee – its Christianity, if you will – is black with the blackness of the North African unconscious of its author.[36]

It is also black because blackened, or singed, by Genet's searing critique – what Derrida calls his 'violent ... radiographic interpretation ... of Golgotha' (147b). Another blazing critique of Christianity at work in *Glas* is that of Feuerbach – whose name, of course, means 'stream of fire'; with this in mind Marx famously proclaims: 'Christians ... there is no other road for you to *truth* ... except that leading *through* the stream of fire.'[37] There certainly are both Christians and churches who go the way of fire in *Ulysses*: witness the church at Sandymount where 'one of the candles was just going to set fire to the flowers' (296); or again, 'the Earl of Kildare [who once] ... set fire to Cashel cathedral' (190). As it happens, the candle is moved to safety and the archbishop whom the Earl intended to kill was not in the cathedral; on these occasions, the church burns and no one is hurt – nevertheless, a terrible potential is glimpsed, a potential encoded in the strangely-phrased reference to 'those incense they burned in the church' (293). This fiery potential has found terrible historical realization; those they burned in the church have, since 1922, come to include not just heretics but Jews – the church, we know, played a significant part in stoking the flames of the Holocaust (literally, 'total-burning').[38] Genet seems mindful of this; as Derrida observes, 'In *Funeral Rites*, the Trinity (the church) represents the eagle of the Reich' (121b). The anti-Semitism that would link church and Reich is distilled in *Ulysses* as 'those jews they said killed the christian boy' (89). The nightmare in which the *Nazis'* 'christian boys' would kill Jews is a future that *Ulysses* also distils, or chances upon: 'that will be,' remarks Martin Cunningham, 'a great race tomorrow in Germany'(80); whilst, for Stephen, 'the bloodboltered shambles in ... [*Hamlet*] is a forecast of the concentration camp'(154).[39] There is, indeed, a very present holocaust upon the mind, or rather the day of *Ulysses* – namely, 'All those women and children excursion beanfeast burned and drowned in New York. Holocaust' (149). Bloom refers to a report that appeared on 16 June 1904 in the *Freeman's Journal*:

> Five hundred persons, mostly children, perished today by the burning of the steamer General Slocum ... in New York Harbour ... The annual St Mark's German Lutheran Church was proceeding to ... Long Island.'[40]

Coming just fifty pages after 'Jews ... killed the Christian boy', this New York holocaust that killed yet more Christian boys is an uncanny doubling of both holocaust past (the killing of Christ) and holocaust future (the killing of the Jews).

One holocaust is far more than enough, but, in the age of mechanical reproduction, doubling is the fate even of holocaust; the New York holocaust is itself mechanically reproduced – via telegraphy and printing press – as a Dublin newspaper report. Equally reproducible is the sacrifice, or holocaust that is the crucifixion: recall of course, Genet's 'violent ... radiographic interpretation ... of Golgotha', an interpretation that Derrida compares to placing 'relics in a kind of developing bath' (196b). Shades of Bloom's 'Easter number of *Photo Bits*' (53) – a line charged with the conceit that, in the age of photographic reproduction, Easter's body-in-bits must suffer yet another dismemberment. Indeed, reading 'Easter number of *Photo Bits*' more closely, it is as if Easter is itself a kind of photography; in which case photographic reproduction belongs to the age of the church, not vice versa. Jean-Michel Rabaté thought of that: in *The Ghosts of Modernity* he reminds us of the story of St Veronica who, meeting Jesus on his way to Golgotha, wiped his sweating face with a cloth upon which there was left an image of Christ's features.[41]

The reproductive magic of photography is, for Roland Barthes, more specifically related to Gethsemene: 'photography,' he writes, 'has something to do with resurrection.'[42] *Glas*, however, maintains the link with the crucifixion, the Golgothan holocaust. This 'blazing,' writes Derrida, 'is not yet philosophy' (242a), but it *is* photography in that a holocaust is so terrible as to demand reproduction – it *must* be remembered, *must* be reproduced. In this sense, one holocaust is *not* enough – a riddle that lies buried in Derrida's dark and difficult talk of 'a holocaust of the holocaust'. It is as if, for Derrida, any 'reflection ... of the holocaust' must be a repetition, must itself *be* a holocaust – anything else would not be faithful to the sheer awfulness of the event. In this sense, holocaust impossibilizes the whole logic of representation and verisimilitude; like *Glas*, holocaust smashes the glass, the mirror in which so much Western culture sees itself.[43]

This, though, is precisely what is believed to happen in every mass in every Catholic church in *Glas* and *Ulysses*. The magic of transubstantiation means that in breaking bread these churches break not so much a sign of Christ's holocaust-ed body but the body itself; and in pouring wine they are pouring out not just a sign of Christ's holocaust-ed blood but the blood itself. Moreover, moving still closer to Derrida's 'holocaust of a holocaust', many of the churches of *Glas* and *Ulysses* recall the Jewish burnt sacrifice with the actual burning of incense – this is, in a sense, fire for fire.

Boat

Incense is carried in a symbolic boat: Buck Mulligan's 'boat of incense' (10) or navette is, as Derrida observes, 'a small metal vessel in the form of a boat. They keep,' he adds, 'incense in it' (208a). Though it is the incense that is supposed to burn, on 16 June 1904 a German Lutheran church sets out in a boat that does itself burn; this is a church that quite literally burns its boats. But then that, in a sense, is the nature of a Lutheran church, a church that in breaking from Rome breaks from a past that, as *Ulysses* reminds us, begins at sea: as Joyce recites, 'Peter, on which rock was the holy church ... founded' is also 'he that holdeth the fisherman's seal' – 'Peter Piscator' (319–20). The church of Rome, as the church of Peter, is made in the image of a ship as well as a rock; but a ship cannot be founded on a rock, it can only founder. Once again, Derrida's prediction: 'the stone [of the church of stone] ... will give rise to another fracture, another ruin'(72a).

The church does, though, survive its own decline – *perte* ('ruin') being an anagram, or ruin of 'Peter.' In *Ulysses*, Stephen declares that 'Peter Piscator lives ... in the house that Jack built' (320); in *Glas* he lives *on* in the house that *Jacques* declares unsafe, declares a ruin – a ruin that survives to the very last line of the Hegel column: 'elle court à sa perte.'[44] Indeed, this ruin of a church is a sea-going ruin; the very last line of the Genet column ends with the word 'debris', the debris – we presume – of what Derrida has just called 'the machine ... of writing', a curious and enigmatic machine that seems to double as a ship:

> ... drop[ping] anchor and ink[ing] in another depth ... Pulleys ... greased ropes grow taut ... the breathing of slaves bent double. Good for pulling. Proofs ready for printing. The cracking whip of the first mate [*contremaitre*] ... So little would have been necessary, the slightest error of calculation ... The machine is still too simple, the pre-capitalist mode of writing.[45]

This writing-cum-printing machine that is also a kind of ship is, if anything, the publishing house of Galilee, the printing-machine that recalls the sea of Galilee – the sea that is, much earlier, punningly encoded as 'la mère galiléenne' (181b), the sea that launched the church.[46]

This final sea of *Glas* is not, though, simply a sea of faith; it is also, in a sense, 'the Atlantic Ocean' (246b). For the Genet column runs aground upon the cryptic words: 'what I had dreaded, naturally, already re-edited itself', words which seem to articulate Derrida's fear of the re-editing that is *translation* – most obviously, translation by a transatlantic press. Derrida wrote *Glas* knowing, of course, that translation into English, or rather American, was inevitable. In this sense, the ruined ship-machine of *Glas* is bound for America; so too is Derrida – the following year, 1975, he makes the first of his annual visits to Yale which, in the wake of *Glas*, inspires that dream of an infinitely playful textuality that goes by the name of American deconstruction. What the end of *Glas* seems to 'know', however, is that the late-1970s American dream of deconstruction would be a dream of a *non-simple, high*-capitalist writing-machine – a machine of infinitely moveable type that was soon to be be realized as the computerized text. This is 'known' to *Glas* if only because the sheer difficulty involved in its typesetting almost necessitates the word-processor, almost requires its invention. It is a debt that is tacitly acknowledged in 'Circumfession', the essay 'projected after *Glas*'; here Derrida makes several references to word-processing and includes a photograph of the text on the screen of his Macintosh computer.[47] To revise Hartman's claim, *Glas* is of the American house of Macintosh.

Or rather, it is of the house of *both* Galilee and Macintosh; for what we enter in *Glas* is a church that, under the impact of modernity, is so 'violently ... redistributed' as to become an anagram or, in the case of Genet, 'an overloaded telephone exchange' in which not just letters but whole 'lines [are] ... moved out of place'(169b). In *Ulysses* this dream, or nightmare, of the modern church as the very model of a crazed and infinitely flexible writing-machine is encoded in 'THE CHAPEL OF FREEMAN TYPESETTERS' (395), whose potential to make thinkable a chapel, or church, of free *type* finds comic realization in those five 'sandwichmen' whose lettered hats can spell out not only 'H.E.L.Y.S.' but every other possible combination; they are, for Bloom, a bizarre kind of priesthood: this 'procession of whitesmocked ... men [with] ... scarlet sashes ... Like that priest they are this morning' (127) – like that priest with 'Letters on his back: I.N.R.I.? No: I.H.S.' (66). In *Glas* and *Ulysses*, the ultimate writing-machine is not just high-capitalist and high-tech but high-church; at times, indeed, the machine *is* the church. Early on in *Glas* this is a bleak vision of a church that is on the side of the philosophical police:[48]

> All the police forces in the world can be routed by a surname, but even before they know it, a secret computer, at the moment of baptism, will have kept them up to date. (7b)

By the time, however, of 'Circumfession' (1991), the high-church computer is a benign and lyrical dream of a self-editing text: an 'angel,' writes Derrida, 'last night took hold of my computer, dooming once more invention to dispossession.'[49]

Something, it seems, has changed in Derrida's relation to the high-church writing-machine, the machine that *is* writing; but then, for Derrida, the very direction of writing has changed course. Whilst *Glas* is finally bound for America, 'Circumfession' is set toward Africa. Derrida is once again preoccupied with *Sa*, or rather SA – this time, though, it is not SA as in U*SA* but SA for *St* Augustine, the Algerian. Here Derrida compares his own sailing from Algiers in 1949 to the young Augustine's much earlier voyage out,[50] whilst the essay ends with a mysterious sea-voyage that, inevitably, makes as if to repeat Augustine's return to Algiers:

> ... you ... whose life will have been so short, the voyage short, scarcely organized, by you with no lighthouse and no book, you the floating toy at high tide and under the moon, you the crossing between these two phantoms of witnesses who will never come down to the same.

In relation to his first voyage, his voyage out, Derrida writes of 'seasickness bad enough to make you give up the ghost', but it seems, come the end of 'Circumfession', that the sea-going Derrida has not given up ghosts. For his ship is a ghost ship, or rather a *holy*-ghost ship – Derrida's 'phantoms of witnesses' come very close to the New Testament's 'great *cloud* of witnesses' (Heb. 12:1), the Church Invisible, or communion of saints, the sainted dead.

For Derrida, the Church Invisible will never be in*di*visible – the phantoms of witnesses will never come down to the same. For Bloom, however, they *will* – or rather we all will; regarding mortality, Bloom offers the simple sentence: 'In the same boat' (87). Bloom is certainly in a very similar boat to Homer's Ulysses, making as he does a journey home that mimics Ulysses's sea-journey back to Ithaca; but it is not the identical boat, not the same boat. Bloom is no more in precisely the same returning boat as Ulysses than Derrida is in precisely the same returning boat as St Augustine; in fact, it is the *same* difference. Ironically, Derrida and Bloom are in the same boat of not being in the same boat.

To absorb difference into a higher order of sameness is an Hegelian movement,[51] a movement which my comparative reading can never fully escape. Nor, though, can Derrida; for 'those two phantoms of witnesses who will never come down to the same' in so doing *are* – in a sense – the same, are in the same boat of *not* being the same. Derrida's boat, for all its refusal of sameness, is still in Hegelian waters – but then Derrida predicts this in *Glas* when he foresees not only 'another fracture, [and] another ruin [but also] ... another relief', another sublation, or resolution, of difference.

What *is* different at the sea-going end of 'Circumfession' is that this Hegelian relief is dramatically reworked in simple and existential terms that very precisely echo Bloom's blunt sentence: 'In the same boat'. For here, the same-in-difference phantoms of witnesses answer not to a philosophical problem but to Derrida's overwhelming human fear that he 'will never have had any witness'. This is the fear to which he confesses immediately before going on to express the conviction that, though utterly alone at sea, he *will* somehow be witnessed, seen. Though this is a 'voyage ... with ... no lighthouse and no book', and though he is but 'a floating toy at high tide', there *are* 'these ... phantoms of witnesses'.

Were it not for the Church Invisible, the church of the dead, the living would themselves, it seems, be invisible. To quote again the New Testament: 'seeing we are compassed about with so great a cloud of witnesses' *we ourselves are seen.*

Notes

1. James Joyce, *Ulysses* (Harmondsworth: Penguin, 1986 [1922]), p. 2; Jacques Derrida, *Glas*, trans. John P. Leavey and Richard Rand (Lincoln: University of Nebraska Press, 1986), p. 208b – translation modified. All subsequent references to these two texts appear parenthetically in the text; when I quote *Glas* in French the page reference is to the original edition published by Éditions Galilée in 1974.
2. Derrida returns to this connection between church and modern communication systems in *The Post Card: From Socrates to Freud and Beyond*, tr. Alan Bass (Chicago: University of Chicago Press, 1987 [1980]), p. 69.
3. 'To curse "by bell, book and candle" is to pronounce "major excommunication." The bell calls attention; the book contains the sentence to be pronounced; the candle is extinguished to symbolise the spiritual darkness into which the excommunicant is cast', Don Gifford and Robert J. Seidman, *Notes for Joyce* (New York: E.P. Ditton, 1974), p. 308.
4. Jacques Derrida, 'Circumfession', in Jacques Derrida and Geoffrey Bennington, *Jacques Derrida* (Chicago: Chicago University Press, 1993 [1991]), p. 56.
5. All references to the Bible are to the Authorised Version.
6. For full details see Herbert Thurston, S.J., *The Holy Year of Jubilee* (London: Sandsand Co., 1900).
7. Fascinating in this connection is the claim that, following the Roman jubilee of 1775, Voltaire declared, 'another such jubilee and it would be all over with philosophy' – Thurston, *The Holy Year of Jubilee*, p. 128.
8. I am writing this essay in the summer of 1999. *Glas*'s twenty-fifth anniversary inspired some to plan a whole conference at Cornell University to be held in October 1999 – unfortunately the conference never took place.
9. Translation modified
10. For further discussion of Derrida, crypts and the church, see my 'Dickens' Cryptic Church: Drawing on *Pictures from Italy*' in John Schad (ed.), *Dickens Refigured: bodies, desires, and other histories* (Manchester University Press, 1996), pp. 5–21
11. As Richard Ellmann writes, 'the name of Joyce is derived ... from the French *joyeux* and

Latin *jocax*, and Joyce ... accepted his name as an omen' – *James Joyce* (Oxford University Press, 1982), p. 12.
12 Quoted in Frank Budgen, *James Joyce and the Making of Ulysses and Other Writings* (London: Oxford University Press, 1972), p. 347.
13 *The Letters of James Joyce*, 3 vols, ed. Richard Ellmann (London: Faber and Faber, 1966), ii.196.
14 See Friedrich Nietzsche, *Twilight of the Idols / The Anti-Christ* [1895], tr. R.J. Hollingdale (Harmondsworth: Penguin, 1968).
15 See 'Plato's Pharmacy' in Jacques Derrida, *Dissemination*, tr. Barbara Johnson (London: Athlone Press, 1981 [1972]), pp. 61–172; Karl Marx, 'A Contribution to the Critique of Hegel's Philosophy of Right. Introduction.' [1843–44], in Karl Marx, *Early Writings*, tr. R. Livingstone and G. Benton (Harmondsworth: Penguin, 1975), p. 244.
16 James Fairhall, *James Joyce and the Question of History* (Cambridge: Cambridge University Press, 1993), p. 46 – the bomb was set off by a Fenian splinter group called the Dynamitards in an attempt to free imprisoned comrades from Clerkenwell Prison.
17 'That fellow' to whom Bloom refers is James Carey (1845–83), one of the Invincibles involved in the Phoenix Park murders; the Clerkenwell bomber is Joseph Casey. Although, the Catholic Church in Ireland was, on the whole, opposed to the violent republicanism of the Fenians, there were some priests who were very sympathetic – most famously, Father Lavelle – see Fairhall, *James Joyce*, pp. 129–31
18 Nietzsche, *Twilight of the Idols*, pp. 196, 191.
19 Werner Heisenberg, *Physics and Beyond: Encounters and Conversations*, tr. A.J. Pomerans (New York: Harper and Row, 1971), p. 41.
20 James Joyce, *Finnegans Wake* (Harmondsworth: Penguin, 1992 [1939]) p.225.
21 See Gillian Beer's excellent '"Wireless": Popular Physics, Radio and Modernism' in B. Spufford and J. Uglow (eds), *Cultural Babbage: Technology, Time and Innovation* (London: Faber and Faber, 1996), p. 160; and David C. Cassidy, *Uncertinty: The Life and Science of Werner Heisenberg* (New York: W.H. Freeman, 1992), p. 455.
22 Mark C. Taylor, *Tears* (Albany: SUNY Press, 1990), p. 42.
23 *James Joyce Letters*, II.195; Carla de Petris, 'Exiles or Emigrants,' in Giorgio Melchiori (ed.), *Joyce in Rome: The Genesis of Ulysses* (Rome: Bulzoni Editore, 1972), p. 80.
24 Taylor, *Tears*, p. 42
25 Jacques Derrida, 'No Apocalypse, Not Now (full speed ahead, seven missiles, seven missives)', *Diacritics* 14 (1984), pp. 26, 31, 23.
26 Quoted in Edmund White, *Genet* (London: Picador, 1993), pp. 228, 29.
27 See ibid., p. 507.
28 Jean Genet, *The Blacks: A Clown Show* [1959], tr. Bernard Frechtman (London: Faber and Faber, 1967), p. 81.
29 I refer, of course, to 'White Mythology: Metaphor in the Text of Philosophy' in Jacques Derrida, *Margins of Philosophy*, tr. Alan Bass (London: Harvester Wheatsheaf [1972] 1982); this title is, of course, given a literal, or post-colonial twist by Robert Young in his celebrated *White Mythologies: Writing History and the West* (London: Routledge, 1990).
30 See Carlo Bigazzi, 'Joyce and the Italian Press', in Melchiori, *Joyce in Rome*, p. 59.
31 The church is St Mary's Chapel of Ease (Church of Ireland) – see Gifford and Seidman, *Notes for Joyce*, p. 413.
32 Jacques Derrida, *The Gift of Death* [1992], tr. David Wills (Chicago: Chicago University Press, 1995) pp. 86, 85,
33 See, for example, Jane Gallop, *Reading Lacan* (Ithaca: New York, 1985), pp. 58–9; and Francis Fukuyama, *The End of History and the Last Man* (New York: The Free Press, 1992).

34 Bennington and Derrida, *Jacques Derrida*, p. 58
35 I refer, of course, to Swinburne's 'Hymn to Proserpine' (1867) – *The Poems of Algernon Charles Swinburne*, 6 vols (London: Chatto and Windus, 1904) 1.69; Geoffrey H. Hartman, *Saving the Text: Literature / Derrida / Philosophy* (London; John Hopkins University Press, 1981), p. 19.
36 For a very interesting discussion of the African, or Algerian Derrida see Lee Morrissey, 'Derrida, Algeria, and "Structure, Sign and Play"', <http://jefferson.village.virginia.edu/pmc/current.issue/9.2morrissey.html>
37 Quoted in Valentine Cunningham, *Everywhere Spoken Against: Dissent in the Victorian Novel* (Oxford; Clarendon Press, 1975), p. 143.
38 As Hans Kung writes, 'Nazi anti-Semitism ... would have been impossible without the preceding two thousand years of 'Christian' hostility to the Jews' – *The Church* (London: Burns and Oates, 1968), p. 137. I am very aware that to refer to the extermination of the Jews not as the Shoah but in terms of the Greco-Christian ecclesiastical notion of *to holocauston*, or burnt offering may well constitute a Christianization of the event – but that, in a sense, is precisely what I mean to do. Interestingly, Simon Critchley raises this issue specifically in relation to *Glas* – see 'A Commentary on Derrida's Reading of Hegel in Glas', *Bulletin of the Hegel Society of Great Britain* 18 (1988), p. 32, n.17.
39 Stephen refers of course to the extremely harsh camps set up during the Boer War (1899–1902) to imprison Boer civilians, including women and children – see Gifford and Seidman, *Notes for Joyce*, pp. 163–4.
40 See ibid., p. 150.
41 'If photography is both ... a resurrection and a haunting ... could we not say – as Beckett once said, jokingly – that the inventor of photograph was not Niepce or Talbot but [St] Veronica' – Jean Michel Rabaté, *The Ghosts of Modernity* (Gainesville: University Press of Florida, 1996), p. 82.
42 Roland Barthes, *Camera Lucida*, tr. Richard Howard (New York: Noonday Press, 1981), p. 82.
43 Shoshana Felman and Dori Laub explore a related question in writing of the Holocaust as 'an event without a witness' – they argue that the 'the inherently incomprehensible and deceptive psychological structure of the event precluded its own witnessing, even by its very victims' – *Testimony: Crises of Witnessing in Literature, Psychoanalysis and History* (London: Routledge, 1992), p. 80.
44 I am acutely conscious that this line constitutes a decidedly feminine ending; unfortunately, I did not feel able to develop this line of thought within the confines of this essay.
45 Translation modified.
46 *Glas* meets Christianity in the sea, there they converge; as Gayatri Chakravorty Spivak points out, in *Glas*, there is an 'expansion of ... IC (Immaculate Conception as well as Categorical Imperative) into the ego (ICH) and Christ the Fish (ICHTHYOS) – '*Glas*-Piece: A *Compte Rendu*', *Diacritics* 7 (1977) p. 27. Hartman in *Saving the Text* makes a similar point, p. 62.
47 Bennington and Derrida, *Jacques Derrida*, p. 97 – see pp. 35, 11.
48 It is this vision of the church that John D. Caputo picks up in when he writes that 'the Church ... [in the end] calls the police' – *The Prayers and Tears of Jacques Derrida: Religion without Religion* (Bloomington: Indiana University Press, 1997), p. 91.
49 Bennington and Derrida, *Jacques Derrida*, p. 238
50 Ibid., pp. 177–80.
51 As Mark C. Taylor writes, 'Hegelian philosophy can be understood as a systematic attempt to secure the identity of identity and nonidentity ... By revealing the Logos of

everything to be the logical structure of identity-in-difference, speculative philosophy is supposed to reconcile opposites without destroying difference(s)' – *Altarity* (Chicago: University of Chicago Press, 1987)

II

THE CHURCH (IN)VISIBLE

... [from] a ... subterranean church ... crowds of phantom-looking men and women ... came hobbling out.
Charles Dickens, *Pictures from Italy*

... the vastness of St Peter's ... spead ... itself everywhere like a disease of the retina.
George Eliot, *Middlemarch*

... here public openness is ... lacking; the hole-and-corner, the dark chamber is Christian.
Friedrich Nietzsche, *Twilight of the Idols*

Fatherhood ... is mystical estate, an apostolic succession ... [o]n that mystery and not on the madonna ... the church is founded.
James Joyce, *Ulysses*

... the post office is a church in which street rendez-vous are given, Notre Dame on Sunday afternoon in the crowd.
Jacques Derrida, *The Post Card*

Chapter 4

The Matter of Faith: Incarnation and Incorporation in Tennyson's *In Memoriam*

Julian Wolfreys

> The extraordinary pun of 'incorporate' [in *In Memoriam*] ... yields an opposite but reciprocal meaning, moving from the bodiless to the bodily ...
> Isobel Armstrong, *Victorian Poetry*

> That in all ages, individuals who have directed their meditations and their studies to the nobler characters of our nature, to the cultivation of these powers and instincts which constitute the man...and distinguish the nobler from the animal part of his own being, will be led by the *supernatural* in themselves to the contemplation of a power which is likewise super-*human*; that science, and especially moral science, will lead to religion and remain blended with it
> Samuel Taylor Coleridge, On the Constitution of the Church and State

When considering the *matter* of faith, Tennyson's relationship to the conventions of Christianity in *In Memoriam*[1] is revealed as being both complex and complexly encrypted. Articulated through irregular and intermittent, though frequently recurring, tropes, Tennyson's discourse on Christianity and his personal negotiation between the systems of Broad Church belief and Christian Typology on the one hand, and his own highly idiosyncratic comprehension of the nature of faith and belief on the other resists as much as it encourages inquiry and analysis. Yet, in Tennyson's 'imaginative act of mourning',[2] peopled and figured by countless phantoms, not only are the various tropes by which faith is expressed endless substitutions for one another; every trope is supplemented within itself. Becoming other, tropes trope themselves, to the extent that one cannot speak with any confidence of originary figures from which troping is an act of transfiguration.

As one such trope, faith is never simply faith in the possibility of the representation of Christ and thus a figure for such representation. Nor is it a controlling trope, a centre around which all other figures orbit. The poet resists the normative grounding of faith in orthodox, church-sponsored representations of Christ, and thereby a lapse into unthinking acceptance. In doing so, he struggles to come to terms with the appropriate language for, as Kant puts it, 'a faith that ought to represent what God is in himself' in an onto-theological consideration of being which maintains both mystery and revelation: 'A little flash, a mystic hint'(XLIV.8).[3] What becomes apparent in reading the indirect embodiment of Christ and Christian faith in the poem through lines such as the one just quoted is that one would be more accurate in speaking of Tennyson's faith as the manifestation of an apophatic discourse driven by a poetics of difference and non-synonymous substitution. In the context of Christian faith, such a poetics becomes discernible in the text as a constant pre-phenomenal marking, whereby faith is articulated through an implicit comprehension of the immanence of incarnation everywhere, yet impossible to represent.

Religious truth, as a matter of faith, and as Isobel Armstrong correctly asserts, is then only ever '"darkly" or obscurely apprehended'.[4] *In Memoriam*'s faith is made manifest through indirection, processes of archival memorialization, anamnesis[5] and a specifically Christian 'analogy of apperception or appresentation',[6] rather than through conventional or canonical Christological modes of representation predicated on the promise of presence or the locatability of some logocentric origin which will either return or to which we will return. To qualify this, however: it is not a matter of dialectical choice in Tennyon's verse, it is not a question of, on the one hand, representation and mimesis, or, on the other, the analogy of apperception or appresentation. Instead, the analogical and apophatic is the apparitional other incorporated and incarnated within Tennyson's borrowings from conventional Christological representation and theological discourse.

Tennyson's is not, though, a negative theology, despite the fact that so many of the lyrics proceed by negation. Indeed, given the poet's resistance to and distrust of philosophical systems, it cannot, properly speaking, be described as a theology at all. Donald Hair has remarked that 'Tennyson's faith [is] unsystematic', while William Brashear, on the same subject, argues for a 'non-rational' articulation of faith: 'The truth would seem that Tennyson "would not formulate" his creed, because he had no creed that could be conceptualized or reduced to principles.'[7] At best, Tennyson's faith is expressed through something like a quasi-theology which comes from within and yet exceeds theology in its comprehension of the limits of language to express the unknown, the other, and to allow the other to manifest itself as a haunting spirit through a language expressing the limit. Of negation, Elaine Jordan suggests that the poem is 'perversely rich in negative qualifiers – nameless, fruitless, countless, sightless'.[8] Thus, negation is not merely denial, it is also the marking of boundary in language, and to which language can go. There are limits, after all, to what can be expressed in words: 'But there is more than I can see/And what I see I leave unsaid' (LXXIV.9–10); 'I leave thy praises unexpress'd ... I leave thy greatness to be guess'd' (LXXV.13,16). Words halt on the brink of representation, choosing instead to bear witness to the unrepresentable as that which is other. Thus the poet halts, saying that he cannot say. *In Memoriam*, we can see, is a fragmented, self-fragmenting text which seeks to find ways of speaking the word of God indirectly, and attempting to do so, what is more, through the constant recourse to the spectral undecidability which haunts even the most assured figures of speech pertaining to the matter of faith, as though speech were itself the constant remarking of the border of apperception. Admitting that one cannot see, that one cannot put into words what one can see, and that one's responsibility is to leave 'unexpress'd' and 'to be guess'd' is to articulate one's faith absolutely and in other words; it is to give oneself over to the incorporate, immanent spirit within which one dwells and which haunts one from within and which yet is to come.

Tennyson makes this clear in the following qualification: 'No visual shade of some one lost,/But he, the Spirit himself, may come' (XCIII.5-6). The distinction is made between the ghost and the spirit, though not explained. At most, one might comprehend the limit at which Tennyson speaks through a fragmenting temporality within the line. The ghost, the revenant, is not our concern here, Tennyson tells us. That is merely the phenomenal, anthropomorphized (and therefore normalized) representation of 'some one' returning from the past. The Spirit is different from the ghost in that it is remarked as the haunting possibility of something other which may or may not make itself apparent, from a temporal moment to come. The analogy of apperception makes the two forms of haunting distinct, broken off from one another by the play on similarity or resemblance which is itself negated as the limit of representation, and further disjointed through the temporal distinction formally marked between the two lines. And the distinction, the fragmentation, is enforced further in that implicit rejection of what may be seen in favour of what may be hoped for, or, in other words, that possibility, the articulation of which expresses faith.

The fragmented condition of the poem extends from its verse organization and subject, to its syntax, and is observed by a number of critics.[9] Its concomitant resistance to readerly unity is, I would suggest, Tennyson's formal recognition that one cannot come face to face with God, but must articulate the incarnation of Christ indirectly (as in the lines just considered), and always in terms which promise to give way to the trace of alterity or haunting in the moment of their utterance. Analogy is, again, one particular modality for allowing the spectral operation its play, as we have seen and will consider further. To quote Donald Hair on this, whose reading is developed from the very ecclesiastical source of Bishop Butler's theory of analogy:

> [the] theory rests upon the assumptions that language and nature are analogous because both proceed from God; that nature gives imperfect evidence of providence; that language is likewise ambiguous and inadequate; and that these inadequacies in both nature and language make necessary our judgement, which sorts out degrees of probability where clear and unequivocal evidence is not to be had. Such assertions of probability are statements of faith.[10]

However, faith itself, to be faith, has also to be spirited away from within itself if it is to operate for Tennyson within the ruined structure of *In Memoriam*.

It therefore seems necessary to pause momentarily to make the following claim: while faith is the principal focus of this essay, it is not to be mistaken as some metaphysical guarantor, the figure *par excellence* of figurality and tropological play in *In Memoriam* any more than are the names of either Arthur Hallam or Christ for that matter. To allow this implication to remain unchallenged would be to place the reading of the poem back into the search for a centre or unifying principle which would, in turn, arrest the 'instrumental possibility of [the] production'[11] of faith's fragmentary revelation *and* mystery. As we have said, faith is but one of many figures which operate the troping machinery of the text according to a paradoxical 'disseminating fission' peculiar to the 'spectral motif'[12] and the spectral logic of which the figure of faith is exemplary. It is possible only to name some of these tropological devices at this point: haunting, light, illumination, dust, veil, ghosts, phantoms, flashes, spirit, spectre, love, tract, type. None of these remain stable in Tennyson's use, even as they all serve in the illumination of faith, even as they enlighten the reader as to faith's power to illuminate, addressing also faith's spectrality and the ghostly effects of incarnation, whereby, paradoxically, it is precisely as a matter of haunting that Christ comes to be embodied through the poet's attention to faith and love. (It is no accident that 'the dark church [is] like a ghost' (LXVIII.15))

This essay concerns itself, then, with certain tensions pertaining to matters of Christianity and theological discourse as these operate in *In Memoriam* in general, and, specifically, through the troping of faith. Such tensions are readable, arguably, not simply as those of Alfred Tennyson, as the working through of personal grief, following the death of Arthur Hallam. Rather, they are tensions peculiar to matters of representation and its limits in the context of early nineteenth-century Christianity. Such tensions are installed throughout *In Memoriam* and are irreducible to a unified semantic or theological horizon concerning the question of Christian belief or the role and parameters of either Christian typology or Christology in early Victorian England. Being irreducible – and, often, irreconcilable or otherwise paradoxical – such discursive and philosophical tensions open within the poem itself, as both a necessary condition of its structures and the aporetic trace which is conventionally termed 'doubt' in criticism of the poem, the reading of which has been determined in large part throughout the twentieth century by T.S. Eliot's comment on the poem that 'Its faith is a poor thing, but its doubt is a very intense experience.'[13]

Things are not so unequivocal. Although the poet's 'prospect and horizon' (XXXVIII.4) has vanished, there remains a 'doubtful gleam of solace' in the songs he loves to sing. It is significant in the context of Tennysonian tropes relating to the question of faith that the adjectival form ('doubtful') modifies, and is modified by, a questionable illumination ('gleam'), which is both figurative *and* literal. While the effect of the line is to put doubt into doubt even as it is expressed, the undecidability of the figure puts into doubt the certainty of the reading to decide how the trope's movement may be calmed. Elsewhere 'doubt' is again related to the disappearance of light, a conventional enough Christian configuration for the loss of faith (XLI.19; XCV.49). Yet this is rendered complicated by the repeated insistence on the spectrality of doubt. We read of 'a spectral doubt' (XLI.19), the 'slender shade of doubt' (XLVIII.7) and 'doubts', we are told, are 'spectres of the mind' (XCVI.13,15). Doubt is therefore doubtful and difficult to read. What is interesting in these figures is that the phantom of doubt arises from within the subject, illuminated as it were by the disappearance of light, whether literal or metaphorical (or both simultaneously). Doubt's intimate relationship with illumination and haunting is traced in the second of the three quotations, not in the figure of doubt itself but in the play in the word 'shade', suggestive of both shadows and ghosts. However, the play does not stop in this oscillation. Shade and its cognate shadow are used by Tennyson as poetic terms for spectres (XXII, XXIII, XXX, XXXIII, XCIII), as euphemistic projections of Death (already spirited as an anthropomorphic trope haunting the poet (XXXV, LXVII, LXXIV)). They are, furthermore, haunted internally, by that which is cast through illumination, a graduated darkness appearing, so to speak, as a result of light. All of which is to cast a shadow on the unequivocal projection of doubt as that which is absolutely distinguishable from faith. Light and shade are both the orbs of the 'Strong Son of God, immortal love,' as the 'Prologue' informs us; they inform and *incorporate* one another. So too, doubt is cognate with faith and not its polar opposite.

Tennyson makes this plain when he remarks: 'There lives more faith in honest doubt,/ Believe me, than in half the creeds' (XCVI.11–12). Faith is incorporate: a spectral figure without presence, it nonetheless *lives on*, incarnate in doubt itself. And this is a *matter* of faith ('Believe me'). Faith persists uncannily in the articulation of doubt with more vitality than in any theological system or programme. Tennyson's affirmation of doubt is also, at the same time, an affirmation of faith, of faith in doubt and faith in faith's immanence in the manifestation of doubt. To go back to the argument concerning Tennyson's tropes, then, doubt does not in itself offer some metaphysical or logocentric valence, albeit of a negative kind, as Eliot's reading implies, nor is it separable from faith. It is, once more, one rhetorical and tropological figure among others by which Tennyson maintains the tensions of the text in his consideration of being, and in the disruption implicit between transformation and transcendence (translation as opposed to sublation), and between a personal a-systematic expression of belief ('There lives more faith in honest doubt') and a more conventional Christian metaphysics of Broad Church discourse. There is in Tennyson's figures the reading of faith's survival as a process of transformations *within* and perhaps even *despite* systems predicated on metaphysics.

The tension between translation and transcendence which opens onto the aporia of faith can be read in the second epigraph, above, from Samuel Taylor Coleridge.[14] Coleridge's language is marked, albeit indirectly, by the onto-theological concerns to which I will have recourse to allude with regard to *In Memoriam*. Coleridge addresses the transcendent possibility of 'man' while locating this *supernatural* spectre *in themselves*. There is thus described a transition which is both sublation – the elevation of 'man' – and incarnation as haunting – the *supernatural*. However, this movement is also partly circular, or perhaps more accurately, reiterative. For where this leads is 'to religion' while 'moral science' will 'remain *blended* with religion' (emphasis added). The imagined Coleridgean notion is internally disturbed within itself, its transcendent promise interrupted by a translation not necessarily figured by transcendence (even while the translation-effect is inscribed specifically within the metaphysical horizon), and this internal crossing, from one state to another, is also a blending, a moment of incarnation. This double movement is described by Tennyson in the poem as 'the same, but not the same' (LXXXVII.14). Coleridge's 'cultivation' of the 'nobler characters of our nature' anticipates and finds its echo in Tennyson's assessment of the progression of humankind, which moves 'from more to more' (CXVIII.17).

However, Tennyson is not content to offer one such echo. Instead, he takes this formula ('from more to more', 'from man to man' (Prologue.25, 35); 'from world to world' (XXI.19); 'from high to higher' (XLI.2); 'from high to higher' (XLIV.14); 'from marge to marge' (XLVI.7); 'from state to state' (LXXII.6); 'from theme to theme' (LXXXIX .33); 'From form to form' (CXXIII.6), 'from place to place' (CXXVI.10)) as a transformative trope which, reworked some thirty or more times, incorporates not only the human condition, but also refigures itself as the articulation of belief in natural, spatial, geographical, geological, intellectual, temporal and mortal transition, establishing as it does so a figurative echolalia of faith's faith in that which is simultaneously unrepresentable, unprogrammable and yet which is immanent in all forms, all phenomena.

Furthermore, these reiterated figures, which establish a performative technicity resistant to any but the most basic systematization, recirculate, redouble and move elsewhere. They speak to a constant disinterrance within the same while remaining outside any properly formalizable apprehension. Can we say, for instance, that the speculation on metaphysical transfer has anything other than a syntactical resemblance to the temporal movement from one year to the next, or the passage from one country to another? And is there not in this figural play an echo or reiteration, albeit of a wholly different kind, of the rhythm and movement of the abba rhyme scheme? To put this another way, is not Tennyson's most profound expression of the transition of humankind to be found in the most basic structural device of the poem as a whole, a rhythmic device which, in seeming to turn back upon itself, initiates and is part of a movement? And is this motion both the figure of apparent unity and closure, while also being, paradoxically, that which maintains a poetry of fragments, in ruins, resistant to a greater unity? There is, however, another way to comprehend the double work of this figure, a doubling which interrupts any straightforwardly discernible structure. 'From _ to _ ' is marked by, and remarks, both spatial and temporal transition, regardless of what comes to fill those blank spaces. We read the implication of a motion from one place, one event, one condition, state of being or emotion to another. We also read temporal transition, inasmuch as, conventionally speaking, one may be said to move from the past to the future. Yet the phrases cited, and those which are not, all complete the phrase by a kind of figural palindrome, so that the motion appears to recirculate, to return to its beginning point, to disrupt and thus paradoxically double itself in its own process. This brings me back to the analogy of apperception or appresentation, that troping wherein is figured 'the same, but not the same'.

Of analogy, Elaine Jordan remarks: '*In Memoriam* works by metaphysical analogies between the human, the divine and the natural – analogies which it does not trust except as a way of working, of keeping going. Metaphysical imaginations of what an individual's state might be after death are matched by a material psychological account of how an individual self is acquired through language.'[15] Jordan's epistemological model of analogical replacement and re-presentation addresses what Armstrong calls 'the constant flux of displacement', that interminable work of mourning *and* faith through deferral, relay, and reiteration. Where Jordan's argument is problematic is in her assumption that the work of analogy is the expression of a lack of trust in the analogy. Tennyson works with analogy, and from within the metaphysics of Broad Church analogical convention, but he strives for a more radical process of analogy which moves expression of faith 'beyond the bounds of Christian orthodoxy',[17] which struggle is itself the dim comprehension of the materiality of language and its limits; the understanding, to cite Armstrong once more, that '"man" is not only a phantasmal classification of "artificial signs" but the very arbitrariness of those signs ensures their instability and collapse.'[18] The only way to work with and in response to this 'collapse' – a collapse, we would suggest, which marks not Tennyson's poem so much as the more conventional, supposed, Victorian crisis of faith – is to put the signs to work in another way, or to put both other signs and the other within the signs to work in the performative expression of faith in the onto-theological persistence of being. The metaphysics of being is still readable, but it is a metaphysics of ruins and in ruins. Such a metaphysics is more appropriate to the analogy of apperception.

Tennyson's employment of analogy as an onto-theologically informed modality is the formal taking place of opening oneself to revelation, to a thinking of God. But, it must be insisted, it is a thinking otherwise. It is an attempt to think the other, the other thought of the other, from within, and as the sign of the limit of ecclesiastical articulations of Christian belief and the representations by which it functions. Like Kant, Tennyson finds it necessary 'to deny *knowledge*, in order to make room for *faith*'.[19] In this, what I have called Tennyson's 'quasi-theology' might also be understood as a non-metaphysical theology, inasmuch as *In Memoriam* relies on the possibility of thinking Christ and God while rejecting the possibility that either can be known. Doubt, as we have seen, is not doubt concerning God or Christ as such, but is that which clears the ground for such a possibility. Analogy maintains the opening, through the various replacements and displacements signalled in the syntax of the 'From _ to _ ' formula. There are two further points to be made about this 'formula of transition', one formal, the other onto-theological.

Metaphysical analogy is reliant on 'a metaphoric transfer of predicates from one subject to another', as Kevin Hart reminds us.[20] Each of the figures bound within the formula of transition addresses, often in the most indirect of analogies, the possible resemblance, the family likeness between humans and Christ, a resemblance which relies on anthropo- and theomorphic counter-incarnation, or the immanence of this possibility. Each figure is thus invested with the possibility of a reading which is, in the words of Werner Hamacher, 'still not yet what it already is'.[21] (This, we might also say, is applicable to an understanding of Tennyson's rhyme scheme, wherein the apparent hermeneutic circle implied in the pattern, offering to represent the connection of *arché* with *telos*, also, always already, opens itself out, disjointing its own completion.) Yet, we can only read the process of analogy indirectly through the basic formal resemblance which its reiteration makes possible. The formula of transition is but one example of what Alan Sinfield describes as 'repetition with difference', which, he adds, 'is the primary strategy of the incremental structure of *In Memoriam*'.[22] This analogical formula is performative in that it builds as it reiterates, and yet resists unity and coherence. The 'building' if it can be called this, is already disrupted by the dissimilarity on which it also relies. There is none but the most basic structural similarity between 'from state to state' or 'from place to place' and 'From flower to flower, from snow to snow' (XXII.4) or 'From April to April'

(XXII.7). Nor could one draw out distinctly that which echoes from these lines to 'From orb to orb, from veil to veil' (XXX.28).

Furthermore, because the terms by which the transitional motion is mapped are without exception the same, a kind of palindromic mapping as we have already suggested, we must ask precisely what increment or transformation can be said or read to take place? How are we to read the difference in 'Spirit to Spirit, Ghost to Ghost' (XCIII.8)? Clearly there is the question of difference at work, however displaced, but in this the analogy operates by apperception rather than direct representation. There is, once again, a comprehension of that which is the same, but not the same. Formally, therefore, Tennyson's reiterations constitute a prephenomenal marking, a material remarking of the text's and language's materiality.[23] Such a materiality belongs to the condition of apophatic discourse signalling the alterity of Christ *incorporate*, while forestalling a fall into anthropomorphism, the lapse that *is*, of course, the official version of incarnation, typical of Victorian Christology. Faith 'calls for another syntax', to use a phrase of Derrida's. Repetition, reiteration and materiality belong to that syntax, in that they precede and exceed 'even the order of predicative discourse'[24] and yet are also distinguishable from a purely negative discourse in the maintenance of a material sublime on the basis of inscription. Incarnation through the acoherence of Tennyson's analogy of apperception constitutes an interruption of received narratives *qua* incorporation of the spirit. The performative materiality of reiteration effects appropriation *and* effacement, as the very alterity and sublime ineffability of Christian faith. Tennyson's tropology becomes irreversibly performative, once perceived in its material efficacy; in doing so, it re-marks itself precisely as that which cannot close itself off and which cannot be closed off through a reading of the tropological as a governable system. 'From _ to _' names this constant transference while it also enacts the motion, and thus gives expression to faith in that which cannot be represented. Tennyson's twisting of analogy is always a performative enunciation of faith in that it attests to the sublime as 'a different order of experience'[25] even as it resists efforts to represent the unrepresentable. Thus, in attending to the materiality of the text through its most fundamental formal properties, Tennyson opens the text for the incarnation of the other.

The formal operation of the material marking of the text also constitutes an effort to prevent a fall into what Kant describes as a vulgar mode of analogy, 'when God is thought of in human shape'.[26] However, in thinking God, Kant remarks that analogy is indispensable. The danger is that the process of analogy, in becoming a process of what he calls '*object-determination* (as a means of expanding our cognition)', is precisely the lapse into anthropomorphism.[27] In employing analogy, Kant warns, we must never 'infer by analogy that what pertains to the sensible must also be attributed to the supersensible'.[28] Anthropomorphism, in the Kantian scheme, is no analogy at all. There is thus a radical separation between like and like, an ineradicable difference by which analogy may be made and yet which cannot be rendered as a unity. Later, as an example of 'sublime analogy', whereby the truth is perceived while the mystery of the divine is maintained in the perception, Kant has occasion to refer to Newton's representation of gravity 'as if it were the divine presence in appearance' with the *caveat* that 'this is not an attempt to explain it.' We are involved in an ethical duty, Kant suggests, the obligation to which 'lies outside the bounds of all our insight'.[29] The thinking of God belongs to the Kantian category of *anthropomorphismus subtilis* in the consideration of onto-theology, 'where human perfections are ascribed to God but without separating the limitations from them'.[30] It is better, says Kant, 'not to be able to represent something at all than only to be able to think of it confused with errors'.[31] Tennyson's formal materiality recognizes the lapsarian dangers attendant in matters of belief, and so the material marking of the text seeks to affirm the sublime through a resistance to the coherence of anthropomorphic or theomorphic representation, in particular any official, ecclesiastical version of incarnation.

One last example of the Kantian propositions readable in Tennyson: the first verse of Lyric CXXIV, which might be read as simply what Tennyson calls 'A contradiction on the tongue' (CXXV.4):

That which we dare invoke to bless;
   Our dearest faith; our ghastliest doubt;
   He, They, One, All; within, without;
The Power in darkness whom we guess;

The structural symmetry of the punctuation both within and across lines halts as much as it impels, making the verse forbidding, and yet a material manifestation of faith. The punctuation also follows the rhyme scheme, so that lines 1 and 4 and 2 and 3 are marked in the same fashion, the former with the single semi-colon as end-stop, the latter doubling the diaeresis. Such division and discontinuity is also inscribed in the semantic tensions of the verse. That which we 'invoke' is that at which we can only guess, given its invisibility. 'It' is thus both what is dearest *and* ghastliest, faith *and* doubt, both within *and* without. The verse thus incorporates its figures, each into the other, in a paradoxical enfolding, which yet works through the maintenance of separation and discontinuity, rather than through the positive process of identificatory equivalence. The materiality of the verse performs what it wishes to express, revealing in the process the mystery of faith while maintaining that enigma through sublime analogy. Faith is taken as greater faith in not appearing to appeal to reason.

Faith is not coherent then, it never can be. Being nothing as such, and yet, strictly speaking, not being *nothing*, faith is phantomatic. Neither there nor not there faith persists. One can never speak of faith singular. Always in ruins, already fragmentary, faith returns and recedes, its traces everywhere. Faith, furthermore, in having no single definition, cannot by definition be defined, for every instance of faith will necessarily differ from every other. Faith thus maintains itself and its precarious possibility by always already having moved on, by having spirited itself into an other manifestation, whereby faith is recognized in the ghostly embodied fragment of the articulation of belief: '... we, that have not seen thy face,/By faith, and faith alone, embrace, /Believing where we cannot prove' (Prologue.2–4). Embodying and even, as the poet puts it, embracing contradiction (the absence of proof is taken as 'proof', if not of Christ, but faith's faith in the other's revenance), faith, distinguished from knowledge in what Eleanor Bustin Mattes describes as a 'Kantian-Coleridgean distinction',[32] appears as the result of illumination and as illumination itself, illumination of faith illuminating itself from within the darkness that we name doubt, and which, mistakenly, we believe to be separate from faith, not a necessary precursor or condition for the ghostly revenance of faith.[33] This is made apparent in James R. Kincaid's symmetrical comments. Kincaid first remarks that 'faith lives in and is assured by doubt.' Later, he inverts this, in a manner appropriate to Tennyson's own troping displacements, suggesting that 'doubt is contained within faith.' Such a commentary on the intimate interconnectedness of faith and doubt and their mutual and reciprocal cross-incorporation – the one as the ghost of the other – is pertinent to Tennysonian quasi-theological tropology and anticipates the reciprocity and deconstructive iterability pertaining to incarnation.

Kincaid's fleeting analysis illustrates Tennyson's understanding of, on the one hand, the immanent power of tropes when one opens oneself to Tennyson's radical version of their fundamental instability, and on the other, the necessity of being open to such oscillation if one is to recognize faith as the *arrivant*. Tennyson, it can be suggested, comprehends and reveals repeatedly to both himself and the reader that what haunts him is not Arthur Hallam, nor the possible loss of Christ, but faith itself, as phantom or phantasm, as Phosphor (IX.10; CXXI.9). Jacques Derrida has remarked on the haunting figure of light, and the connection between light and the phantom, or phantasm articulated in the Greek *Phos* (the root, meaning light or illumination, is common to each of the terms, implicated as it is in *phainesthai*, *phantasma*); for Derrida, phantasm – in the context of theological discourse – is that which institutes an originary taking place and which, '*commands or begins discourse and takes the initiative in general ... in the discourses of revelation ... or of a revealability*'.[34] Like faith and doubt, illumination and haunting are closely, intimately, interwoven, the one in the other, neither having precedence, and both appearing with such frequency throughout *In Memoriam*, always in terms of faith.

It is for this reason that the troping of light, enlightenment, illumination, plays such an important part in *In Memoriam*. Yet light is not stable. Not only does it come and go, it is also always different from itself. There is, for example, the 'Calm and still light on yon great plain' (XI.10). Is this literal, a simple moment of descriptive narration? A manifestation of the pathetic fallacy in the context of the lyric? Perhaps – but then we read, 'O Father touch the east, and light/The light that shone when Hope was born' (XXX.31–2). There is clearly a discernible trembling between the certainties of literal and metaphorical. God the father brings illumination of a spiritual (metaphorical, figural) nature through the touch, but the touch is already refigured as the literal rising of the sun in the east. Thus the spiritual illumination, given momentary personification in the figure of the father, is overwritten, even as it overwrites, in a process which makes undecidable a reading of the figure of light as either straightforwardly literal *or* figural. Across the lines the two instances of light suggest how the figure of light is doubled from within itself. Light illuminates its tropological processes. Then there is that light in which 'We lose ourselves' (XLVII.16), which is the same, but not the same as 'my light' which 'is low' (L.1). The former is the Spirit, while the latter is the spirit; the one haunts the other, and it is through the ghost of a chance that difference maintains itself and is barely perceived. What the troping of light illuminates is undecidability, transference and recurrence. Yet faith is, arguably, discernible, if we comprehend to what extent the poem relies on the tropological pushing at the limit of language in the service of a radicalized incarnation.

Figural recurrence is remarked especially in relation to the subject's reflection upon himself and the embodiment of the disembodied other – whether we momentarily bring such a figure to rest in the desired image of either Arthur Hallam or Christ – through the constant return of faith as that which haunts subjectivity as the spectral possibility of an onto-theology, the incorporation of all beings into a Being to come or, as Tennyson has it, 'to be' (XXVI.12; CIII.35; CVI.32; CXVI.16; CXXIX.9). The return of the deferred temporal horizon – where, in destabilizing substitutions, 'indifference', 'that great race', 'Christ', 'some strong bond', and the 'Strange friend', refigure the spectral event – intimates the haunting to-come as the event of Christian incarnation within the poetic subject.[35] Michael Wheeler, who suggests that the hope for 'the Christ that is to be' reflects 'the Johanine emphasis upon incarnation in the poem', has argued that Tennyson, developing a 'theomorphic conception of man in the poem' developed from Coleridge, Maurice, Jowett, and, of course, Hallam, saw the question of Christianity in terms of a 'future state, grounded in possibilities, rather than demonstrations or proofs'.[36] Yet the movement of incorporation we are reading in the various exchanges and reiterations of 'to be' are not merely the expression of a metaphysical hope, the desire for a future transcendence as the horizon of faith; nor is this simply a one-way spiritual street. For, as we witness, and as the poet bears witness throughout *In Memoriam*, incarnation, the spectral manifestation of Christ incorporate, always already takes place in an untimely fashion.

For example, the line 'Strange friend, past, present, and to be' is haunted within itself by a destabilizing structural anachrony of dislocation, displacement and redoubling of the friend whose uncanny quality is precisely that of revenance as the incarnation of faith. The ghostly figure of the 'Strange friend' might be stabilized momentarily by reading it as the ghost of Arthur Hallam. However – and this is typical of *In Memoriam's* continuous process of iteration and doubling, where figures are, to use Tennyson's phrase once again, 'the same, but not the same' (LXXXVII.14) – Lyric CXXIX never names Hallam. Instead it partakes of the euphemistic apperception of Christ typical of Broad Church representation, speaking of the 'Dear friend' and the 'Dear Heavenly friend' (1,7). Yet, if the verse does indeed partake of the 'eternal present of Victorian hymnody',[37] it is precisely the ghostly persistence and the polytemporal trace of the 'Strange Friend' which disrupts and makes discontinuous, if not impossible, the very idea of an eternal present which is not fractured from within itself by the constant recurrence of spectral anachrony. At the same time, the quality of strangeness renders strange the humanizing impulse behind the figure of the 'friend'. Tennyson's faith requires that he open himself and remain open to receive the spectre with hospitality; strangeness however estranges and thereby resists any inclination to anthropomorphic slippage. Thus a phantomatic force is idiosyncratically installed within early Victorian convention. Of course, as a strategy of normalization, critics have argued that Hallam figures in the poem as an incarnation of Christ, that he serves also as an androgynous figure for the typically Victorian representation of the androgynous or feminized Christ, and thus is composed by Tennyson according to conventional nineteenth-century Christological patterns.[38]

While this may be true in part, there is still to be read in this representation a resistance to representation of any one figure or a possible stability of representation. The play between the ecclesiatical conventions of hymnody and the intimate appeal to the personal installs an irresolvable aporetic tension. The aporia opens through the stanza's transformative play: between, implicitly, Arthur and Christ, and, explicitly, 'human' and 'heavenly' (6, 7); transition or translation also is to be read between 'far' and 'near' (2), the instances of 'past, present, and to be', and the image of the poet's dream in which he 'mingle[s] all the world in thee' (12), a line which actually inverts incarnation. The line of Lyric CXXIX which most forcefully performs the taking place of figural disfiguration is that which begins the second of the three verses: 'Known and unknown; human, divine' (5). Tennyson insists on the paradoxical, unending cross-incorporation and counter-incarnation between figures, and does so in the lyric temporally and spatially. He does so, moreover, in a manner which indirectly reveals, yet again, the limits of Broad Church representation (implicitly but particularly in relation to the limits of Christological imagery and the representation of Christ's body), while refusing any stable location or privileged position. Thus the articulation of faith works performatively through the visible mutability of the figural architecture of the lyric. Faith is articulated through the subject's ability to let go of the stabilizing referent or image, while at the same time saying – to whom? Christ? Hallam? – 'Mine, mine, for ever, ever mine' (8). If the friend is strange, this response, riddled with proprietorial desire, the formal reiteration of which hints that it will never be completed, is equally strange. It resembles nothing so much as a palindrome in ruins. It almost completes itself, it seems to promise a structural symmetry; however, haunted by a loss which its reiterations seek to deny, it remains incomplete, breaking up into its own fragments. Finally, with regard to Lyric CXXIX and the undecidability regarding the 'Strange friend', it should be noted that the unidentifiable figure who haunts this verse is 'Loved deeplier, darklier understood' (10) . Recalling the 'Prologue', it should be remembered that both 'love' and 'darkness', unstable figures in themselves which recur throughout *In Memoriam*, are intimately enfolded into the question of faith.

There is, then, always a reciprocal reiterative experience at work in the poem, albeit as a series of discontinuous events which are neither wholly singular nor wholly programmed or systematic, and yet lawlessly partake of the singular and the systematic. While the Son of God may be refigured as love, love, like faith, is never defined or stable. And neither is darkness, which, as with so many other figures in the poem is at times apparently literal, while at others seemingly metaphorical, and, occasionally and disconcertingly, both. Once more, it is important to note how such distinctions themselves (the reading of a figure as unequivocally 'literal' or 'metaphorical') refuse to remain in place and belong to the more general sense of discontinuity and disruption. Thus Tennyson's language operates constantly through transformation, translation and disinterrance, in a continuous process of crossing and dissolution of boundaries, whether these belong to subjectivity, time, or as the translation of Christ into love attests, the conventional comprehension of Christianity itself. Hence, to reiterate, the haunted nature of faith, a figure which, despite the modest poverty in which it is presented by Tennyson in what is conventionally called the 'Prologue', exceeds itself throughout *In Memoriam*, and thus remains difficult to comprehend in its true light.

What is revealed in *In Memoriam* is, then, revelation itself, revelation in other words and not as representation or the manifestation of some simple, or simply determinable, anterior presence, originating authority, empirical proof or truth belonging to or otherwise authorizing or guaranteeing 'little systems' (Prologue.17). To cite Michael Wheeler again, 'Like Coleridge, Tennyson was weary of Christian evidences.'[39] For such evidential, church-sponsored truth would not be that which is revealed but, instead, knowledge, and knowledge, Tennyson confidently informs us, is empirically grounded, it is 'of things we see' (Prologue.22). *In Memoriam* therefore struggles with the very grounds of any official, ecclesiastical Christology which implicitly operates through mimesis. Faith, on the other hand, is precisely that which 'we cannot know' (Prologue.21). The impossibility of knowledge concerning the 'Strong Son of God, immortal Love' (Prologue.1), is exactly the precondition of faith. Faith, like the son of God, cannot be represented because it is not available to sight, it is incorporate, and as already suggested, never single. It is no accident that the 'single church [is]/ ... folded in the mist' (CIV.3–4), folded double as it were. And, as if to make this point as clearly as possible, Tennyson opens the poem with the line just quoted, whereby, through a process of translation, Christ is *dis*embodied in being named 'immortal Love'. Here there is no body of Christ. Thus, from coming to terms with the impossibility of Christological representation, faith grows. It is invisible and yet illuminates, a light emanating from the Son of God as a 'beam in darkness' (Prologue.24). Moreover, in recognizing this, we apprehend how not only is Christ Love, but also illumination. Love illuminates. Christ illuminates, but faith also illuminates, and what it brings to light is the light of the other. Such enlightenment, while coming from an other place, comes from and dwells within. What therefore must be negotiated through the revelation of faith-as-incarnation is a kind of spectral onto-theology which, to paraphrase and cite Derrida on onto-theology, is that which dismisses or rejects religion as a 'little system', the 'petty cobwebs we have spun' (CXXIV.8), while, paradoxically, it is that which also 'perhaps ... informs ... the theological and ecclesiastical, even religious, development of faith'.[40]

So, in conclusion, to return to the 'Prologue', to its opening line: 'Strong Son of God, immortal love'. As Michael Wheeler and Donald Hair have pointed out, the image of God as love is taken by Tennyson from Arthur Hallam's *Theodicaea Novissima*, an essay first read by Hallam to the Cambridge Apostles in 1831, and in which Hallam both configures God as Love and associates love with incarnation.[41] It has been the case, generally, that Tennyson's 'Prologue', written after the rest of *In Memoriam* in 1849, as is well known, is regarded as a somewhat conventional gesture towards the institutionalized discourse of Broad Church theology, and that, more cynically, the lyric was written to appease, and thereby win over, the future Mrs Tennyson (and, more importantly, her father). Yet, within this seemingly conventional lyric, apparently wholly consonant with Broad Church Anglicanism of the mid-Victorian period, there is this spectral dissonance, a spiritual oscillation or resistance *incorporated* into the articulation of faith. It is an affirmative resistance, moreover, of the 'faith that comes of self-control, ... And all we flow from, soul in soul' (CXXXI.9,12), which opens constantly to the spirit of Christ as Love and to the ghost of Arthur Hallam; such faith opens to both, and to the trace of both as the haunting instance of disembodied, yet incarnate alterity at work. The same, but not the same, faith is the arché-origin before the beginning, and is, therefore, inscribed at the end of composition as the disruption of orthodoxy and in deference to eschatological deferral and differentiation. Which double motion we find inscribed in the instance that Tennyson appears to take leave of Arthur: 'I hear it now, and o'er and o'er,/Eternal greetings to the dead; And "Ave, Ave, Ave," said,/ "Adieu, adieu," for evermore' (LVII.13–16). The endless act of hearing marks the subject as one who cannot choose but be open to a mode of communication from the other, itself without end. Differing articulations in rhythmic reiteration, different from one another, in three different languages and from different locations, give the lie to finality. And, as Derrida reminds us, invoking Emmanuel Levinas, 'The greeting of the *à-Dieu* does not signal the end ... The *à-Dieu* greets the other beyond being.'[42] In such an insistence, and in the reception and response which informs the radical separation *and* proximity between self and other, are the signs or matter of Tennyson's faith.

Notes

1. All citations from *In Memoriam* are taken from Christopher Ricks, ed., *Tennyson: A Selected Edition* (Berkeley: University of California Press, 1989), pp. 331–484.
2. Peter Schwenger, *Fantasm and Fiction: On Textual Envisioning* (Stanford: Stanford University Press, 1999), p. 23.
3. Immanuel Kant, *Religion within the boundaries of mere reason* (1793) tr. George di Giovanni, *Religion and Rational Theology*, tr. Allen W. Wood and George di Giovanni (Cambridge: Cambridge University Press, 1996), pp. 39–216, p. 167. Hereafter, *Religion*.
4. Isobel Armstrong, *Victorian Poetry: Poetry, Poetics and Politics* (London: Routledge, 1993), p. 261.
5. Michael Wheeler, *Death and the Future Life in Victorian Language and Theology* (Cambridge: Cambridge University Press, 1990), p. 264.
6. Graham Ward, *Barth, Derrida and the Language of Theology* (Cambridge: Cambridge University Press, 1995), p. 151. The phrase cited is coined by Edmund Husserl in his *Cartesian Meditations* 'in an attempt', as Ward puts it, 'to answer the question of how, given his own commitment to a transcendental subjectivity, there can be an experience of and an acknowledgement of someone else'. It is precisely this Husserlian or phenomenological problematic of mediation which we encounter in Tennyson's recourse to analogy throughout *In Memoriam*. On the subject of analogy in the poem, see Christopher Craft, *Another Kind of Love: Male Homosexual Desire in English Discourse* (Berkeley: University of California Press, 1994), p. 53; Donald S. Hair, *Tennyson's Language* (Toronto: University of Toronto Press, 1991); Wheeler, *Death and the Future Life*, p. 230; Elaine Jordan, *Alfred Tennyson* (Cambridge: Cambridge University Press, 1988), p. 123.
7. Hair, *Tennyson's Language*, p. 122; William R. Brashear, *The Living Will* (The Hague: Mouton, 1969), p. 96.
8. Jordan, *Alfred Tennyson*, p. 115.
9. On the poem as a series of fragments resistant to unification, see Hair, *Tennyson's*

Language, pp. 89–95; Timothy Peltason, *Reading In Memoriam* (Princeton: Princeton University Press, 1985) pp. 5, 14. Isobel Armstrong reads the 'fragmented syntax' of particular lyrics (p. 264). Elaine Jordan regards the question of unity as a problem (p. 109).
10 Hair, *Tennyson's Language*, p. 101.
11 Jacques Derrida, *Archive Fever: A Freudian Impression* (1995) tr. Eric Prenowitz (Chicago: University of Chicago Press, 1996), p. 17.
12 Ibid., p. 84.
13 T.S. Eliot, 'In Memoriam', *Essays Ancient and Modern* (London: Faber and Faber, 1936), pp. 200–201.
14 Samuel Taylor Coleridge, 'On the Constitution of the Church and State, According to the Idea of Each', (1829) in John Morrow, ed., *Coleridge's Writings on Politics and Society. Volume 1* (Princeton: Princeton University Press, 1991): pp. 152–220. The passage cited is from pp. 173–4.
15 Jordan, *Alfred Tennyson*, p. 123.
16 Armstrong, *Victorian Poetry*, p. 254.
17 Wheeler, *Death and the Future Life*, p. 239.
18 Armstrong, *Victorian Poetry*, p. 264.
19 Immanuel Kant, 'Preface to the Second Edition'(1787), *Critique of Pure Reason*, tr. and ed. Paul Guyer and Allen W. Wood (Cambridge: Cambridge University Press, 1997), p. 117.
20 Kevin Hart, *The Trespass of the Sign: Deconstruction, Theology and Philosophy* (Cambridge: Cambridge University Press, 1989), pp. 130–31. Hart provides a useful overview and critique of onto-theology, from Kant, through Heidegger and Derrida (pp. 75–96).
21 Werner Hamacher, *Pleroma: Reading in Hegel*, (1978) tr. Nicholas Walker and Simon Jarvis (Stanford: Stanford University Press, 1998), p. 3.
22 Alan Sinfield, *Alfred Tennyson* (Oxford: Basil Blackwell, 1986), p. 115.
23 For the consideration of a materiality of inscription, and for the specific thinking of a materiality that forestalls anthropomorphism and the normalization of analogy, I am indebted to Paul de Man's consideration of materiality in Kant's third *Critique*, in *Aesthetic Ideology*, ed. Andrzej Warminski (Minneapolis: University of Minnesota Press, 1996), pp. 70–90. I am also indebted to the various considerations of de Man's late work, particularly on the matter of materiality, in Tom Cohen, Barbara Cohen, J. Hillis Miller and Andrzej Warminski, eds, *Material Events: Paul de Man and the Afterlife of Theory* (Minneapolis: University of Minnesota Press, 2000). The phrase 'materiality without matter' is used by the editors as the subtitle for their introduction, and is taken from Derrida's contribution to the collection.
24 Jacques Derrida, 'How to Avoid Speaking: Denials' (1987) tr. Ken Friedan, in Sanford Budick and Wolfgang Iser, eds, *Languages of the Unsayable: The Play of Negativity in Literature and Literary Theory* (New York: Columbia University Press, 1989), pp. 3–70, p. 4.
25 De Man, *Aesthetic Ideology*, p. 75.
26 Immanuel Kant, *Lectures on the philosophical doctrine of religion* (1817) tr. Allen W. Wood, *Religion and Rational Theology*, tr. Allen W. Wood and George di Giovanni (Cambridge: Cambridge University Press, 1996), pp. 335–452, p. 385. Hereafter *Lectures*.
27 Kant, *Religion*, p. 107.
28 Ibid., p. 107.
29 Ibid., p. 165.
30 Kant, *Lectures*, p. 385.

31 Ibid., p. 385.
32 Eleanor Bustin Mattes, *In Memoriam: The Way of the Soul: A Study of Some Influences that Shaped Tennyson's Poem* (New York: Exposition Press, 1951), p. 114. Michael Wheeler, discussing the theological thought of Maurice, Coleridge and Jowett, refers to the latter's arguments as 'Kantian' in tone (p. 228). Wheeler also points to the ways in which Tennyson's argument in the poem for the 'immortality of the soul' is 'derived from Kant (partly from reading Goethe and listening to Hallam)' (*Death and the Future Life*, p. 240).
33 James R. Kincaid, *Tennyson's Major Poems: The Comic and Ironic Patterns* (New Haven: Yale University Press, 1975), pp. 81, 99.
34 Jacques Derrida, 'Faith and Knowledge' (1996) tr. Samuel Weber, in Jacques Derrida and Gianni Vattimo, eds, *Religion* (Stanford: Stanford University Press, 1998), pp. 1–78, p. 6. One might also usefully connect Derrida's assertion to another – namely, that one ought to be able to begin with haunting (*Specters of Marx*, (1993) trans. Peggy Kamuf (New York: Routledge, 1994) p. 175).
35 Referring to the Epilogue, Eleanor Bustin Mattes argues that the 'progress of the universe toward some remote goal' has nothing 'specifically Christian' in it (p. 91). In reading this, she is correct in observing the idiomatic aspect of Tennyson's expression of faith, already commented on above.
36 Wheeler, *Death and the Future Life*, pp. 223, 224, 228.
37 Ibid., p. 247.
38 On Hallam's androgyny and the Victorian perception of an androgynous Christ, see Richard Dellamora, who describes Hallam as a 'male Beatrice' (*Masculine Desire: The Sexual Politics of Victorian Aesthetics* (Chapel Hill: University of North Carolina Press, 1990), p. 10). See also Craft (*Another Kind of Love*) and Diane Long Hoeveler, *"Manly-Women and Womanly-Men": Tennyson's Androgynous Ideal in The Princess and In Memoriam*, Michigan Occasional Papers XIX (Spring 1981).
39 Wheeler, *Death and the Future Life*, p. 228.
40 Derrida, 'Faith and Knowledge', p. 15.
41 Wheeler, *Death and the Future Life*, p. 230; Hair, *Tennyson's Language*, p. 98.
42 Jacques Derrida, *Adieu to Emmanuel Levinas*, (1997) tr. Pascale-Anne Brault and Michael Naas (Stanford: Stanford University Press, 1999), p. 13.

Chapter 5

'A City Without a Church':
The Origin of Species, the Tree of Life and the Apocalypse

Kevin Mills

'The polity of nature'

In *The Origin of Species* (1859), Charles Darwin described nature as a 'polity' with 'districts' and an 'economy', in which the structural features of beehives, for example, are compared to the work of architects, masons and painters.[1] But what place, if any, did the Church occupy in this City of Nature? The text of the *The Origin*, for the most part, seems to occlude the body of Christ. This might betoken a belief, on Darwin's part, that the Church was not relevant to the natural processes which he described, nor those processes relevant to the Church. But for T.H. Huxley, Darwin's publicist and defender, the advent of such theories as that of evolution by natural selection was of deep significance for the beliefs of religious people. He envisaged the 'drowning' of religious souls beneath what he characterized as 'the advancing tide of matter'.[2] Materialist descriptions of natural phenomena, in Huxley's metaphor, seemed to overwhelm spiritual possibilities. On this account the Church must be seen as that Pauline paradox, a 'spiritual body', which had no place in the newly material order of nature.

But materialist arguments led in other directions simultaneously. For some Christians, Darwinian theory served as a confirmation of their belief that God never intervenes in a natural order the laws of which he fixed in advance. A.L. Moore, for example, argued that 'there are not, and cannot be, any Divine interpositions in nature, for God cannot interfere with Himself ... *For the Christian theologian the facts of nature are the acts of God.*'[3] But the nature of nature is still very much in doubt here. In 1860 Darwin himself pointed out certain natural phenomena which would present 'the Christian theologian' with some uncomfortable data: 'I cannot persuade myself that a beneficent and omnipotent God would have designedly created the Ichneumonidae with the express intention of their feeding within the living bodies of Caterpillars... .'[4] It seems unlikely that Moore's version of nature included a detailed knowledge of the parasitic egg-laying habits of a certain species of wasp. Natural theology is seldom so punctilious. This highlights the fact that the meaning given to 'nature' depends upon the value-system within which it is studied or described. The value attached to the body, whether of Christ or of a simple organism, will, to some extent, be determined by the level of observation and the concomitant mode of description applied to natural phenomena.

If Darwin's highly differentiated natural world was, for all its closely observed detail, constructed on an urban model, then it should come as no surprise to find that the Church, while it is not altogether absent, is well hidden in the recesses of *The Origin*. The rapid growth of Victorian conurbations quickly outstripped the Anglican Church's ability to erect new buildings and to adapt its parochial system of government to meet newly-expanded urban requirements. Large areas of Britain's mid-nineteenth-century cities, the urban model for Darwin's natural architecture, were (temporarily) without churches. Both Marx and Engels noted the urbanity of Darwin's characterization of the natural world, its reflections of industrial, capitalist civilization.[5] According to Engels: '... the struggle for existence is simply the transference from society to animate nature of Hobbes's theory of the war of every man against every man and the bourgeois economic theory of competition, along with the Malthusian theory of population.'[6] The metaphoric profile of *The Origin* tends to support Engels' view. Darwin does, for instance, sound Hobbesian much of the time: he refers to 'battle within battle' (61), 'the great battle of life' (64), 'the war of nature' (66); he speaks of 'the war' between males competing for females, and refers to some carnivorous animals as 'well armed' (73–4). He employs the phrases 'the great battle for life' (106), 'the struggle for life' (167), and 'the struggle for existence' (191); he frequently uses the language of invasion and extermination, of victory and defeat, and of supplanting. He is, however, careful to point out that he uses this terminology 'in a large and metaphorical sense' (53). Even so, its sheer pervasiveness tends to undermine this claim of control over its inferences.

Darwin's conflictual language betrays the cultural context of the *The Origin*. Walter Houghton traces what he calls 'the worship of force' in Victorian culture, through the work of Thomas Carlyle and Charles Kingsley, to the 'self-righteous intolerance' of Puritanism, and the religious insecurities of the most aggressive writers of the age.[7] Such aggression found its way into the poetry of both Browning and Tennyson: ' ... it lighten'd my despair', says the protagonist of *Maud* (1855), 'When I thought that a war would arise in defence of the right.' While the initial public enthusiasm for the Crimean Campaign (1854–56) is reflected in Tennyson's poem, it was not only military ambition which fuelled this cultural belligerence. In *North and South* (1855), Elizabeth Gaskell hints at an undercurrent of violent domination in the process of industrialisation: '... we have many among us,' boasts the industrialist John Thornton, 'who ... could spring into the breach and carry on the war which compels, and shall compel, all material power to yield to science.'[8] While Darwin cannot be held responsible for the widespread cultural emphasis on force, his text illustrates the point that metaphors, whatever the intention underlying their production, are never confined by the voluntary limits which govern their deployment.

As Engels suggests, at times Darwin's language also betrays its socioeconomic and political provenance: he speaks often of 'colonisation', of specialization and the division of labour, and of 'kingdoms' and 'economies'. The stressing of the central theme of genealogy is also politically significant in a text produced by a member of a highly class-conscious society, especially when such a theme employs the pre-Mendelian phrase 'allied in blood' to indicate real affinities in nature (see, for example, 340–43).

Part of the fascination of reading *The Origin of Species* lies in an imaginative response to such metaphorical language. Nor is this a perverse 'literary' reading of a scientific text. *The Origin* itself is very concerned with the status of its own language, recognizing the metaphoricity which it hopes to overcome. The overcoming of metaphors is the ongoing dream of scientific discourse. As one historian of Darwin's age and ideas puts it: 'To arrive at a just interpretation of the controversy over Darwinism, the inquiring historian must *cut through the cake of metaphor* which encrusts the subject' (emphasis added).[9] That one cannot very easily dispense with metaphor, even when dealing with scientific matters, is apparent in this very claim: language is too blunt an instrument, it seems, to penetrate to the underlying reality. The very language which asserts the importance of removing the encasing layers of metaphor from the core of scientific truth merely adds another layer of encrustation.

Consideration of the role of metaphor in Darwin's work leads Gillian Beer to conclude that 'Metaphor depends upon species and upon categorisation.' We might be equally convinced by Ricoeur's insistence in *The Rule of Metaphor* that, as the trope of resemblances or analogies, metaphor also *gives rise* to such classification.[10] Thus a dialectic of metaphor and classification is implied which leads to the conclusion that 'cutting through the cake of metaphor', as well as being a kind of oxymoron, is a peculiarly self-defeating notion when it is applied to a text whose theme is analogy and speciation.

The Church Invisible

The body of Christ, according to Paul, is the special creation of the Holy Spirit: 'For by one Spirit are we all baptized into one body' (1 Cor. 12:13). Such specific acts of individuation with regard to bodies are very much the target of Darwin's work. Again and again he makes his point in favour of natural selection by contrasting it with the explanation of the same facts by appeal to special creation: 'This grand fact of the grouping of all organic beings seems to me utterly inexplicable on the theory of creation' (380, *passim*).

That Darwin is not concerned with human evolution in *The Origin* does little to stave off the sense (confirmed by his *Descent of Man* in 1871) that mankind's antecedents were, from this point on, to be thought of as having greater affinities with apes than with angels. Bodies, whether of arthropod or anthropoid, whether of crustacea or of Christ, are mere localized hardenings in the primordial soup. The Church might still have appeared as the product of divine intervention at some point in the evolutionary process, but Darwin shows no glimmer of interest in such a possibility. However, he is keen to obviate any miraculous incursions into the realm of nature. He writes, rather dismissively, that the observer who rejects the theory of natural selection can only explain geographical distribution by calling in 'the agency of a miracle' (285).

The Church does appear, momentarily, in the final chapter of *The Origin*, in the guise of 'a celebrated author and divine' – that is, the Reverend Charles Kingsley – who had written to Darwin to express his approval of the latter's 'noble conception of the Deity'. Given the absence of the Church from the preceding account of natural processes, this ecclesiophany seems almost miraculous. The awkward coalescence of theology and science creates a degree of rhetorical unease, largely by virtue of what is left unsaid. 'I see no good reason,' writes Darwin defensively, 'why the views given in this volume should shock the religious feelings of any one' (388). Now the only reason for mentioning the shocking of religious feelings is the assumption that some religious feelings will be shocked, comprehensively. The 'should' in Darwin's pre-emptive strike at his potential religious detractors is crucial: it is a judgement about the validity of certain conceptions of creation and of nature, especially the creation of mankind in God's image. Darwin is sure that some religious feelings will be shocked, but they *should not be*, they have no right to be. This is the only moment in *The Origin* at which an addressee is visible; one might almost conclude that it was written *to the Church*. It certainly suggests that while the Church was absent from the natural processes Darwin described, it was a significant force in the shaping of his theory.

In the event, the Church was (and remains, to some extent) divided over Darwin. James R. Moore has done a very thorough job of tracing the lines along which Christian opinion split in what he calls the post-Darwinian controversies.[11] Darwin's words, hinting at a fear of religious objections yet able to cite religious approval, betoken a divided Church, a broken body. The invisibility of the Church in the polity of nature, then, is not the same as its complete absence. When, at last, it appears in the final, prophetic chapter of *The Origin*, as a scene of potential conflict between the 'celebrated author and divine' and people with shocked religious feelings, it is perceived as both a threat and an ally. Its place is unclear. This ambivalence is due not only to Darwin's own worries about the religious significance and the likely impact of his theory, but also to the strange ambiguity of the notion of the Church as a body. Paul theorized various kinds of bodies: 'all flesh is not the same flesh ... celestial bodies, and bodies terrestrial ... There is a natural body, and there is a spiritual body' (1 Cor. 15:39–44). What kind of body is the Church? Is it a body of evolved human flesh – a 'body terrestrial'? Or, is it the special creation of the Holy Spirit – a 'celestial body'?

The Tree of Life

At the centre of Darwin's churchless conurbation, the 'polity of nature', stands the Tree of Life:

> The affinities of all the beings of the same class have sometimes been represented by a great tree. I believe this simile largely speaks the truth ... As buds give rise by growth to fresh buds, and these, if vigorous, branch out and overtop on all sides many a feebler branch, so by generation I believe it has been with the great Tree of Life, which fills with its dead and broken branches the crust of the earth, and covers the surface with its ever branching and beautiful ramifications. (106–7)

The Tree of Life as it appears in *The Origin* refers both to the material, developmental processes of natural selection, and to the diagram by means of which

Darwin sets out to represent these processes. According to Gillian Beer, Darwin demetaphorized this image by showing that biological descent does, in reality, branch out through time, forming widely ramose system networks: 'He did not simply adopt the image of the tree as a similitude or as a polemical counter to other organisations. He *came upon* it as he cast his argument in the form of a diagram ... It was substantial, a condensation of real events, rather than a metaphor.'[12] But if there is such a process of demetaphorization at work in Darwin's text, which metaphor is thus substantiated?

Perhaps the most obvious candidate, in the context of a discourse on origins, is the tree as it appears in Genesis. If this is the intended target, then the process is more a matter of demythologization – a profoundly ecclesial gesture in the mid-nineteenth-century context – than of demetaphorization. One effect of the publication of *The Origin* was to prompt a rethinking of Christian cosmogony and soteriology – even if the Creator remained after the rejection of a literal six-day creation, it became very difficult to hold on to the idea of a primeval Fall into sin. It seems, then, appropriate enough to see Darwin's tree as a demythologized version of Edenic origins. But there are other candidates: the Tree of Life also appears in Proverbs, Ezekiel and Revelation. Since Darwin's argument in *The Origin* tends to elide the difference between the trees of life and of knowledge, turning scientific data into a diagram labelled *Arbor Vitae*, then the book of Proverbs is perhaps the most relevant biblical model: 'She [Wisdom] is a tree of life to them that lay hold upon her' (3:18).

However, if as I have argued (following Engels and Marx), Darwin's nature is modelled on civilization, then his Tree of Life is perhaps best understood in relation to the tree in Revelation, the tree which stands at the centre of a city – the New Jerusalem (Rev. 22:2). This might prompt a reinterpretation of the apocalypse: the New Jerusalem would no longer symbolize the citadel of millenial expectation; rather it would become a figure for the natural world in the process of becoming. The war, famine and disease of apocalyptic vision could be reimagined as aspects of the struggle for existence, and the last judgement might serve as a metaphor for natural selection. Improbable as it may seem, one strand of theological evolutionism tends towards such an explanation. Ernst Benz, assessing the thought of Teilhard de Chardin, writes: 'The idea that all lines of evolution converge in point Omega, leads, without fail, to the idea of *Universal Redemption*. Humanity thus absorbs the Church and final judgement becomes identical with the selection process of evolution in which much is sacrificed and eliminated.'[13] The Church vanishes. It is 'absorbed' in a soteriologically undifferentiated humanity. Much the same might be said of Henry Drummond's interpretation of the Apocalypse, and of most liberal strands of nineteenth-century theology.

Ironically, the very text in which the demetaphorization of the Tree of Life is propagated became a spur to the Church to *remetaphorize* its own discourse on origins and ends. This can be seen clearly in the work of Henry Drummond, Charles Kingsley, F.D. Maurice and Teilhard de Chardin among many others. Furthermore, the very process of demetaphorization by which natural history is supposed to supplant natural theology, the scientific interpretation supposed to supplant the ecclesial, is unstable. This is not just because natural observation, as practiced in

The Origin, is shot through with the mores of Western, industrial civilization, but also because the Tree of Life is not a single metaphor; it is a whole species. Among its many functions, it represents the Church to itself, so that when liberal theology absorbs the Church in humanity, the Church's self-image is fused with Darwin's diagram of natural selection (as the map of human development), and vice versa. Both become apocalyptic foreshadowings of the Church's disappearance, and the scientific heuristic device is no longer distinguishable from the mythic metaphor. The process of demetaphorization which turns the Tree of Life into a diagram of natural selection doubles as a process of remetaphorization by which the diagram of natural selection, in the guise of the Tree of Life, figures the Church.

Demetaphorization is vital to the argument of *The Origin*, and forms the core of the final, prophetic chapter: 'The terms used by naturalists ... will cease to be metaphorical, and will have a plain signification' (392). The classification of genera and species, according to Darwin, will be based (henceforth) on descent rather than on analogy. But, of course, analogy could not but remain a vital clue to descent: 'I should infer from analogy that probably all the organic beings which have ever lived on this earth have descended from some one primordial form ...' (391). Since the very process of classification is a matter of analogous thinking, Darwin's demetaphorization can never completely succeed. His metaphor-ridden text bears witness to the difficulty. If this is so then the Tree of Life not only remains figural, but stands as a figure of the non-reducibility of metaphor to genealogy: a metaphor of metaphors.

This metaphoricity is rendered even more intractable by the fact that the tree metaphor has its own natural-historical genealogy. Dov Ospovat has traced the image from the point at which evolutionary thought broke with Cuvier's teleological method. In 1828, Karl Ernst von Baer used 'the branching conception' as the basis for his interpretation of the facts of embryology; Martin Barry wrote of the 'tree of animal development', and Henri Milne Edwards developed the case for embryologically determined classification by employing the same metaphor.[14] According to Ospovat, Darwin effectively reinterpreted the 'branching conception' by thinking of it in terms of divergence: the diversification of groups inhabiting single regions. The 'struggle for existence' enforced this diversification so that different varieties could make use of diverse food-sources. In a gesture which might bring to mind Paul's description of the distinct functions allotted to members of the body of Christ (1 Cor. 12), Darwin described this in terms of the division of labour in modern industrial conditions: 'The advantage in each group becoming as different as possible, may be compared to the fact that by division of ... labour most people can be supported in each country ....'[15] But he also returned the branching conception to metaphorical status by naming it 'the Tree of Life'. So, while the process of plotting biological genealogies might seem to be a kind of demetaphorization of the Tree of Life, the genealogy of the tree metaphor suggests that the allusion to the Tree of Life is actually a process of remetaphorization.

The inexorability of this return of/to the metaphor becomes even more evident when the demetaphorizing drive is turned towards language. In 'Darwin and the Growth of Language Theory', Gillian Beer traces the reciprocal relationship which grew up between the theories of evolution and of language development in the second half of the nineteenth century.[16] In *The Origin*, Darwin uses the example of linguistic filiation to illustrate the genealogical arrangement of the natural system: 'The various degrees of difference in the languages from the same stock, would have to be expressed by groups subordinate to groups; but the proper or even only possible arrangement would still be genealogical' (342). As Beer observes, the terms describing language and descent are interchangeable in Darwin's illustration. She goes on to argue that whereas this sharing of terms was, in the period of Darwin's enquiries, 'only a metaphorical link between evolutionary theory and language theory', it has since become substantive. Experimental study of the linguistic capabilities and communication systems of non-human primates has established the connectedness of genetic and linguistic versions of filiation.[17]

Hans Aarsleff notes that the nineteenth century saw 'language study ... beginning to form an alliance with geology'.[18] Lawrence Frank insists that, given Lyell's comparison between the fossil record and a 'demotic ... curious document', 'it is no wonder that Darwin's Tree of Life in *The Origin of Species* looks, curiously, like a Tree of Language.'[19] According to Beer, 'the branching diagram of Darwinian theory shares its pattern with that of the comparative grammarians of the earlier nineteenth century.'[20] That 'shared pattern' implicates this secondary substantiation of metaphor in the movement of remetaphorization.

The tangled web of affinities in which language itself appears as a yet-to-be-substantiated metaphor, has no locatable centre; which is to say that the Tree of Life belongs to no genre. It always appears as a branching-off from itself of a discipline in search of supplementation. As metaphorical representation of the very surplus of meaning which characterizes metaphor, the Tree of Life exceeds the confines of the demetaphorizing discourse. Since it is at the same time metaphorical, meta-metaphorical, metalinguistic and substantiated non-metaphorical process, and is always at work beneath every genealogical enterprise, it may be described as a figure of textual *différance*: an always displaced, non-originary origin. Described in this way, as the reification within a discourse of the hidden movement which is its very possibility, the 'Tree of Life' is named only by means of a catachresis. But this prophetic trope, which calls the yet-to-be-revealed by the name of the apparent, and which comes to us already interpreted by the Church and its texts, is our only resource in tracing the processes of speciation, classification and metaphor.[21]

Observations

The double movement of demetaphorization and of remetaphorization which can be traced in *The Origin*, as the genealogy of species interweaves with the genealogy of the very metaphor employed to depict genealogy, is possibly delusory from top to bottom. Darwin's use of the tree diagram is, after all, susceptible to the criticism which Hillis Miller has levelled at *Middlemarch*: the 'web of affinities' which it traces, like Eliot's social fabric, may be an effect of the eye which perceives it.[22] While this is a criticism which could be levelled at almost any text, it is peculiarly appropriate to the case of *The Origin*, since, for Darwin, the eye is not altogether trustworthy. In defending the possibility of the evolution of such a 'perfect organ',

Darwin expressed a strong doubt about the adequacy of the eye to correct 'the aberration of light' (164). Despite this caveat (designed to bring the eye within the ambit of evolutionary development) Darwin's dependence upon his own eyes could hardly have been more clearly stated. Throughout *The Origin* he encourages the reader to 'look at' certain phenomena, uses phrases such as 'when we see' both literally and metaphorically; he refers to 'careful observers' (161), 'good observers' (230), 'observations I have made' (219), and organisms which have 'passed under my own eyes' (246). The list could be extended almost indefinitely.

It is as if a peculiar blindspot in Darwin's work allows him to claim the ability to 'see in the dark', as it were: 'In the dim obscurity of the past we can see that the early progenitor of all the Vertebrata must have been an aquatic animal... .'[23] Despite this dimness, obscurity and confinement to the past, the eye, for all its avowed inadequacies, has the power to penetrate the vagaries of formal analogy and to uncover the unimaginably extended progress of human evolution. The weakness of the ubiquitous eye is also attested by the presence of its mechanical extensions – the telescope (154), the camera lucida (196) and the microscope (200). The telescope is brought in as a seemingly inevitable comparison with the eye: 'It is scarcely possible', says Darwin, 'to avoid comparing the eye to a telescope.' This is a curiously incestuous image which involves a 'power always intently *watching* each slight accidental alteration ... and carefully *selecting* each alteration which ... may in any way, or in any degree tend to produce a distincter image' (154, emphasis added). Natural Selection is thus personified: it 'watches' and 'selects'; it must be a 'good observer' gifted with a more reliable eye than it can hope to produce in the organisms which it moulds. The prosopopeia and the metaphor combine to make the empirical project a simultaneously self-generating and self-undermining enterprise. Darwin, the observer, cannot look himself in the eye.

With this in mind, the continual references to looking, seeing and observing, render epistemologically questionable the appearances of resemblance between organisms, the formal analogies upon which Darwin's whole project is based. In his *Autobiography*, Darwin explicitly voiced a similar worry about religion: '... can the mind of man, which has, as I fully believe, been developed from a mind as low as that possessed by the lowest animal, be trusted ... ?'[24] The mind and the eye, as is attested by many optical metaphors for thought, are not always wholly distinguishable. Darwin's distrust of the former is of a piece with his bio-scepticism about the latter. Perhaps, then, the disappearance (or, at least, the relegation) of God in the evolution of Darwin's own thought,[25] and the invisibility of the Church in his 'polity of nature' are understandable as blindspots. Even if Darwin could have excised all references to the Creator from a possible version of *The Origin*, could he have managed without the telescope, the absence of which he characterized as 'scarcely possible'? The telescope, as has been observed, implies a watcher with an infallible eye – an organ, which is, by Darwin's own reckoning, not to be found among the developmental achievements of natural selection. The indispensibility of the telescope suggests something beyond the scope of the evolutionary process, something invisible to the human eye because behind it, simultaneously revealed and concealed by it: intimations of apocalypse.

Observing the Apocalypse

An apocalypse is an uncovering, a revelation to the eyes of an observer of what has been veiled up to this point. As an account of what has been revealed, John's Apocalypse continually draws attention to the experience of seeing: the phrase 'and I saw' (*kai eidon*), or a near equivalent, occurs with striking frequency throughout the text. From the opening chapter with its promise of universal observation ('every eye shall see him' – 1:7), and its description of the incendiary eyes of the glorified Christ (1:14), to the blessed vision of the righteous whose eyes shall see God's face, in the final chapter, Revelation is a book full of eyes, of looking, watching and beholding.

Among the Churches to whom John was told to write, the Laodicean Christians stand out as people with serious eye-problems: '... thou ... knowest not that thou art ... blind ... I counsel thee to ... anoint thine eyes with eyesalve, that thou mayest see' (3:17–18). They suffer an 'aberration of light' – a double blindness which means that they cannot see that they cannot see; rather like Darwin, when he claims to be able to penetrate the darkness of the immemorial past. The peculiar blessing promised to them if they 'overcome' is appropriate: 'To him that overcometh will I grant to sit with me in my throne ...'; that throne is surrounded, according to 4:6, with beasts 'full of eyes before and behind'. Given this contrast between defective human eyes and the oversufficiency of divine vision (neatly summarized by the diminutive English title: 'Revelation'), human finitude is visible as an horizon – it is determined by the eye. The Apocalypse is precisely that which uncovers what the unaided human eye is unable to see: that which must be revealed.

The centrality of the eye to Darwin's famous work is one aspect of its apocalyptic tone. The power of observation is crucial in uncovering the secret knowledge of 'the origin of species – that mystery of mysteries' (3). From among its manifold descriptions of organisms and organs, the eye emerges as representative of both the power of natural selection and its weakness, and natural selection thus appears as both the triumph and the tragedy of the human eye. So too the Church, for it is at once both the Church Visible and the Church Invisible. Revelation encrypts this duality – making the Church Invisible appear before the Church Visible, while cloaking both in the figures of apocalyptic rhetoric. Where Darwin calls in telescope, camera lucida and microscope, John appeals to angelic guides, and where Darwin relies on the invisible 'watcher' who oversees the evolutionary development of the human eye, John surrounds himself with the many eyes of God.

Emanating from the focal point of the human eye, 'a web of affinities' (to borrow Darwin's own phrase) is spun between *The Origin* and the biblical Apocalypse. The persistent warfare observed in Revelation is matched by the ubiquitous rhetoric of struggle, battle and extermination in *The Origin*. With the reference to the Reverend Charles Kingsley in the final chapter, this sense of struggle inevitably evokes Victorian notions of 'muscular Christianity' and of the 'Church Militant'. Furthermore, just as Darwin saw his deployment of contemporaneous military language as metaphorical, so John reinterpreted an apocalyptic tradition of eschatological 'holy war' by redeploying its bellicose imperatives in a metaphorical sense. According to Richard Bauckham: 'In the eschatological destruction of evil in

Revelation there is no place for real armed violence, but there is ample space of [sic] the imagery of armed violence.'[26]

Again, while natural selection determines survival in *The Origin*, the 'supernatural selection' of divine judgement determines survival in the Apocalypse. In each case, survival is registered in the (human) body. In *The Origin*, the surviving body is marked by its beneficial adaptations, while in the Apocalypse both God's people and those who belong to the beast are marked in their flesh (Revelation 7:3, 13:16). Both texts deal with the question of human destiny, and both do so by (dis)placing humanity from the centre of their descriptions. Both end with more or less prophetic utopian visions. Time takes on the character of a non-linear plot in both texts. 'Darwin's account of the origin of species', according to Gillian Beer, 'ranges to and fro through time in a way that disturbs any simple sequence or chain.'[27] The same could be said, *mutatis mutandis*, of the book of Revelation.

One connotation of apocalypse (*the* connotation for many people) is the end of the world as we know it. On this account Darwin's work might be perceived as the end of the world as God's special creation, and as the end of man as its crowning achievement made in God's own likeness. At the most profound level of comparison, both texts seek some means of predicting ends or outcomes, especially the outcome of 'the great battle of life'. In each case this involves 'replotting observed relations of cause and effect or of possibility ... perceiving underlying patterns by means of analogy ... ' and acknowledging 'a world beyond the compass of our present knowledge'.[28]

For Henry Drummond (1851–97), one of the early thinkers of Christian evolutionism, nineteenth-century cities were unmistakable intimations of 'a world beyond the compass of our present knowledge': a world from which the Church will have vanished. He read into the Apocalypse a kind of civic evolution which would transform 'London, Berlin, New York, Paris, Melbourne, Calcutta' into the 'cities of God' (99). This process would eventually eliminate the Church which has 'literally stolen Christ from the people' (113). In the 'struggle for existence', the Church is a loser: 'the Church with all its splendid equipment, the cloister with all its holy opportunity, are not the final instruments for *fitting* men for Heaven. The City, in many of its functions, is a greater Church than the Church' (122, emphasis added). The city has become the matrix of salvation, supplanting the Church. Just as Darwinian theory implies that each positive adaptation in an organism helps not only to ensure its success but also to hasten its own obsolescence in the march of evolutionary progress, Drummond's vision is that the Church is the driving force behind its own ultimate extinction: ' ... the great use of the Church is to help men to do without it' (118). The Church, then, is viewed as a kind of temporary shelter, constructed to cater for Christian inadequacies rather than to display the glory of God.

Clearly, the rise of the great, unchurched Victorian cities is a cultural factor in this interpretation. A strong sense of the ecclesial body's failure to adapt to these changed conditions of existence, and of the concomitant mass desertion of the mid-century Church by the common people (registered by the census of 1851), can be felt in Drummond's urban prognosis: 'The masses will never return to the Church till its true relation to the City is more defined. And they can never have that most real life of theirs made religious so long as they rule themselves out of court on the ground that they have broken with ecclesiastical forms' (119).

Drummond centres his new New Jerusalems on the Tree of Life: 'In the midst of the streets there should be a tree of Life.' The strange juxtaposition of literal cities and metaphorical trees, destabilizes the images of both city and Church (in fact, Drummond's text slides between three or four different meanings of the word 'Church' – building, set of rituals, people, even the paradoxical 'City without a Church'). Is this because, like the evolutionary process itself (in which Drummond implicates the Church), the Church has no single, non-analogical meaning? It is a Tree of Life – a material developmental process which has branched out through time, from a single antecedent form into a multiplicity of communions, denominations, factions, recombinations, sects, cults, and even new religious movements.

Like the New Jerusalem in which the Tree of Life grows, the Church is also caught between heaven and earth, between existing as a celestial and as a terrestrial body. This is part of Drummond's difficulty: 'The Church is a Divine institution because it is so very human an institution' (118), he says, indicating its double nature. He also depicts the Church as an outmoded institution with which we do not associate Christ: 'We never think of Him in connection with a Church. We cannot picture Him in the garb of a priest or belonging to any of the classes who specialise religion ... What have ... the vestures and the postures to do with Jesus of Nazareth?' (110–11). Again, this ambivalence is evident in his sense of mission: while, on the one hand, he calls for the urbanization of the Church, on the other hand he issues a challenge to 'Christianise capital; dignify labour', and to 'church' the City (104).

In Drummond's text, then, City and Church are woven together in another web of affinities, and this web is not altogether distinguishable from the Tree of Life. Drummond's version of evolution, it must be admitted, owed more to Herbert Spencer than to Darwin, but his interpretation of the Apocalypse, with its sense of urban/ecclesial evolution and its depiction of the future of human life based upon cities at the heart of which the Tree of Life grows, does suggest certain affinities with *The Origin of Species*.

The Tree of Life might serve further as a metaphor for the 'web of [metaphorical] affinities' which entangles these texts. In Revelation, it first appears as a promise to the Church (Rev. 2:7). Each expression of the apocalyptic Church is identified with a city ('To the Church of Ephesus [etc.] write ...'). Drummond thus insists that 'Christianity is the religion of Cities', and that John's vision makes this clear in a way 'which no eye can mistake' (94–5). The process by which human cities evolve into the Cities of God leads us back to that unreliable organ – the eye. The human eye must be sharp enough to catch the analogy (or the 'real affinity') between the New Jerusalem and London, Berlin, New York, etc., in order to 'discern a new London shaping itself through all the sin and chaos of the City' just as it 'was given to John to see a new Jerusalem rise from the ruins of the old' (99). But the weakness of the eye, as noted by Darwin, returns to unsettle further the troubled relationship between City and Church in Drummond's text: 'The distinction between secular and sacred is a confusion and not a contrast; and it is only because the secular is so intensely sacred that so many eyes are blind before it' (102). One is blind to the sacred because it is so secular, and yet one is able to see the New Jerusalem in

London! Again, as in *The Origin*, the eye is deemed capable of seeing the right analogies, while, simultaneously, its inadequacy is highlighted.

When Darwin introduced *The Origin of Species* as a revelation of 'that mystery of mysteries' (3), he may have only subconsciously echoed the prophetic language of some biblical passages. The same may be true of the final chapter in which he makes various predictions about the future of biological study, foretells the 'coming day' when a certain present blindness will be overcome (390), dimly foresees a 'considerable revolution in natural history' (391), and predicts the opening of 'a grand and almost untrodden field of inquiry' (392). This may not be consciously prophetic or apocalyptic, but the Church, though largely invisible, is present in the background, and perhaps Darwin's deployment of a (de)metaphorized Tree of Life is a shadow thrown across his pages by the Church and its ultimate text: Revelation.

If Revelation is the Church's vision of the end, *The Origin* has come to represent the end of the Church's vision. But origins and ends are always interwoven. Revelation has many affinities with Genesis, and Darwin's consideration of *origins* ends with a chapter in which the *future* tense predominates. While it does not predict the End, this chapter does contain a strong teleological suggestion: '... as natural selection works solely by and for the good of each being, all corporeal and mental endowments will tend to progress towards perfection' (395). Since natural selection is a genealogical theory, the uncovering of this future perfection depends on the uncovering of the past, and on the covering over of an analogy between past and future. This might be what Darwin would have called a 'real affinity', but since the whole project of moving from analogy to real affinity is bound up in the dialectic of speciation and metaphor (which genealogy fails to resolve), we can never be sure that the elision of the (possible) gap between analogy and real affinity is ever more than a metaphorical resistance to metaphor.

If Darwin thought of the 'Tree of Life' as having been demetaphorized by the discovery of the process of natural selection, his text can be read as equally involved in the remetaphorization of the same process. Further, it is caught in a web of metaphoricity centred on the human eye – an eye which looks out at nature from within the city, and projects its aberrant light onto the impenetrable opacity of the scene. The city, the Church and the natural world all inhere in the meta-metaphorical image of the Tree of Life, weaving the End which the Church has given to itself into the fabric of Darwin's materialist discourse. It is an image which connects *The Origin of Species* with the Apocalypse, the terrestrial with the celestial, the city with the Church, the physical with the spiritual, and natural origins with spiritual ends.

Notes

1 Charles Darwin, *The Origin of Species*, ed. Gillian Beer (Oxford: Oxford University Press, 1996), pp. 185–91. Page references to this work are given, henceforth, in the text.
2 T.H. Huxley, 'The Physical Basis of Life', *The Fortnightly Review*, Feb. 1869, p. 143.
3 Quoted in James R. Moore, *The Post-Darwinian Controversies: A Study of the Protestant struggle to come to terms with Darwin in Great Britain and America, 1870–1900* (Cambridge et al.: Cambridge University Press, 1979), p. 261.
4 Charles Darwin, letter to Asa Gray (22 May 1860), in *The Life and Letters of Charles*

Darwin, ed. Francis Darwin, rev. edn (London: John Murray, 1888), vol. 2, pp. 310–12, p. 312.
5   See *Marx and Engels on Malthus*, ed. Ronald L. Meek, tr. D.L.R.L. Meek (London: Lawrence and Wishart, 1953), pp. 171–88.
6   Friedrich Engels, letter to Lavrov (12 November 1875), in ibid., pp. 175–8, p. 176.
7   Walter E. Houghton, *The Victorian Frame of Mind, 1830–1870* (New Haven: Yale University Press, 1957), pp. 196–217.
8   Elizabeth Gaskell, *North and South* (Oxford: Oxford University Press, 1982), p. 81.
9   M. McGiffert, 'Christian Darwinism: The Partnership of Asa Gray and George Frederick Wright, 1874-1881', PhD diss., Yale University, 1958 – quoted (approvingly) in Moore, *The Post-Darwinian Controversies*, p. 13.
10 Gillian Beer, *Darwin's Plots: Evolutionary Narrative in Darwin, George Eliot and Nineteenth-Century Fiction* (London et al.: Routledge and Kegan Paul, 1983), p. 94; Paul Ricoeur, *The Rule of Metaphor: Multi-disciplinary studies in the creation of meaning in language*, tr. R. Czerny, K. McLaughlin and J. Costello, S.J. (London: Routledge and Kegan Paul, 1978), pp. 22–4.
11 Moore, *The Post-Darwinian Controversies*, passim.
12 Beer, *Darwin's Plots*, p. 38.
13 Ernst Benz, *Evolution and Christian Hope: Man's Concept of the Future from the Early Fathers to Teilhard de Chardin*, tr. Heinz G. Frank (London: Victor Gollancz, 1967), p. 229.
14 Dov Ospovat, *The Development of Darwin's Theory: Natural History, Natural Theology, and Natural Selection, 1838–1859* (Cambridge et al.: Cambridge University Press, 1981), pp. 116–28.
15 Charles Darwin, quoted in ibid. p.181. I am grateful to John Schad for pointing out the Pauline parallel here.
16 Gillian Beer, *Open Fields: Science in Cultural Encounter* (Oxford: Clarendon, 1996) pp. 95–114.
17 Ibid., pp.112–13.
18 Hans Aarsleff, *The Study of Language in England, 1780–1860* (Minneapolis: University of Minnesota Press, 1983), p. 208.
19 Lawrence Frank, 'Reading the Gravel Page: Lyell, Darwin, and Conan Doyle', in *Nineteenth-Century Literature* 44 (1989), pp. 364–87, p. 367.
20 Beer, *Open Fields*, p. 108.
21 Jacques Derrida's treatment of the subject of metaphor's relationship to philosophical texts is in view here, specifically his argument that since the term *metaphor* is itself metaphorical every definition will repeat the term to be defined. So, philosophy can never fully define nor control metaphor: 'Classical rhetoric ... cannot dominate, being enmeshed within it, the mass out of which the philosophical text takes shape. Metaphor is less in the philosophical text (and in the rhetorical text coordinated with it) than the philosophical text is within metaphor. And the latter can no longer receive its name from metaphysics, except by a catachresis' – Jacques Derrida, *Margins of Philosophy*, tr. Alan Bass (Brighton: Harvester Press, 1982), pp. 207–71, p. 258.
22 J. Hillis Miller, *The Form of Victorian Fiction* (Notre Dame: University of Notre Dame Press, 1968), pp. 118–19. Hillis Miller focuses on the well-known image of the pier-glass in *Middlemarch*. He suggests that the candle-flame which produces the effect of making random surface-scratches on the pier-glass appear to form a 'concentric arrangement' might be thought to elucidate the role of the author in organising characters and events into a social fabric. Similarly, Darwin's perception that nature can be truly represented by a tree might be an effect of his observational techniques.
23 Charles Darwin, *The Descent of Man*, 2 vols (Princeton: Princeton University Press, 1981), II, p. 389.

24 *The Autobiography of Charles Darwin*, (ed.), Nora Barlow (London: Collins, 1958), p. 54.
25 In his *Autobiography*, Darwin intimates that at the time when *The Origin* was written he was a 'theist', and that sometime later he became an 'agnostic' (p. 54).
26 Richard Bauckham, *The Climax of Prophecy: Studies on the Book of Revelation* (Edinburgh: T & T Clark, 1993), p. 233. Bauckham's argument, here, is that John sought to characterize faithfulness to Christ to the point of martyrdom as an active engagement with the forces of evil rather than as passive resistance, and that the military metaphor of apocalyptic tradition well served this purpose.
27 Beer, *Darwin's Plots*, p. 65.
28 Ibid., p. 90. Beer, at this point, is actually pointing out the features common to scientific theorizing and the making of fiction. While she does note the prophetic function of major scientific theories (also claimed by the novel – 'which seeks to register emergent forms for consciousness before they are capable of manifesting themselves within a society' – p. 91), she makes no mention of the apocalyptic affinities evident in her own description.
29 Henry Drummond, 'The City Without a Church', in *The Greatest Thing in the World and other essays* (London and Glasgow: Collins, n.d.), pp. 91–124. Although I can find no publication date for this collection, the introduction suggests that a date between 1885 and 1890 is quite likely for the writing of 'The City Without a Church'. Page references to this work are given, henceforth, in the text.

Chapter 6

Candlesticks in the Miasmal Mist: The Church and T.S. Eliot

Martin Warner

I

> The Apostles speak, or have always been supposed to speak, of a *Church*, a one Catholic Church, as established, or about to be established, on this earth. They connect that Church with the gift of a Spirit, who is called the Holy Spirit, who, it was said, should dwell in the Church as He did not in the world who was to purify the hearts of its members. Where is this Church? What does History say of it? What do our eyes tell us about it?
>
> Frederick Denison Maurice, *Theological Essays*[1]

The words F.D. Maurice put in the mouth of a critical Unitarian point to a nest of problems which was to preoccupy T.S. Eliot, from the relatively early (1917) sardonic comparison of the 'merely flesh and blood' hippopotamus with the 'True Church' (which 'can never fail / For it is based upon a rock'), through the 1934 choruses for 'The Rock' (where the local community of the 'forever decaying' Church has distinguished itself by exporting 'capital / And several versions of the Word of GOD'), to 'Little Gidding's (1942) 'marred foundations we forgot, / Of sanctuary and choir'.[2]

Taken by itself, 'The Hippopotamus's double-edged appropriation of Théophile Gautier's image to mock 'both the grotesque image of humanity and the institution of "the True Church"'[3] could well be dismissed as no more than a playful *jeu d'esprit*.[4] But, as Martin Scofield notes, 'there is a seriousness in the scepticism', and the poem's placing in a series that moves from 'Gerontion' to Sweeney in Oedipus' death grove suggests a deeper movement of thought.

Its New Testament epigraph addresses 'The Hippopotamus' to the church of the Laodiceans,[5] best remembered for being the only one of the seven churches picked out wholly negatively in the Revelation of St John the Divine:

> I know thy works, that thou art neither cold nor hot: I would that thou wert cold or hot. So then because thou art lukewarm, and neither cold nor hot, I will spue thee out of my mouth. Because thou sayest, I am rich, and increased with goods, and have need of nothing; and knowest not that thou art wretched, and miserable, and poor, and blind, and naked: I counsel thee to buy of me gold tried in the fire, that thou mayest be rich ... As many as I love, I rebuke and chasten: be zealous therefore, and repent.[6]

One remembers the Pauline contention that 'the love of money is the root of all evil',[7] and notes that in a 1937 broadcast talk Eliot suggests that 'Perhaps the dominant vice of our time, from the point of view of the Church, will be proved to be Avarice.'[8]

With this clue it is worth looking more closely at the critique of the Church in 'The Hippopotamus'. By contrast with the gross, vulnerable and errant 'potamus, who despite his best efforts 'can never reach / The mango on the mango-tree', 'fruits of pomegranate and peach / Refresh the Church from over sea', for 'the True Church need never stir / To gather in its dividends' and therefore 'can sleep and feed at once'(49). The relative advantages are reversed in the concluding vision with the unmusical 'potamus grotesquely 'performing on a harp of gold' among the saints and 'martyr'd virgins' above, 'While the True Church remains below / Wrapt in the old miasmal mist'(50).

Given this reversal, we are invited to treat the claim that the latter 'can never fail' as ironic, and its apparently harmonious rejoicing 'at being one with God' as a symptom of potentially damnable complacency associated, as with the Laodicean church, with increase of goods. The joke against the Church in large part depends, as A.D. Moody remarks, 'on the absurdity of such grossness entering into heaven',[9] but when later Eliot embraced the Church and sought to contribute to building a Christian society in his adopted country, what had been a sceptical 'playing with theological notions ("with a puzzled and humorous shifting of the pieces")'[10] provides the materials for an at least partially self-addressed denunciation of complacency and the idolatry of riches. 'The events of September 1938', he wrote, referring to those surrounding the dishonorable 'peace with honour' of Munich, gave rise in himself and many others to 'a feeling of humiliation, which seemed to demand an act of personal contrition, of humility, repentance and amendment':

> We could not match conviction with conviction ... Was our society, which had always been so assured of its superiority and rectitude, so confident of its unexamined premises, assembled round anything more permanent than a congeries of banks, insurance companies and industries, and had it any beliefs more essential than a belief in compound interest and the maintenance of dividends?[11]

Given such a radical questioning, the wealth of the Church must itself come under judgment.[12]

II

How the Church can be both 'one with God' and under judgement presents a problem as old as the New Testament. Moody's curious claim that 'The Hippopotamus' 'explodes the clichés upon which the established Church rests'[13] suggests that it may be worth excavating behind them, for it is remarkably difficult to give a coherent and accurate account of the Church that is faithful to all the orthodox requirements. Not only is it, as the body of Christ, involved in the paradoxes attendant upon incarnation, but the sinlessness attributed to Jesus as the Word incarnate can only by an astonishing *tour de force* be attributed to the historical church which is only too obviously 'Wrapt in the old miasmal mist'.

Of course, simply taking the dominant moral, political, economic, or indeed linguistic or literary, assumptions of one's own culture and period as providing established criteria by which to judge the Church or Scripture is necessarily problematic, for from the Church's scriptural point of view the 'world' with its assumptions is itself under judgement; a society that took seriously the new moral geometry of the Gospels would look very different from any we have seen. But this does not provide the historical Church with *carte blanche*, as the Reformers spectacularly insisted; St Paul maintained that the existence of conscience bears witness to the moral law being written into human nature,[14] and it has always been recognized that the Church's teaching must be brought into positive relation with the informed and sensitive consciences of those who are prepared to learn from it

At the level of the individual, St John advocated the confession that leads to forgiveness and that walking 'in the light' which involves love of God and brother rather than love of 'the world', for 'if we say that we have no sin, we deceive ourselves.'[15] From New Testament times onwards, the borderline between the pastoral problem, of encouraging repentance and walking in the light, and the disciplinary one, of excluding from the congregation those who continue to walk in the darkness and apparently refuse to accept the need for serious repentance, has been a delicate one. The issues arising from the recurrent rigorist reactions to the growing institutionalism of the Church became acute when Imperial favour was extended to Christianity under Constantine in the fourth century. In the modern period, the competing claims of rigorism and a liberalizing 'casuistry' were dramatized in Pascal's *Lettres provinciales* (1656–57), and in Eliot's own native and adopted countries rigorism has been best known in its Puritan versions. The tension is probably inevitable; as Eliot's friend Charles Williams put it:

> The contention is always sharp. The Rigorous view is vital to sanctity; the Relaxed view is vital to sanity. Their union is not impossible, but it is difficult; for whichever is in power begins, after the first five minutes, to maintain itself from bad and unworthy motives. Harshness, pride, resentment encourage the one; indulgence, falsity, detestable good-fellowship the other.[16]

But while there are clearly serious issues of moral and pastoral theology, and of Church discipline, raised by the sinfulness of human beings as individuals, it is at the collective level that some of the most difficult intellectual problems arise, at once theological and philosophical. St Augustine had to confront, for example, isolationists such as the fourth-century Donatists who denied that a body that accepted as a bishop one who had collaborated with the (previously) persecuting civil power could itself be the Church. For Augustine such isolationism (which effectively reduced the 'true' Church to Africa) was a betrayal of its mission to the world and a failure to read the providential signs of the times: 'The clouds roll with thunder, that the House of the Lord shall be built throughout the earth: and these frogs sit in their marsh and croak – We are the only Christians!'[17]

In this dispute the claim of the Church to be 'catholic', universal in scope as well as doctrine, seems to find itself in tension with its claim to be 'holy', a tension which itself puts in doubt its claim to be 'one', a doubt St Augustine sought to meet, in part, by reference to its fourth mark, as set out in the Nicene Creed, that of being 'apostolic'. The challenge presented to the Church by the evidence of its apparent collective failures to 'walk in the light' takes us back to its own self-understanding.

III

The Church as it appears in the New Testament is the new Israel. The Greek term 'ecclesia', employed by Matthew in reporting Christ's declaration 'Upon this rock I will build my church; and the gates of hell shall not prevail against it',[18] is used in the Septuagint to mean 'the people of God', called or assembled together by appointment. The term is a favorite designation for the Christian community by St Paul,[19] is widely used in Acts and Revelation, and also appears in the epistle to the Hebrews, but there are a number of other terms, descriptions and images for that community, perhaps most obviously 'flock', 'vine', 'light', 'bride' (all with Old Testament antecedents), 'the body of Christ', 'the temple of God', 'the children of God', 'the household of God', 'the people of God' and 'the Israel of God'. Paul Minear has identified some eighty analogies and designations for the Christian community in the New Testament, in addition to the one that has become dominant in Christian thinking, the body of Christ.[20]

The image in terms of which the Laodicean church is called to repentance is that of light or, more specifically, a candlestick which raises a candle so that it can give light.[21] 'Ecclesia' is used to designate not only the new Israel but also a localized community; the geographically scattered churches, however, are seen as local embodiments of the whole household of God. This is particularly clear in St Paul, who writes of 'the church which is at Corinth' and not 'the Corinthian church'.[22] Analogously, for the visionary of Revelation the seven golden candlesticks 'are' the 'seven churches which are in Asia', each candlestick a particular local church, but they are grouped about the 'one like unto the Son of man' who 'walketh in the midst' of them, who has authority over them, and the light of whose face is 'as the sun shineth in his strength': 'the churches burn as candles around him, but his own radiance is greater.'[23] Their unification around a single center 'in the Spirit' is what is primary, not their terrestrially diverse locations. To the extent that they behave unspiritually, therefore, the local churches offend against their own principle of unity and are thereby under judgement: 'He that hath an ear, let him hear what the Spirit saith unto the churches.'[24]

From very early times, the Church has read its scriptures through Trinitarian eyes, and in this perspective there need be no conflict in the book of Revelation's tendency to attribute specific words of judgement at once to Christ, the Spirit and the Almighty. But if the Christian community at, say, Laodicea is a local embodiment of the whole Church, if the Church is Christ's body, and if the union of Christ, the Spirit and the Almighty is so close that the action of one can be the action of all, some of the problems that underlie Maurice's Unitarian challenge can be reformulated. How does the Trinitarian unity differ from that between Christ and his body the Church? How could the action of the Church ever, even as it 'gathers in its dividends', differ from that of Christ himself? Or, to put the matter in reverse, if Christ can sit in judgement on the Laodicean church and threaten to 'spue thee out of my mouth', does this show that it is not part of the true Church, or that the union of Christ with his Church has not the unity we associate between an individual and his or her own body, or that we should construe such rejection on the analogy of amputation? The first option points in the direction of a distinction between the 'visible' and the 'invisible' Church, adumbrated in Augustine and developed by the Reformers, but scripturally difficult; the second seems to invalidate scripture, and the third would appear to read the promise that 'the gates of hell will not prevail against it' as guaranteeing that the main body of the Church will remain as sinless as its judge. The final option, of course, returns us to Maurice's challenge: Where is this Church? What does History say of it? What do our eyes tell us about it?

If the Church is the new Israel, it may be worth considering how the Old Testament construed the old Israel's relation to its God. The basis of this relationship was, of course, the Covenant, and covenants can be broken; in its exploration of Israel's failure to live up to its calling one set of descriptions and images has particular resonance in the New Testament, that concerning the love between husband and wife. In Revelation, Christ tells the seven churches that 'as many as I love I rebuke and chasten', and the acted parable of the opening chapters of Hosea provides an analogy; when Israel the unfaithful 'wife' returns to the Lord he declares 'I will betroth thee unto me for ever' as in Revelation's concluding vision of 'the bride, the Lamb's wife'.[25] Analogously Paul (or Deutero-Paul) uses the relationship between Christ and the Church as a model for marital relationships:

> Husbands, love your wives, even as Christ also loved the church, and gave himself for it ... that it should be holy and without blemish. So ought men to love their wives as their own bodies. He that loveth his wife loveth himself. For no man ever yet hated his own flesh; but nourisheth and cherisheth it, even as the Lord the church. For we are members of his body, of his flesh, and of his bones.[26]

Ideally, the love of Christ and his bride is reciprocal, but until the time of the new heaven and the new earth,[27] that of the bride, or at least of her local instantiations, may be at best 'lukewarm' – as the Old Testament model acknowledged. This, however, does not prevent Christ loving it as himself as, analogously, husbands should love even errant wives 'as their own bodies'. The unity between an individual and his or her own body invoked in the image of the Church as the body of Christ is, it would appear, less than straightforward.

Such unsettling of the 'Church as body' image by that of the 'Church as wife' – unsettling to the extent that Christ's body becomes female – points to a broader feature of the Pauline corpus, and indeed of theological thought and expression more generally, that much of it represents the art of balancing – and indeed contrasting – images, models, analogies and parables.[28] As Paul Minear argues, 'the phrase "the body of Christ" is not a single expression with an unchanging meaning. Paul's thought remains extremely flexible and elastic'[29] – and hence dynamic, even explosive.

In Ephesians, not only are members of the Church 'members of [Christ's] body', but Christ is also 'the head of the church'. A somewhat literal minded way of taking this analogy might be that the human members of the Church relate to Christ as the rest of a human body does to its head, but this image hardly squares with the extended account of the 'one body' in I Corinthians where ear, eye and nose are seen as different organs coordinate with hand and foot.[30] Rather, the figure of Christ as the head of the Church 'not only signifies the dependence of the Church on Christ for life and strength, but asserts his sovereignty over it',[31] an account which harmonizes well with the relation of the golden candlesticks to the 'one like unto the Son of man'.

Further complexity emerges if one presses the claim that the body has 'nourishment ministered' by 'the Head', for it is not just the Church which is termed 'the body of Christ', but also the broken eucharistic loaf: *Hoc est enim corpus meum* ('This is my body').[32] The bread is presumably the body of Christ in a different sense than the Church is, members of the Church are not here seen as engaging in auto-cannibalism; the members of the ecclesial body of Christ are nourished through Christ's sacramental body, thereby participating in the transformation achieved by that death and its sequel.

John Robinson goes one step further, arguing that *soma* ('body') be interpreted corporally, 'as the extension of the life and person of the incarnate Christ beyond His resurrection and ascension'.[33] But this, of course, is to return us to our central problem: in what sense can the Church be conceived as 'the extension of Christ's personality'? Even if we do not follow Robinson's reading, we are still faced with the problem of the sense in which those who partake of Christ's body and blood participate in the transformation supposedly wrought by Christ. In what sense are members of the Christian community 'one body in Christ'?[34]

IV

Augustine's answer was to prove seminal for Western Christendom:

> It is good ... that all the whole and holy society of the redeemed and sanctified city be offered unto God by that great Priest who gave up His life in so mean a form for us to make us members of so great a head ... We are one body with Christ, as the Church celebrates in the sacrament of the altar ... wherein is shown that in that oblation the Church is offered.[35]

The validity of the rites of the Church, he elsewhere argues, is guaranteed by their apostolicity, being the rites of the organization connected through the Apostolic Sees, and hence through episcopal succession, with the Apostles. Through these rites the Church participates in the holiness of Christ and the loving unity of the Trinity, the notion of 'participation' being given a strongly neo-Platonic flavor; those who administer them strive imperfectly to realize, or participate in, this holiness and unity, thereby exemplifying a shadow of the reality, of the true Jerusalem. The two symbolic cities of Babylon and Jerusalem have always existed, being founded respectively on the two possibilities of human motivation: love of self, and love of that perceived as good (with attendant self-forgetfulness or death to self) – the former the principle of the city of Satan, the latter of the city of God. The two cities are inextricably mixed, though, even within the Church, the tares growing with the wheat until the day of judgement. For Augustine, the world-wide unity of the Catholic Church is a shadow of the 'sanctified city'[36] but, as with the historical Israel, 'membership of them cannot in itself make men perfect: the dividing-line between the two "cities" is invisible', because it involves each man's capacity to love.[37] Augustine implies that not all members of the Church are true members, which is how the Reformers came to insist on the distinction between the visible and invisible Church. For Augustine, however, matters are not so simple, since he argues that the invisible Church is grounded in the visible sacramental body: the notorious tag *Salus extra Ecclesiam non est* ('There is no salvation outside the Church') comes from his treatise on baptism, through which the visible Church is entered.[38]

Much, though not all, of Augustine's teaching was still 'live' in the Church of England when Eliot was received into it in 1927. The Article (XIX) on the Church in its Thirty-Nine Articles identifies the Church with the visible Church, though H.J. Bicknell's commentary (first published 1919) concedes that the 'edges' of the visible Church 'are blurred'.[39] Against this it should be noted that one of its formative theologians, Richard Hooker, maintained a distinction between 'that Church of Christ, which we properly term his body mystical' and 'this visible Church'.[40] The 1947 Report on *Catholicity* to which Eliot was a co-signatory commented that

> Though his doctrine of the Church was influenced by the Calvinist idea of an invisible Church, Hooker broke away from Calvinist presuppositions in making the Incarnation the centre of his theology, in linking the Sacraments directly with the Incarnation, and in rejecting the tendency to draw a closed circle around the inward and spiritual. Hooker was a pioneer.[41]

Bicknell invokes, in good Augustinian fashion, 'the description of the Church in the Nicene Creed as "One, Holy, Catholic, and Apostolic"', and remarks that 'these four "notes" are intimately connected with one another and depend on the truth that the Church is the Body of Christ ... [which] includes the body which is "militant here on earth" and also the faithful dead.'[42] He also draws attention to the so-called 'Lambeth Quadrilateral' according to which visible unity must be based on general acceptance of 'the Scriptures, the faith of the Nicene Creed, the Sacraments of Baptism and Holy Communion, and the episcopate with its historic functions and continuity'[43] – the latter of course an updating of Augustine's reading of apostolicity.

Turning to 'the tension between the Divine nature of the Church and the sinfulness of its members', the *Catholicity* Report remarks that 'St Paul did not cut the knot by anticipating later doctrines of the "invisible Church"', and aligns itself with 'the apostolic writers [who] cling to the paradox that the Church both is the Body of Christ, and also consists of sinful and fallible members'. The paradox, however, can hardly be said to be resolved; appeal is made to the 'wholeness' of the primitive Church's vision 'wherein the strain of the Church's paradox does not weaken the Christian's belief in what the Church is. In all its aspects, the primitive "wholeness" is the "wholeness", not of an *ideal* but of something that *is*.'[44] The status of a belief that the Church is 'whole', as distinct from its wholeness being an ideal, remains unclear.

The obscurity of this appeal may be in part 'placed', however, by reading it in the light of the work of Michael Ramsey, a contributor to the Report and later, of course, Archbishop of Canterbury. In *The Gospel and the Catholic Church*, published in 1936, Ramsey had argued that such paradoxes should be rooted in the paradox of Calvary itself.

> The heavenly status of the Church can hardly be exaggerated, but it is a sovereignty of dying and risen life, it is apprehended through faith in the Cross, and its power is known in humiliation, and neither the resurrection of the Christ nor the place of the Church beside him can be perceived by the mind of the world. But though the Church has died and risen, the end is not yet; and, by one of the many paradoxes of the New Testament, there is a dying and a rising still to be experienced, and the Church is the scene of dying and rising in every age of history.

He identifies both 'the inner conflict with sin and the outer bearing of pain' as ways in which 'the Church is a scene of continual dying', a struggle in which tribulation may be 'transformed into a pain which is creative ... This reconciling work of God is the history of the Christian Church.'[45] On this account, the scandal of the Church is subsumed within the scandal of the Gospel:

> The relevance of the Church can never be any easier than was the relevance of the Messiah ... 'My God, My God, why hast thou forsaken me?' So ended his earthly life, but in the manner of its end and in the 'why?' uttered on Calvary, there was present the power of God ... His Church on earth is scandalous, with the question-marks set against it by bewildered men and with the question-mark of Calvary at the centre of its teaching; yet precisely there is the power of God found ... Of course it is scandalous, of course it is formed of sinners whose sinfulness is exposed by the light of the Cross, of course there is an awful question-mark at its centre. These things must needs be, if it is the Body of Christ crucified and risen from the dead.[46]

It is no doubt salutary to be reminded that the place of the Church cannot 'be perceived by the mind of the world',[47] but Ramsey suggests at least one possibility for palliating the paradox of the sinfulness of the holy body. If the Church is indeed scandalous in the light of the Cross, but in its conflict with sin is a scene of continuing dying – not least dying to itself – then in its given holiness it has no room for pride and much for humility and contrition, through which alone holiness and sin may be reconciled. This was the conclusion of Charles Williams, in his remarkable 'History of the Holy Spirit in the Church' (1939). Drawing attention, *inter alia*, to the 1920 Lambeth Conference 'Appeal' of the bishops of the Anglican Communion, he remarks that 'the last virtue which the organization of Christendom can achieve is humility', and concludes:

> For the first time a 'great and sacred synod', formally convoked, formally speaking, admitted its own spiritual guilt. 'It has seemed good', they said, in almost those words, 'to the Holy Ghost and to us' that we should confess that we have sinned. If Christendom indeed feels intensely within itself the three strange energies which we call contrition and humility and doctrine, it will be again close ... to the Descent of the Dove.[48]

From this perspective, the scandal of the True Church of 'The Hippopotamus' is that, while it may be strong on doctrine, it displays neither contrition nor humility.

V

Where they bear on the Church, Eliot's prose writings are hardly at the impressive intellectual and spiritual level of Ramsey and Williams. Indeed, one of the minor oddities of his deeply flawed Page-Barbour lectures published (and then deliberately never republished) as *After Strange Gods* is his attitude to the criticism that there is 'an apparent incoherence between my verse and my critical prose ... It would appear that while I maintain the most correct opinions in my criticism, I do nothing but violate them in my verse.' His response is simply that 'in one's prose reflexions one may be legitimately occupied with ideals, whereas in the writing of verse one can only deal with actuality.'[49] His insistence that insincerity with respect to the actuality of one's experience is a mark of bad poetry is, indeed, interesting and plausible, but the divorce of ideals from actuality is far from unproblematic,[50] and the thought that Eliot's poetry violates the 'correct opinions' of his prose is allowed, one hopes ironically, to stand.

After Strange Gods: A Primer of Modern Heresy (1934) attempts to explore contemporary culture in terms of extensions of such concepts as orthodoxy and heresy whose normal home is the Church. There would appear to be a recognizably Augustinian perception of the Church's mission to the world behind the project, but little heed is given to the dangers implicit in its advocacy of social arrangements that can all too easily be seen as primarily achievable by the methods of Augustine's city of Babylon – a problem long ago complained of by the Donatists. Notoriously, in defending the cultural desirability of a 'living tradition', including 'unity of religious background', to facilitate intelligent discrimination, he writes of the desirability of homogeneity in a population; 'a spirit of excessive tolerance is to be deprecated' he remarks, shortly after claiming that 'reasons of race and religion combine to make any large number of free-thinking Jews undesirable.'[51] Whether or not the primary target is 'freethinking' or Jews as such, the words were plainly untimely in 1933 when the lectures were given, however far thoughts of persecution were from Eliot's mind, and he has been properly criticized for them. But beyond this, Eliot's master concepts seem ill-suited to their task; he admits the wide difference between 'tradition' and 'orthodoxy' while insisting on their affinity, but it may be that that very insistence, leading to an attempt to articulate 'tradition' in the light of the concept of 'orthodoxy', involves incoherence. Orthodoxy can be constructed or striven towards, but hardly tradition,[52] and if we drop the notion of orthodoxy here the 'heresy' of Eliot's subtitle is evacuated of content.

Eliot's later *The Idea of a Christian Society* (1939) is more judicious, and with a different focus. He is concerned with the possibility of a 'Christian society' in countries such as England where there was already a certain degree of homogeneity, and he explicitly rejects any suggestion of 'forcible suppression' where this does not apply. He identifies three ways in which the Church must relate to contemporary society: the ecclesiastical hierarchy must have a 'direct and official relation to the State'; its organization, such as a parochial system, must be 'in direct contact with the smallest units of the community'; and its theologians must stand in a positive relation to 'the Community of Christians'. This latter community is a looser version of Coleridge's clerisy which is able 'collectively to form the conscious mind and the conscience of the nation'.⁵³ As the Church may properly rebuke the State, so 'the hierarchy of the Church may be under attack from the Community of Christians, or from groups within it: for any organisation is always in danger of corruption and in need of reform from within.'⁵⁴ But the Church is supposed to be more than simply an organization, let alone its hierarchy, and whether the Church itself may be properly rebuked is a matter left unaddressed.

In the Church of England, as we have seen, this issue has provoked disagreement between those, following Hooker, who distinguish the mystical from the visible Church and those, following its Thirty-Nine Articles, who make no such distinction. Eliot's praise of the 'intellectual achievement' of Hooker and contention that 'the achievement of Hooker and Andrewes was to make the English Church more worthy of intellectual assent'⁵⁵ might lead one to expect him either to side with Hooker in this debate or to dissent respectfully and with reasons. The reality is startling. He takes as his key illustration of Hooker's virtues his 'definition of the Church in the second book of the "Ecclesiastical Polity". ("The Church of Christ which was from the beginning is and continueth until the end.")'. This is astonishingly careless.⁵⁶ Not only does the discussion of the Church belong to the *third* book, but here it is the visible Church which 'continued from the first beginning of the world to the last end', which is carefully distinguished from 'The Church of Christ', a term to be applied either to Christ's 'body mystical' or, where to the visible Church, to that part which has come into existence 'since the coming of Christ'.⁵⁷ Eliot's unchecked memory gets the details exactly wrong, though the description of Hooker's qualities he uses the misquotation to illustrate, 'clarity and precision on matters of importance', is exactly right; one remembers that the subtitle indicates that the book of essays in which it appears is primarily concerned with 'style and order'.

This suggests that it may be unprofitable to seek in Eliot's prose writings for ecclesiological wrestling with the challenge of 'The Hippopotamus'. As so often with Eliot, it is his poetry that cuts deepest, as he wrestles to articulate the 'actuality' of his experience – employing what he later described as poetic 'philosophical structure': 'an organisation, not merely of successive responses to the situation, but of further responses to [the poet's] own responses', a description which, as I have argued elsewhere, fits *Four Quartets* with some precision.⁵⁸ With respect to the Church, clearly, this experience must be conceived as at least in part communal, and it is in the last three (1940–42) of his *Four Quartets* that he most fully seeks to interrogate communal experience, relating local to universal and past to present, with an eye to the possible transfiguration and even redemption of the mundane.

In 'East Coker', the community invoked is that of his English ancestors, but the 'wisdom of age' is largely rejected so long as it is dominated by self-concern – fear 'Of belonging to another, or to others, or to God' (179). It is only in risking everything ('Through the dark cold and the empty desolation'(183)), as had those who had left for the New World ('Out at sea the dawn wind / Wrinkles and slides'(178)), that genuinely new possibilities emerge and we can move from 'In the beginning is my end' to 'In my end is my beginning' (177, 183). Rather than second-hand reliance on 'the quiet voiced elders', 'The only wisdom we can hope to acquire / Is the wisdom of humility'(179); humility, one remembers, had been identified by

Williams the previous year as 'the last virtue which the organization of Christendom can achieve'.[59]

The community of 'The Dry Salvages' is more factitious. Although his own early experience by the Mississippi and sailing off Gloucester, Massachusetts is evoked, his imaginative extension of it to encompass that of the chorus of 'anxious worried women'(185) and the wider American experience is just that – imaginative rather than part of his own 'actuality'. The strongest sense of first-hand communal feeling comes with what is only available, unspecifically, 'for most of us': 'the unattended / Moment, the moment in and out of time'; 'the rest', we are told, 'Is prayer, observance, discipline, thought and action'(190). Taken together these enable the 'Incarnation' to be named ('Here the impossible union / Of spheres of existence is actual') as 'The hint half guessed, the gift half understood'. The poetry appears to fold back on itself, so that if this Christian community is to be conceived in terms of 'the household of God', it will itself participate in the 'impossible union' as a 'gift half understood' and its prayer evince the humility of section IV, of the 'one Annunciation', seeking to conform its will to that of the 'Queen of Heaven' who experienced that impossibility in her own body – 'Figlia del tuo figlio' (189), Dante's 'Daughter of thine own son'.

But there is another community implicit in these poems that only comes fully into focus in 'Little Gidding', that of Eliot and his compatriots, bound together in an unanticipated form of 'homogeneity', as they participate in a desperate war. In 'East Coker', this experience infiltrates the language and sensibility – witness 'undisciplined squads' and 'the years of *l'entre deux guerres*'(182); likewise, in 'The Dry Salvages' the naval blockade seems present – witness 'the drifting wreckage'(185), and 'pray for those who were in ships'(189); whilst in 'Little Gidding' we have a direct evocation of Eliot's experience of fire watching in London: 'Dust in the air suspended'(192), 'water and fire', and 'the dark dove with the flickering tongue'(193). This experience provides a major part of the poem's drive, with the 'dark dove' transposed in the climactic final lyric into 'The dove descending breaks the air / With flame of incandescent terror'(196). United with this communal experience is Eliot's personal experience of one of those 'places / Which are also the world's end'(192), where a community of Christians dedicated to 'prayer, observance, discipline, thought and action' had, with its 'broken king'(191), met defeat as he and his fellows now faced it. This final Quartet seeks to unite personal experience – the poetry responding to the poet's own immediate responses – with that of a community through the perspective of significant history seen as 'a pattern / Of timeless moments', identification with which makes it possible for a 'people' to be 'redeemed from time'(197). Such 'redemption', however, is not without cost; it involves purgation through 'the moments of agony' here presented under the figure of 'fire'.

The community of Little Gidding was itself a local embodiment of the Church, but so too were some of 'those who opposed them' (as indeed were some of the enemy in 1942) who also showed themselves prepared to die for their beliefs, thereby pointing us beyond self-concern (to, indeed, Augustine's City of God). In 'The Dry Salvages' such actions 'fructify in the lives of others'(188), and in 'Little Gidding' both 'those who opposed them / And those whom they opposed', 'United in the strife which divided them', have left us 'A symbol perfected in death'. In this perspective, the experience of sacrifice is as essential as the ecstatic 'moment in and out of time' ('The moment of the rose and the moment of the yew-tree / Are of equal duration'(197)) and the aspired-to 'condition of complete simplicity' is one 'Costing not less than everything'(198).

There is a double movement: 'We die with the dying', for 'See, now they vanish, / The faces and places, with the self which, as it could, loved them, / To become renewed, transfigured, in another pattern'(195), so that 'We are born with the dead'(195). The self must vanish for transfiguration to be possible, a possibility only available in and through the community. The community invoked is, primarily though not exclusively, that of the Church with its spiritual teachers which, in its 'intersection of the timeless / With time', is called to embody 'death in love / Ardour and selflessness and self-surrender', though 'most' of its members 'are only undefeated / Because we have gone on trying'(192–3). In a self-addressed passage of 'communal' dialogue the poet acknowledges 'things ill done and done to others' harm / Which once you took for exercise of virtue', and the need both to 'pray they be forgiven' and of purgation through 'refining fire' (194–5). Since the personal in this final Quartet aspires to the communal, the poetry suggests that the Christian community of the Church requires that which Williams considered as needful to face 'The dove descending', and which was notably lacking in the complacent True Church of 'The Hippopotamus' – namely contrition.[60]

There are many false voices in the *Quartets* which Eliot could not disown but sought to overcome (most obviously that of the 'eminent man of letters', no longer externalized as it had been in his prose). The final perceptions are won (some perhaps more securely than others) not primarily by argument but through poetic and imagistic meditation on and response to his own initial responses. However, if the language of theology is significantly imagistic and parabolic, then the approach of the *Quartets* may be as appropriate as that of a Hooker or a Ramsey. The pilgrimage from the close of the first Quartet – 'Quick now, here, now, always – / Ridiculous the waste sad time / Stretching before and after'(176) – to the final resolution – 'Quick now, here, now, always – / A condition of complete simplicity (Costing not less than everything)'(198) – involves a transformation of Eliot's own sensibility, in part made possible by the 'actuality' of his wartime experience as a member of a community under siege. The pilgrimage is also the index of a transfiguration from the perception of the True Church comparing badly with the grotesque (a harp-playing hippopotamus) to a vision in which 'The marred foundations ... / Of sanctuary and choir' point to a 'symbol perfected in death'.

Notes

I am grateful to the editor for a number of suggestions on the basis of an earlier draft of this essay, most of which I have accepted.

1. Frederick Denison Maurice, *Theological Essays*, ed. E.F. Carpenter (London: James Clarke, [1853] 1957), p. 263.
2. *The Complete Poems and Plays of T.S. Eliot* (London: Faber and Faber, 1969), pp. 49,

152, 193. All subsequent references to Eliot's poetry are to this edition and appear parenthetically in the essay.
3   Martin Scofield, *T.S. Eliot: the poems* (Cambridge: Cambridge University Press, 1988), p. 94.
4   Eliot himself might be construed as encouraging such a dismissal, distinguishing between poems that were not really 'serious', like 'The Hippopotamus', and serious ones such as 'Sweeney Among the Nightingales' – see Peter Ackroyd, *T.S. Eliot*, (London: Hamish Hamilton, 1984), pp. 92, 343. But what counts as poetically 'serious' here is not exactly clear; one notes that Ackroyd aligns the former group with 'satiric argumentation', the latter with 'dramatic and verbal intensity' – a criterion which would curiously prejudge, for example, the seriousness of Rochester's 'Satyre against Reason and Mankind'.
5   Taken from Colossians 4:16.
6   Revelation 3:15–19. I have normally, as here, used the Authorised Version [AV] translation (used by Eliot for his epigraph to 'The Hippopotamus'), with an eye to the Revised Version [RV] with its margin, and occasional reference back to the originals.
7   1 Timothy 6:10.
8   Published as an Appendix to Eliot's *The Idea of a Christian Society* (London: Faber and Faber, 1939); see p. 97.
9   A.D. Moody, *Thomas Stearns Eliot: Poet* (Cambridge: Cambridge University Press, 1980), p. 63.
10 Scofield, *T.S. Eliot*, p. 94.
11 Conclusion to Eliot's, *The Idea of a Christian Society*, p. 64.
12 I refer, in the first instance, to the wealth of the established Church of England, an organization to which Eliot belonged and without which, he believed, 'no Christianisation of England can take place' (*The Idea of a Christian Society*, p. 47); but Eliot also has in mind the wealth of 'Christendom as a whole' (p. 46) and of the Church more generally as it 'gathers in its dividends'.
13 Moody, *Thomas Stearns Eliot: Poet*, p. 63.
14 Romans 2:14–15.
15 1 John 1:8.
16 Charles Williams, *The Descent of the Dove: A Short History of the Holy Spirit in the Church* (London: Faber and Faber, [1939] 1955), p. 31.
17 Augustine, *Enarrationes in Psalmos* XCV 11; translation taken from Peter Brown, *Augustine of Hippo* (London: Faber and Faber, 1967) p. 221.
18 Matthew 16:18; the saying plays an ironic role in 'The Hippopotamus'.
19 The standard English translations render *ecclesia* as 'church' in its New Testament occurrences.
20 Paul S. Minear, *Images of the Church in the New Testament* (London: Lutterworth Press, 1960).
21 The RV margin plausibly prefers 'lampstand'; Revelation 1:20; compare Matthew 5:15–16 and Zechariah 4:1–2.
22 1 Corinthians 1:2; 2 Corinthians 1:1.
23 Revelation 1:10–2:1; Austin Farrer, *The Revelation of St John the Divine* (Oxford: Clarendon Press, 1964), p. 66.
24 Revelation 2:22.
25 Hosea 3:19 (and see also Ezekiel 16:8–14); Revelation 21:9. On this model, unfaithfulness to the Covenant, especially as represented by idolatry, is figured as the defilement of adultery.
26 Ephesians 5:25–30.
27 Revelation 21:1–2.

28 Perhaps the most influential philosophico-theological restatement of this theme emerged from the Anglican stable around half a century ago in the work of Austin Farrer, Ian Crombie, Ian Ramsey and others. Farrer was a fellow contributor with Eliot to the Report on *Catholicity* presented to the Archbishop of Canterbury in 1947.
29 Minear, *Images of the Church*, p. 173.
30 1 Corinthians 12:12–30.
31 F.J. Taylor, 'Body' in *A Theological Word Book of the Bible*, ed. Alan Richardson (London: SCM, 1950), p. 35.
32 1 Corinthians 11:24–7.
33 John A.T. Robinson, *The Body* (London: SCM Press, 1952), pp. 57–8. It should be noted that the linguistic underpinnings of this whole line of argument have been subjected to severe criticism by James Barr, *The Semantics of Biblical Language*, (Oxford: Oxford University Press, 1961), pp. 34–8. Barr's linguistic arguments seem decisive; how far this touches Robinson's broader theological claim is another matter.
34 Romans 12:5.
35 Augustine, *The City of God*, tr. R.V.G. Tasker, 2 vols (London: Dent, Everyman Library, 1945), vol. 1, pp. 279–80.
36 'The holy city, new Jerusalem, coming down from God out of heaven, prepared as a bride adorned for her husband', Revelation 21:2.
37 Peter Brown, *Augustine of Hippo*, p. 323; chapters 19 and 27 give convenient sets of detailed references for much of the web of textual authority supporting this paragraph.
38 *De Baptismo*, IV. xvii.24. Caution however is necessary here, since for Augustine the Donatists had valid sacraments yet were outside the visible community of the Church; Augustine is here resisting the Donatists' attempt to interpret Cyprian's similar dictum in an exclusivist manner.
39 H.J. Bicknell, *A Theological Introduction to the Thirty-Nine Articles of the Church of England*, 3rd edn, ed. H. J. Carpenter (London: Longmans, 1955), p. 245. The first edition was published in 1919 and very quickly became the standard work on the Articles in Anglican theological colleges; it remained so well after Eliot's death and is still in use today. Carpenter's third edition, from which the quotation is taken, is an update and expansion 'on conservative lines' (p. v).
40 *The Works of that Learned and Judicious Divine, Mr Richard Hooker*, ed. John Keble, 3 vols, 3rd edn (Oxford: University Press, 1845), Vol. I, Book III, ch. I, sects 2–3, pp. 338–9.
41 E.S. Abbot *et al.*, *Catholicity: A Study in the Conflict of Christian Traditions in the West* (London: Dacre Press, 1947), p. 50. The fourteen signatories included Eliot himself, Farrer (as already noted), Carpenter (subsequently to update Bicknell *op. cit.*), and Michael Ramsey, later Archbishop of Canterbury.
42 Bicknell, *A Theological Introduction*, p. 234.
43 Ibid., p. 244.
44 Abbot, *Catholicity*, pp. 12 and 16–17.
45 Arthur Michael Ramsey, *The Gospel and the Catholic Church*, 2nd edn (London: Longmans, [1936] 1956), pp. 39–41.
46 Ibid., pp. 4–5.
47 Ramsey is of course echoing 1 Corinthians 1:23–4, where the preaching of the Cross is 'unto the Greeks foolishness ... but unto them which are called ... the power of God'.
48 Williams, *Descent of the Dove*, pp. 232–3.
49 T.S. Eliot, *After Strange Gods: A Primer of Modern Heresy* (London: Faber and Faber, 1934), p. 28.
50 The difficulty of the *Catholicity* Report's contrast of an ideal with 'something that is', noted above, throws some light on this.

51 Eiot, *After Strange Gods*, pp. 19–20.
52 Anthony Julius comments tartly on the project that, 'within Eliot's terms of reference', 'the only traditions that can be created are bogus ones'; see his *T.S. Eliot, Anti-Semitism and Literary Form* (Cambridge: Cambridge University Press, 1995) pp. 255, 156.
53 Eliot, *The Idea of a Christian Society*, pp. 43–5.
54 Ibid., pp. 47–8.
55 'Lancelot Andrewes', in Eliot's *For Lancelot Andrewes: Essays on Style and Order* (London: Faber & Gwyer, 1928), pp. 16–17.
56 Ibid., p. 17; remarkably, the passage remains uncorrected in Eliot's *Selected Essays* (London: Faber and Faber, 3rd edn, 1951) p. 343, even though the typographical conventions have been changed.
57 Hooker, Vol. I, Book III, ch. I, sects 2–3, pp. 338–9. Prior to Book III the Church has significant mention only at I, xv, 2 and II, v, 7; neither passage is relevant.
58 T.S. Eliot, 'Scylla and Charybdis', *Agenda*, 23, 1–2 (1985), p. 20; lecture delivered 1952. See also Martin Warner, *A Philosophical Study of T.S. Eliot's FOUR QUARTETS* (Edwin Mellen Press: New York, 1999).
59 The 'nurse' of the lyric of section IV is often read as an image of the Church; if this is right, it is worth noting that her primary characteristic is that she is 'dying'. The whole lyric enacts the reversal of 'worldly' values.
60 One remembers that at the conclusion of *The Idea of a Christian Society* (p. 64) with contrition and humility went repentance and amendment.

Chapter 7

Christ's Breaking of the 'Great Chain of Being'

Slavoj Zizek

For God so loved the world that he gave his one and only Son, that whoever believes in him shall not perish but have eternal life.' (John 3:16)

How, exactly, are we to conceive of this basic tenet of the Christian faith? Problems emerge the moment we comprehend this 'giving of his one and only Son', that is, the death of Christ, as a sacrificial gesture in the exchange between God and man. If we claim that, by sacrificing that which is most precious to Him, His own son, God redeems humanity, buying off its sins, then there are ultimately only two ways to explain this act: either God Himself demands this retribution, that Christ sacrifice himself as the representative of humanity to satisfy the retributive need of God his father; or God is not omnipotent, that He is, like a Greek tragic hero, subordinated to a higher Destiny. His act of creation, like the fateful deed of a Greek hero, brings about unwanted dire consequences, and the only way for Him to re-establish the balance of Justice is to sacrifice what is most precious to Him, His own son – in this sense, God Himself is the ultimate Abraham. The fundamental problem of Christology is how to avoid these two readings of Christ's sacrifice that impose themselves as obvious:

> Any idea that God 'needs' reparation either from us or from our representative should be banished, as should the idea that there is some kind of moral order which is above God and to which God must conform by requiring reparation.[1]

The problem, of course, is *how exactly* to avoid these two options, when the very wording of the Bible seems to support their common premise: Christ's act is repeatedly designated as 'ransom', by the words of Christ himself, by other biblical texts, as well as by the most prominent commentators of the Bible. Jesus himself says that he came 'to give his life as a ransom for many'(Mark 10:45); Timothy 2:5–6 speaks of Christ as the 'mediator between God and humanity ... who gave his life as a ransom for all'; and St Paul, when he states that Christians are slaves who have been 'bought at a price' (Cor. 6:20), implies that the death of Christ should be conceived as purchasing our freedom. So we have a Christ who, through his suffering and death, pays the price for setting us free, redeeming us from the burden of sin; if, then, we have been liberated from captivity to sin and the fear of death through the death and resurrection of Christ, *who demanded this price? To whom* was the ransom paid? Some early Christian writers, clearly perceiving this problem, proposed a logical, if heretic, solution: since Christ's sacrifice delivered us from the power of the Devil (Satan), then Christ's death was the price God had to pay to the Devil, our 'owner' when we live in sin, in order that the Devil set us free. Again, therein resides the deadlock: if Christ is offered as a sacrifice to God Himself, the question arises why did God demand this sacrifice? Was He still the cruel jealous God who wanted a heavy price for His reconciliation with humanity which betrayed Him? If the sacrifice of Christ was offered to someone else (the Devil), then we get the strange spectacle of God and Devil as partners in an exchange.

Of course, Christ's sacrificial death is easy to 'understand', there is a tremendous 'psychological force' in this act: when we are haunted by the notion that things go fundamentally wrong and that we are ultimately responsible for it, that there is some deep flaw inherent in the very existence of humanity, that we are burdened by a tremendous guilt which we can never properly repay, then the idea of God, the absolutely innocent being, sacrificing Himself for our sins out of infinite love for us and thus relieving us of our guilt, serves as the proof that we are not alone, that we *matter* to God, that He *cares* for us, that we are protected by the Creator's infinite Love, while at the same time infinitely indebted to Him. Christ's sacrifice thus serves as the eternal reminder and incitement to lead an ethical life – whatever we do, we should always remember that God Himself gave His life for us.... However, such an account is clearly insufficient, since one has to explain this act in *inherent* theological terms, not in the terms of psychological mechanisms. The enigma remains, and even the most sophisticated theologians (like Anselm of Canterbury) tended to regress into the trap of legalism. According to Anselm, when there is sin and guilt, there must be a satisfaction, something must be done by which the offence caused by human sin will be purged. However, humanity itself is not strong enough to provide this necessary satisfaction – only God can do it. The only solution is thus the incarnation, the emergence of a God-man, of a person who is simultaneously fully divine and fully human: as a God, He has the *ability* to pay the required satisfaction, and as a man, he has the *obligation* to pay.[2]

The problem of this solution is that the legalistic notion of the inexorable character of the need to pay for the sin (the offence must be compensated for) is not argued for, but simply accepted – the question here is a very naive one: why does God not *directly* forgive us? Why has He to obey the need to pay for the sin? Is not the basic tenet of Christianity precisely the opposite one, the suspension of this legalistic logic of retribution, the idea that through the miracle of conversion a New Beginning is possible, through which the past debts (sins) are simply erased? Following an apparently similar line, but with a radically shifted emphasis, Karl Barth provides a tentative answer in his essay on 'The Judge Judged in Our Place': God as a Judge first passed a judgement of humanity, and then became a human being and paid Himself the price, took upon Himself the punishment, 'in order that in this way there might be brought about by him our reconciliation with him, and our conversion to him'.[3] So, to put it in somewhat inappropriate terms, God became man and sacrificed Himself in order to set the ultimate example that would evoke our sympathy for Him and thus convert us to Him. This idea was first clearly articulated by Abelard:

The Son of God took our nature, and in it took upon himself to teach us by both word and example even to the point of death, thus binding us to himself through love.[4]

The reason Christ had to suffer and die is here not the legalistic notion of retribution, but the edifying religious-moral *effect* of his death on us, sinful humans: if God were to pardon us directly, this would not transform us, making us new, better – it is only the compassion and feeling of gratitude and debt elicited by the scene of Christ's sacrifice that have the necessary power to transform us... . It is easy to see that something is amiss in this reasoning: is this not a strange God who sacrifices his own son, that which matters most to him – just to impress humans? Things become even more uncanny if we focus on the idea that God sacrificed His Son in order to bind us to Himself through love: what was at stake was then not only God's love for us, but also his (narcissistic) desire to *be loved* by us, humans. In this reading, is God Himself not strangely akin to the mad governess from Patricia Highsmith's 'Heroine', who sets the family house on fire in order to be able to prove her devotion to the family by bravely saving the children from the raging fire? Along these lines, God first causes the Fall, that is, He provokes a situation in which we need Him, and then redeems us, by pulling us out of the mess for which He Himself is responsible.

Does this then mean that Christianity *is* a flawed religion? Or is a different reading of the Crucifixion feasible? The first step to take in order to get out of this predicament is to recall Christ's statements which perturb – or, rather, simply *suspend* – the circular logic of revenge or punishment destined to re-establish the balance of Justice: instead of 'An eye for an eye!', we get 'If someone slaps your right cheek, turn to him also your left cheek!' The point here is not stupid masochism, humble acceptance of one's humiliation, but the endeavour to *interrupt the circular logic of the re-established balance of justice*. Along the same lines, Christ's sacrifice, with its paradoxical nature (it is the very person *against whom* we, humans, have sinned, whose trust we have betrayed, that atones and pays the price for our sins), suspends the logic of sin and punishment, of legal or ethical retribution, of 'settling the accounts', by bringing it to the point of self-relating. The only way to achieve this suspension, to break the chain of crime and punishment/retribution, is to assume the utter readiness to self-erasure. And *love*, at its most elementary, is nothing but such a paradoxical gesture of breaking the chain of retribution. So the second step is to focus on the terrifying force of someone accepting in advance, and pursuing, his own annihilation – Christ was not sacrificed by and for another, he sacrificed *Himself*.

The third step is to focus on the notion of Christ as the mediator between God and humanity: in order for humanity to be restored to God, the mediator must sacrifice himself. In other words, as long as Christ is here, there can be no Holy Ghost, which *is* the figure of the reunification of God and humanity. Christ as the mediator between God and humanity is, to put it in today's deconstructionist terms, both the condition of possibility *and* the condition of impossibility between the two: as mediator, he is at the same time the obstacle which prevents the full mediation of the opposed poles. Or, to put it in the Hegelian terms of the Christian syllogism: there are two 'premises' (Christ is God's Son, fully divine, and Christ is man's son, fully human), and to unite the opposed poles, to arrive at the 'conclusion' (humanity is fully united with God in the Holy Spirit), the mediator must erase himself out of the picture. Christ's death is not part of the eternal cycle of the divine incarnation and death, in which God repeatedly appears and then withdraws into himself, into his Beyond. As Hegel put it, what dies on the Cross is *not* the human incarnation of the transcendent God, but *the God of Beyond Himself.* Through Christ's sacrifice, God Himself is no longer beyond, but passes into the Holy Spirit (of the religious community). In other words, if Christ were to be the mediator between two separated entities (God and humanity), his death would mean that there is no longer a mediation, that the two entities are apart again. So, obviously, God must be the mediator in a stronger sense: it is not that, in the Holy Spirit, there is no longer the need for Christ, because the two poles are directly united; for this mediation to be possible, *the nature of both poles must be radically changed* – in one and the same movement, they both must undergo a transubstantiation. Christ is, on the one hand, the vanishing mediator/medium through whose death God-Father himself 'passes into' the Holy Spirit, and, on the other hand, the vanishing mediator/medium through whose death human community itself 'passes into' the new spiritual stage.[5]

These two operations are not separated, they are the two aspects of one and the same movement: the very movement through which God loses the character of a transcendent Beyond and passes into the Holy Spirit (the spirit of the community of believers) *equals* the movement through which the 'fallen' human community is elevated into the Holy Spirit. In other words, it is not that, in the Holy Ghost, men and God communicate directly, without Christ's mediation; it is rather that they directly coincide: God is *nothing but* the Holy Spirit of the community of believers. Christ must die not in order to enable direct communication between God and humanity, but because *there is no longer any transcendent God with whom to communicate.*

As Boris Groys recently remarked, Christ is the first and only fully 'ready made God' in the history of religions: he is fully human, and thus indistinguishable from other ordinary men – there is nothing in his bodily appearance that makes Him a special case.[6] So, in the same way Duchamp's pissoir or bicycle are not objects of art because of their inherent qualities, but because of the places they are made to occupy: Christ is not God because of his inherent 'divine' qualities, but because, precisely as fully human, he is God's son. For this reason, the properly Christian attitude apropos of Christ's death is not the one of melancholic attachment to his deceased figure, but that of infinite joy. The ultimate horizon of the pagan Wisdom is melancholy – ultimately, everything returns to dust, so one must learn to detach oneself, to renounce desire. If there was ever a religion that is *not* melancholic, it is Christianity, in spite of the false appearance of the melancholic attachment to Christ as the lost object.

Christ's sacrifice is thus in a radical sense *meaningless*: not an act of exchange, but a superfluous, excessive, unwarranted gesture aimed at demonstrating His love for us, for the fallen humanity. It is like when, in our daily lives, we want to show someone that we really love him, and we can only do so by accomplishing a superfluous gesture of expenditure. Christ does not 'pay' for our sins – as was made clear by St Paul, *it is this very logic of payment, of exchange, that, in a way, IS the sin,* and the wager of Christ's act is to show us that *the chain of exchanges can be interrupted*. Christ redeems humanity not by paying the price for our sins, but by demonstrating to us that we can break out of the vicious cycle of sin and payment. Instead of paying for our sins, Christ literally *erases* them, retroactively 'undoing' them through love.

It is against this background that one should measure the radical difference which, in spite of superficial resemblances, separates Christianity from Buddhism.[7] Although both Christianity and Buddhism assert the individual's ability to establish a direct contact with the Absolute (the Void, the Holy Spirit), bypassing the hierarchical structure of cosmos and society, Buddhism remains indebted to the pagan notion of the Great Chain of Being. In Buddhism, even the most heroic person among us is like Gulliver whom the Lilliputians have tied down with hundreds of ropes: we cannot escape the consequences of our past acts, they drag behind us like shadows and, sooner or later, they catch up with us, we have to pay the price. Therein resides the kernel of the properly pagan tragic vision of life: our existence itself is ultimately the proof of our sin, something one should feel guilty of, something that disturbs the cosmic balance, and we pay the price for it in our ultimate annihilation, when 'the dust returns to dust'. What is of crucial importance here is that this pagan notion involves the short-circuit, the overlapping between the 'ontological' and 'ethical' dimension, best rendered in the Greek word for causality (*aitia*): 'to cause something' also means 'to be guilty/responsible for it'. Against this pagan horizon, the Christian 'Good News (Gospel)' is that it is possible to suspend the burden of the past, to cut off the ropes which tie us to our past deeds, to clean up the slate and begin from the zero-level. There is no supranatural magic involved here: this liberation simply means the separation between the 'ontological' and the 'ethical' dimension: the Great Chain of Being can be broken at the *ethical* level, sins can not only be pardoned, but also retroactively erased with no traces left, a New Beginning is possible.

The properly dialectical paradox of paganism is that it legitimizes social hierarchy ('each in his/her/its own place') with reference to the notion of a universe in which all differences are ultimately rendered worthless, in which every determinate being ultimately disintegrates into the primordial Abyss out of which it emerged. In symmetrical contrast, Christianity predicates equality and direct access to universality precisely through asserting the most radical Difference/Rupture. Therein resides the gap that separates Christianity from Buddhism: according to Buddhism, we can achieve liberation from our past deeds, but this liberation is only possible through radical renunciation to (what we perceive as) reality, through liberating ourselves from the very impetus/thriving ('desire') that defines life, through extinguishing its spark and immersing ourselves into the primordial Void of Nirvana, into the formless One-All. There is no liberation in life, since, in this life (and there is no other), we are always enslaved to the craving that defines it: what we are now (a king, a beggar, a fly, a lion ...) is determined by our acts in our previous lives, and after our death the consequences of our present life will determine the character of our next reincarnation. In contrast to Buddhism, Christianity puts its wager on the possibility of the radical Rupture, of breaking the Great Chain of Being, already in *this* life, while we are still fully alive. And the new community found on this Rupture *is* the living body of Christ.

Notes

1 Gerald O'Collins, *Christology* (Oxford: Oxford University Press, 1995), pp. 286–7.
2 I rely here on Alister E. McGrath, *An Introduction to Christianity* (Oxford: Blackwell, 1997), pp. 138–9.
3 Ibid., p. 141.
4 Ibid., pp. 141–2
5 See G.W.F. Hegel, *Vorlesungen ueber die Philosophie der Religion* (Frankfurt: Suhrkamp Verlag, 1969), Vol.II, p. 287–306.
6 From a private conversation with Boris Groys in Karlsruhe, 22 October 1999.
7 The following paragraph is intended as self-criticism with regard to Slavoj Zizek, *The Fragile Absolute* (London: Verso Books, 2000).

III

THE CHURCH SUBJECTIVE

... sitting in any of the churches towards evening is like a mild dose of opium.
Charles Dickens, *Pictures from Italy*

This head [is] more than churches.
Walt Whitman, 'Song of Myself'

The church can sleep and feed at once.
T.S. Eliot, 'The Hippopotamus'

... psychoanalysis ... the church to which I don't belong.
James Joyce, in Richard Ellman, *James Joyce*

The Church is ... woven from imaginary, erotic, carnal and sensual elements. It's superb.
Michel Foucault, in David Macey, *The Lives of Michel Foucault*

Chapter 8

Christendom and the Police: Kierkegaard Inside the Panopticon

Jeremy Tambling

Confessional Autobiography

In 1848, the year of revolutions, and the moment when bourgeois reaction became most apparent, Søren Kierkegaard produced one of his provocative titles. Kierkegaardian titles, like *The Concept of Irony, Either/Or, The Concept of Dread* (*The Concept of Anxiety* in its weaker formulation), or *The Sickness Unto Death* suggest the power of delimiting, of drawing a margin, of thinking in unitary terms. In *The Point of View for My Work as an Author: A Direct Communication, Report to History* (1848), a similar definition of interest looks on offer. He describes his 'whole authorship' and says that it all pertains to Christianity, 'to the issue: becoming a Christian, with direct and indirect polemical aim at that enormous illusion Christendom, or the illusion that in such a country all are Christians of sorts'.[1] Such definiteness; but it is almost the last time we shall be able to comment on it in Kierkegaard.

Kierkegaard's writings began, he says in *The Point of View*, with *Either/Or* (1843), a pseudonymous work by 'Victor Eremita'. He goes on to list his works, up to what he thinks of as the pivotal moment of *Concluding Unscientific Postscript* (1846). After that, he says, come only the religious writings, for in 1847 – the year of *The Communist Manifesto*'s assessment of bourgeois culture – he began his critique of 'Christendom'.[2] In *Concluding Unscientific Postscript*, written by 'Johannes Climacus', Kierkegaard claimed the authorship of his pseudonymous works, which had previously circulated in Copenhagen under the names of: Victor Eremita, Constantin Constantius, Johannes de Silentio, Johannes Climacus, Vigilius Haufniensis, Nicolaus Notabene and Inter and Inter. *Concluding Unscientific Postscript* and *The Point of View for My Work as an Author* seemed to draw a line under all these pseudonyms, and under the principle of writing which Johannes Climacus calls 'indirect communication'.[3] *Concluding Unscientific Postscript* contains in its title the word 'concluding' because it brings to an end the literary pseudonymous pieces, and 'unscientific' because it is fragmentary, and, *contra* Hegel, Kierkegaard does not believe that knowledge can be a systematic science. Indirect communication, which may be negative communication,[4] acknowledges that no utterance can be immediate; it recognizes the effects of irony, it knows that all speech is allegorical (literally: speaking other). It knows that, as with irony where there is no true speech which irony conceals, speech may relate to illusion only.

Perhaps, though, nothing really changed in Kierkegaard's writing. In deconstructive terms, even the name Søren Kierkegaard is as much a fiction, a non-origin, a non-centre, as pseudonymous as any other name. Nor did pseudonymous writings stop appearing (under the names Inter and Inter, and Anti-Climacus). *The Point of View for My Work as an Author: A Direct Communication*, which his brother, Peter Christian Kierkegaard published in 1859, four years after S.K.'s death, and which Kierkegaard presented as a justification for his work, is a text that has received much attention from deconstruction.[5] Its title, despite its definiteness, begins the possible ambiguities. Direct communication? Since the original manuscript was lost, it is not even definite that the name Søren Kierkegaard appeared on the title-page, while Peter Christian's comment on his brother's text seems apt: 'one might almost be tempted to think that even what was signed S.K. might not be for certain his final words, but only a point of view.'[6]

The supposedly 'direct communication' of *The Point of View* is that 'I am and was a religious author.'[7] But the first part of that book dwells on the equivocalness or duplicity of the whole body of texts which have appeared so far, turning on the question of whether the writer can be called an aesthetic or a religious author.[8] No decision can be made here. The question can only be left for the reader to sort out: fixing a genre cannot be done at the level of discussing intention, even if that intention could be considered unambiguous. Besides, *The Point of View* should also be considered within the genre of confession, which, for Michel Foucault, is the dominant mode of Christianity and which, in nineteenth-century bourgeois society, was being realized in spatial terms in the Panopticon, with its encouragement to self-scrutiny, self-surveillance, and attention to the mind as needing to be disciplined. Kierkegaard can accuse his society of living in untruth, and he can also, as he says, adopt the position of a *flâneur* in Copenhagen,[9] but he is not as free as that description implies. Indeed, for Walter Benjamin, the *flâneur* is never free but is, instead, part of the commodification of bourgeois life.[10] For Benjamin, the crowd acts like an intoxicant for the *flâneur*; Kierkegaard, however, hates the crowd, which in some ways is the same as Christendom – he declares that 'the crowd is untruth.'[11] Yet perhaps it held more attraction for him than he would admit. When Kierkegaard announces that 'what I write here is for orientation and attestation – it is not a defence or an apologetics',[12] he opens the question as to how far he is really outside the Christendom he judges so intensely. As a *flâneur*, he may be nostalgic for the crowd which is Christendom. Though he declares that he is not writing a confession, he also knows that he has also been accused of misanthropy, and he certainly offers a partial autobiography.[13] There *are* elements of confessional autobiography at work, which make Kierkegaard's text reactive, not simply spontaneous, and the distinction he would like to make between himself and Christendom involves a disavowal on his part of the connectedness of the two.

In *The Point of View*, Kierkegaard argues that there is a dialectic working throughout his writings, and lists their titles to establish the fact; this, though, means the provocative omission of *The Concept of Irony* (1841) and *From the Papers of One Still Living* (1838) – Kierkegaard supports his argument by framing his authorship selectively and deceptively. Such ambiguity is characteristic of the way that the church, or 'Christendom', is constructed in his texts. The undecidability, or playfulness that has been found in Kierkegaard's 'indirect communication' – that it is all indirect, signed or not, and that there is never any question of direct communication in this body of writing – should be remembered when thinking about Kierkegaard as a confessional writer, or reading arguments aligning him to authoritarianism, and to a judgmental single-minded utterance. This indirection is the starting-point of my essay, which reads Kierkegaard on the bourgeois formation he called 'Christendom'.

Any reference to confession must imply Foucault's analysis of that bourgeois culture as disciplinary and evoking a state of heightened self-consciousness as awareness of others looking – all of which disrupts the spontaneity Kierkegaard calls 'immediacy'. Kierkegaard's awareness of being under the eye of others, while attempting to pass judgement on the bourgeois state, can be compared in its results with the anger it produces in, for example, Thomas Carlyle, a writer equally anxious to diagnose what he thinks is missing in bourgeois culture. Carlyle interprets that culture as mechanical, through and through, and as lacking means of transcendence; it is in him an increasing source of bitterness and anger, starting from the early 'Signs of the Times' (1829). Carlyle fears that there can be no alternative to what he calls 'the condition of England', which he hates so intensely.[14] However reactionary his views, and it is not a question of justifying them, Carlyle has no comprehensive term for what he criticizes. In contrast, Kierkegaard begins by delimiting it, perhaps, by giving a name to error, hoping to fix it just as Albion, in William Blake's *The Four Zoas*, is fixed to form 'the limit of contraction', the fixed boundaries of error.[15] Kierkegaard calls his culture 'Christendom'.

'The object riddled with error'

What does Kierkegaard mean by the term 'Christendom'? Kierkegaard's Denmark was still predominantly rural, with a population of a million, only 121,000 of whom lived in Copenhagen.[16] In 1848, the country shifted from being an aristocratic and absolutist state to a constitutional monarchy with power possessed by its legislative assembly, which was elected by a universal male suffrage. Given this political formation, Alastair Hannay annotates 'Christendom' as 'the term used by Kierkegaard to refer to the corrupted form of Christianity represented by the life and institutions of the Danish Church'.[17] John Elrod, in fact, equates it with the 'modern Danish state' itself, 'the religiously legitimated modern liberal state'.[18] For Bruce Kirmmse, who stresses Kierkegaard's political forwardness, Christendom is 'the traditional aristocratic-conservative synthesis ... which was the time-honoured and comfortable marriage of the "horizontal" element of traditional society and the "vertical" element of religious transcendence'.[19] Since Danish citizenship was restricted to those who were baptized and confirmed members of the Church, the assumption implied in 'Christendom' is that the church maps onto the state exactly. The assumption licensed a nationalism which came into prominence as Denmark went into war against Prussia (1848–50) over the border states of Schleswig-Holstein.

But the Danish Church – what Kierkegaard calls Christendom – is still, even for him, the only church that there is. Christendom's existence was as an 'immediate' state, for the Danish subject was born into it. As Kierkegaard puts it in his journals, 'throughout Christendom, the dialectical element has been abolished.'[20] Being within Christendom could never give a point of cognition by which to know any other state. There could be no question of being outside Christendom, or of beginning a new church. Though Kierkegaard singles out individual pastors and bishops for satire, he cannot make the distinction between Christianity and the church that, say, William Blake can when his poetry assumes the immanence of Christ and of Christianity within the world-system dominated by Urizen and when he argues that a change of perception – 'the doors of perception' being cleansed (*The Marriage of Heaven and Hell*) – could alter everything.

Adapting Derrida, who says there is nothing outside the text, it might be said that, for Kierkegaard, there is nothing outside Christendom. But Kierkegaard has already delimited a system in calling it 'Christendom', even though it may be 'an enormous illusion'. In selecting it as *the* illusion, he still assumes that something is to be found from Christendom, that it *is* the place to look. In contrast, Carlyle gives up on Christianity, though his writings retain its vocabulary; and Blake similarly, before him, does not define his discursive limits by reference to the church or to the power of the church in the world – indeed, 'The Divine Image'[21] thinks outside such Eurocentric limits. In writing of Christendom, Kierkegaard chooses his area of thought very deliberately, for Christendom provides the substance of his polemic; this means that, while he may pronounce it an enormous illusion, he still has nowhere else to go. It also means that there is virtually no transcendence to be glimpsed from Kierkegaard's texts, only a commitment to further inwardness – which cannot be communicated directly – and to individualism.

Hope might come only from the uncanny quality of 'repetition' which, in an implicit oxymoron, is declared in *Repetition* (1843) to be 'the new category that will be discovered':

> When the Greeks said that all knowing is recollecting, they said that all existence, which is, has been; when one says that life is a repetition, one says: actuality, which has been, now comes into existence. If one does not have the category of recollection or repetition, all life dissolves into an empty, meaningless noise. Recollection is the ethical view of life; repetition the modern.[22]

Repetition does not get the subject out of the textual system which is Christendom, but, because repetition is inseparable from difference,[23] it discovers difference within that system. Without repetition, the narrator says, life dissolves into the materiality of an empty, meaningless noise: undifferentiated. But the difference that repetition discovers cannot be articulated. At the end of *Repetition*, the young man, whose emotional trials have been the subject of the text, feels that he has had the repetition he wanted, which looks like the achievement of transcendence, which is what repetition is said to be.[24] This jubilation is followed, however, by the 'Concluding Letter by Constantin Constantius', the older narrator, which leaves the reader with the question of whether the young man can be said to have really had such an experience as getting out of the 'universal' state and into the exceptional. In posing the problem, the older narrator articulates what is already clear: that an experience of repetition can still only ever be presented within textual form, a form where things have been already said; so that whatever repetition has taken place is already contained within an existing discourse. How, then, can the experience be exceptional, new?

For Kierkegaard, the Christian state, as opposed to the pagan, *is* the modern, and modernity involves repetition as opposed to recollection. Recollection implies the power of memory, and the possibility of holding on to individual experience and using it; in contrast, repetition does not necessarily escape the system in which the individual is found. Thus the limit but also the interest of Kierkegaard's thought is that it cannot, and will not, separate itself from repeating the doublenesses of the Christendom that he opts for – its existence as illusion and error, and also as the church, however that might be described. It therefore commits itself to the impossibility of distinguishing truth and falsehood. In a footnote to one of the supplements to *The Point of View*, Kierkegaard says that 'it is impossible to attack "the system" from a point within the system'; he adds that there is only one point outside that, namely 'the single individual'. The reader who is inclined to criticize him must reflect, says Kierkegard, that 'he still has not really become the single individual which I myself do not pretend to be', adding that to be 'the single individual is beyond a human being's powers'.[25] If Kierkegaard is so fragmented that he cannot be a single individual, then how can he be a Christian? And indeed, he can only equivocally claim to be a Christian.[26] He says of the task of writing to proclaim Christianity that it cannot start with 'I am Christian – you are not a Christian – but this way: You are a Christian, I am not a Christian.'[27] This articulation he calls deceptive, but that is part of the duplicity of all Kierkegaard's writing. In the present age of 'reflection' – where identity is established by identification with what others do – there can only be 'communication ... in reflection – therefore [as] indirect communication':

> The communicator is defined in reflection, therefore negatively, not one who claims to be an extraordinary Christian or even claims to have revelations (all of which is commensurate with immediacy and direct communication) but the opposite, one who even claims not to be Christian – in other words, the communicator is in the background, helping negatively, since whether he succeeds in helping someone is indeed something else. The issue itself is one belonging to reflection: to become a Christian when in a way one is a Christian.[28]

To be caught in a textual system such as Christendom is to be held in something like Saussure's definition of language as a system of differences without positive terms. Knowing in an age of reflection means that no knowledge is other than differential, and that there is no Christianity outside the error-filled existing system of Christianity. Christianity, like Christ, would be the utterly other, quite unknowable, even if its traces may be located in Christendom. As a modern, Kierkegaard works with the crowd which is 'untruth'.

Here the best commentary is that of Walter Benjamin who says that 'sundering truth from falsehood is the goal of the materialist method, not its point of departure ... Its point of departure is the object riddled with error.'[29] For the modern Christian there is, perhaps, no alternative but to work with the materialist method, and this is the discovery at the heart of Kierkegaard's text: that he cannot, for all his inclination to begin with 'truth', ever do more than hope to arrive at the goal which he would like to take as his origin. He cannot do better than Blake, who sees things in terms of 'contraries' – to do which assumes that they can be identified and separated – but who then discovers the reversibility of all such terms, even innocence and experience, and therefore their inseparability. It is Urizen in Blake who looks for 'a joy without pain',[30] in other words for a state – or a church – which can be exclusively one thing and not another. The sphere of Christendom, however, is that of talk – 'chatter' – which Peter Fenves reads as suspending the distinction between speech and meaning.[31] The Christian can never know anything apart from that sphere.

The Philosopher and the Police

Consciously or not, Kierkegaard's writing is, therefore, double; it operates on both sides of an argument where neither side is sustainable except through its differences from another position. In a journal entry of 14 February 1850, Kierkegaard considers what the church would be – if it was even possible to think of it as separated from Christendom – and compares it to a criminal fraternity:

> The world of crime forms a little society of its own, on the outside of human society, a little society which ordinarily has an intimate solidarity not altogether common in the world, perhaps also because each one individually feels expelled from human society. Similarly, with the society of Christians. Each individually – by accepting Christianity ... that is, by accepting the absurd, indeed staking his life on it – has said farewell to the world, has broken with the world. The society of those who have voluntarily placed themselves outside society in the usual sense of the word is all the more intimate precisely because each individually feels isolated from 'the world.' But just as the company of criminals must take good care that no one enters into the society who is not branded as they are, so with the society of Christians: they must see to it that no one enters into this society except that person whose mark is that he is radically polemical towards 'society' in the usual sense. This means that the Christian congregation is a society consisting of qualitative individuals and that the intimacy of the society is also conditioned by its polemical stance against human society at large.[32]

In civil society, the criminal has been branded, written upon; for, as Foucault's *Discipline and Punish* contends, society makes the subject the criminal by constructing a personality and a personality type on the basis of behaviour it wishes to marginalize. Does the analogy hold with the 'Christian', supposing the existence of such a person? For Kierkegaard, the Christian has not been branded, but he brands himself in his writing – as though writing were, like confession, an act of self-criminalizing – through the mark of polemicizing against society. The Christian congregation, each individual in it, is defined by negating the world's 'nonsense' through listening to 'the absurd'. The absurd is the unharmonious. If it may be defined in Kierkegaardian terms as 'the voice of the other that summons our voice',[33] then that which is heard as the voice of the other is unmusical. The writing of the Christian implies a commitment to the disjointed, the out-of-tune and harsh.

In Kierkegaard's church, every individual writes and, as *The Point of View* states, 'every religious author is *eo ipso* polemical, because the world is not so good that the religious can be assumed to have triumphed or to be in the majority. A triumphant religious author who is *in vogue* is *eo ipso* not a *religious* author. The essentially religious author is always polemical ....' In considering the question 'which comes first, the branding or the polemicism?' it seems that the latter is the result of an antagonism which has been formed from the attitudes of the crowd. The essentially religious author demonstrates that he is right and that what he says is true – not nonsense – when he answers that '"I demonstrate it by this, that I am persecuted; it is truth, and I demonstrate it by this, that I am laughed to scorn."'[34] This sequence of thought assumes that an author is constituted as a particular kind of author by the attention he has received. The criminal is branded, the religious author persecuted – and the evidence for this inheres in the response he receives; if he were not persecuted he would not be right, if people did not laugh at him what he says would not be true. The author is thus branded like the criminal, for his polemicism originates from a public reaction, from the point of view of the normalizing crowd. The church, if it could exist, would consist of essentially religious – that is, polemical – authors.

Kierkegaard wants to maintain two positions: that being polemical starts from the point of view of the crowd, and that the church and the criminal world may be put together, since the constituents of both have been marginalized. In Kierkegaard's world, the criminal world – or church – is hermetically sealed: to be branded is its form of baptism. In *The Sickness Unto Death* (1849), Kierkegaard says that when someone in the modern world feels the need for solitude, that is a positive sign that the person still possesses spirit. 'Group people' – the crowd – feel no need for solitude:

> In antiquity as well as in the Middle Ages there was an awareness of this longing for solitude and a respect for what it means; whereas in the constant sociality of our day we shrink from solitude to the point (what a capital epigram!) that no use for it is known other than as a punishment for criminals. But since it is a crime in our day to have spirit, it is indeed quite in order to classify such people, lovers of solitude, with criminals.[35]

The punishment to which Kierkegaard refers is solitary confinement, the system connected with Panopticism that was introduced on a quasi-scientific basis in England and America in the nineteenth century. Kierkegaard must be aware of the irony that the silent and separate systems which enforced solitude were the product of Protestant thinking – in particular, of Quaker discipline in, for example, Philadelphia. Christendom produces its own ideal (that is, solitude) as a form of punishment. But Kierkegaard elides an argument when he says 'it is a crime in our day to have spirit.' Such overstatement, creating a branding where none exists, and so as rhetoric undoing itself, is needed to get to his other argument – that Christians are like criminals in that they are associated with solitude, with not going with the crowd. But there is another argument hovering here: that the criminal (condemned to solitary confinement) is nonetheless also definable as the person who likes solitude, that enjoyment of solitude is likely to lead to criminality.

Kierkegaard's alliance with the criminal is not accidental, but part of a more general 'self-contradiction'.[36] In the journals for 1847, written in the decade that produced Poe's detective Dupin and the detective story, Kierkegaard says that once his only wish had been 'to become a police official. It seemed an occupation for my restless, scheming mind. I had the idea that among the criminals there were people to contest with: shrewd, vigorous, fly fellows.'[37] Kierkegaard as the self-describing *flâneur* is also the detective, which is a combination that Benjamin puts together in relation to nineteenth-century city existence.[38] Kierkegaard says he only gave up the idea when he realized that police cases were 'usually only a matter of a few shillings and some poor wretch'. The dream he abandoned was of entangling with criminals and therefore being, like the classic (Oedipal) detective, both policeman and criminal at once. It was a dream of collapsing the division, of taking away the law that inscribes difference. The same dream puts together church and criminal fraternity.

Kierkegaard frequently returns to images of policing, and often is on both sides of the criminal/police divide. In *The Present Age* (1846), after commenting on 'envy' as the 'negatively unifying principle' of a 'passionless and very reflective age' – an age marked by everyone needing to take their character from the way others see them – he writes that

> ... the individual must first of all break out of the prison in which his own reflection holds him, and if he succeeds, he still does not stand in the open but in the vast penitentiary built by the reflection of his associates ... it is reflection that does this and not tyrants and secret police.[39]

The similarity of this to Nietzsche's account of *ressentiment* as the power motivating bourgeois culture needs no underlining, but the Foucauldian implications of 'reflection' are even closer. The Panopticon, a system which engineers envy (urban space cultivates *ressentiment*), is the place for endless reflection, endless consideration of the self in relation to others and construction of the self's inadequacy in relation to the imagined faults of others. Kierkegaard has stated precisely the power mechanisms that activate nineteenth-century Christendom: Christendom equals the Panopticon.

A little later, however, Kierkegaard will have it that, in the face of the 'levelling process' of modern society, great men, 'like plain-clothes policemen ... will be *unrecognizable*'.[40] They will be unrecognizable as great men. Difference in our modern state of indifference reduces to tiny differences; but nonetheless, why does Kierkegaard want to become one of the secret observers, like the warder at the centre of the Panopticon, or like Mr Bucket, the plain-clothes policeman of *Bleak House* – much less ambiguous, much less Oedipal, than Dupin ? In the next moment there is a slide of the image: the unrecognized are now called 'secret agents'. Similarly, *The Point of View* refers to Kierkegaard's activities as those of a spy observing or a private operator.[41] Adorno, in his study of Kierkegaard, comments on the idea of spying as an aspect of Kierkegaard's own bourgeois formation, as a figure cultivating inwardness and, for that reason, surrounded by images of domestic interiority which confirm him as a figure of bourgeois culture.[42] Less negatively, however, it can be said that the secret agent is on both sides of the Panoptical structure at once, most liable to the melancholia of self-contradiction, and a modern culture-hero in that spying works only in the element of 'the object riddled with error'. If truth and error are indistinguishable, everyone becomes a double agent.

Nonetheless, Kierkegaard takes the police-image seriously. He recuperates it in saying that the movement of *Concluding Unscientific Postscript* demands that people go 'back' – adding 'and even though it is all done *without authority*, there is still something in the tone that is reminiscent of a policeman when he says to a crowd: Move back! That is indeed why more than one of the pseudonymous writers calls himself a policeman, a street inspector.'[43] Kierkegaard's editors annotate this last comment by reference to *Repetition and Stages on Life's Way*. In the short pamphlet *On My Work as an Author* Kierkegaard summarizes his position: '"Without authority" to make aware of the religious, the essentially Christian is the category for my whole work considered as an author ... From the very beginning I have enjoined ... that I was "without authority."'[44] Paradoxically, coercion and recognition of lack of authority go together, as perhaps they do also in Carlyle; though in Kierkegaard's books the acknowledgement that he has no *author*ity, or en*title*ment is signalled in every crazy pseudonym and impossibly rational title. Kierkegaard – the name means 'churchyard' – is his own grave-digger as well as the grave-digger of his age: a figure of posthumous existence, just as so many of his writings are posthumous.

Kierkegaard, Dickens, Carlyle

However casually voiced, Kierkegaard's desire to be a policeman maps the commentator on Christendom onto the realist novelist of the nineteenth century – who is also like the policeman in his surveillance of a whole society. In particular, it links him to Charles Dickens in *Bleak House* (1852–54), a work of the same moment as the later Kierkegaard, which is also interested in trying to chart an amorphous system as extensive as a textual system. Dickens's Chancery could be compared with Kierkegaard's Christendom. Chancery is also a Panoptical structure and, in both cases, Christendom and Chancery, the issue is one of attempted and frustrated surveillance, whose failure, in Kierkegaard's case, leads to further and further melancholia.

The desire to exercise surveillance and control is born out of melancholia, as well as being, of course, productive of melancholia in the person under surveillance. In Dickens the melancholia turns to anger, and to other strategies of accommodation with the age to negotiate that anger. In Dickens's mentor, Carlyle, there is a total negation of 'the present age' and an increasing impotence as a result (he could not, for instance, finish the *Latter-Day Pamphlets* which were intended to be a comprehensive account of the age). Carlyle's frustration leads to a further spiralling authoritarianism in an attempt to assert the control he was losing. The anger produces a loss of control which is visible in Carlyle's scabrous images, examples of the return of the repressed which surface in allegorical names such as Teufelsdröckh ('Devil's Dung'), the tormented soul of his *Sartor Resartus*. In this allegorical naming there is no Carlylean transcendence of the material. What appears in Carlyle's hostility is not only his passion but his abjection. This, used, of course, in Julia Kristeva's sense, is both an hysterical revulsion from, *and* attraction to, the overwhelming materiality of the age from which Carlyle needs to separate himself to avoid the Kierkegaardian state of the young man of *Repetition* whose hysteria – traditionally, 'the female malady' – is marked by the way that 'his whole person screams'.[45]

Clearly, the anxieties about control are also gender-based, as they are in Constantin Constantius commenting on the melancholia of the young man of *Repetition*, and in the desire to be an agent of surveillance. In *Repetition*, the ironist Constantin Constantius initiates the text with his 'Report' and confesses that it 'is often distressing to be an observer – it has the same melancholy effect as being a police-officer.'[46] The word 'melancholy' will be noted. In this 'novel', if it may be called that, Love makes the young man melancholic in bringing him out of his spontaneity, his immediate state, and he rounds on Constantin Constantius, as though he were like the Panoptical warder. He says that Constantius has 'subjugated ... every passion, every emotion, every mood under the cold regimentation of reflection'.[47] The young man, who identifies himself in his melancholia with Job, identifies Constantius with one of Job's comforters. But this is not quite true of Constantin Constantius, any more than lack of feeling was true of the passionate Carlyle. Rather, the ironic stance he adopts is a melancholic repression of feeling. Both the young man, who becomes a poet in becoming a lover, and Constantin Constantius are melancholics. It is not 'better', speaking only in terms of psychology or psychoanalysis, to be a warder in the Panopticon than to be the exposed prisoner: both are subjects of reflection, neither seem to have the power of free action.

Constantius' own doubleness appears at the end, in his act of policing when, in his 'Concluding Letter', he laments the dearth of good readers and identifies himself with Clement of Alexandria in 'writing in such a way that the heretics are unable to understand it'.[48] This implies that the text, whose genre he cannot specify as though it were a Bakhtinian mixed genre, is allegory, or indirect communication; but the word 'heretic' also carries with it the reminder that any church – and even though Christianity is not the ostensible subject of *Repetition*, the point still emerges – is both inclusive and exclusive. It polices the truth, and controls what Foucault calls 'the discourse of truth'.[49]

However, even before he begins writing about Christendom in 1847, Kierkegaard also shows, in Constantius, that the critique of Christendom is itself a kind of policing. The very selection of 'Christendom' as a discourse comprising illusion and error is a commitment to policing, just as belief in a true church is inseparable from the wish to dominate. To think of a church outside Christendom runs, at once, both the risk of criminalizing *and* policing. Witness, the judgmentalism of Kierkegaard's *The Sickness Unto Death* – his most Carlylean text – where his target is the spiritlessness of the bourgeois philistine:

> ... so-called Christendom (in which all are Christians by the millions as a matter of course, and thus there are just as many – exactly just as many – Christians as there are people) is not just a shabby edition of the essentially Christian, full of printer's errors that distort the meaning, and of thoughtless omissions and admixtures, but is also a misuse of it, a profanation and prostitution of Christianity.[50]

Accusations of spiritlessness in others are, in Carlyle or Kierkegaard, a form of spiritual elitism, allowing for a censoriousness whereby the sins of the spiritless are said to not even constitute 'sin in the strictly spiritual sense'.[51] But Kierkegaard's rhetoric in any case undoes itself. Why is Christendom called 'so-called'? Because it is not true Christianity? Or because it is not true Christendom? Who is calling it anything if not the writer with the compulsion to dominate? Images of different editions of a book always lead to problems of identifying a true origin: indeed, they disallow the idea of a single origin. They suggest that from the beginning Christianity is always already a corrupt, or disseminated, text.

A fascinating contradiction runs throughout Kierkegaard: namely, his wish to see the true church as a criminal fraternity and his equal wish – even though he can be ironic about it – to judge Christendom as though from the standpoint of the police. Perhaps Benjamin's citation of Goethe (via Bulwer Lytton) is apt: that every person, the best as well as the most wretched, carries around a secret which would make him hateful to all others if it became known.[52] The requirement of secrecy makes everyone tend to merge with the crowd, and if, as Kierkegaard argues, 'the category of sin is the category of individuality',[53] then the crowd becomes the means whereby guilt in relation to God may be escaped. Christendom, paradoxically, is the place to be to escape awareness of sin since it is the place to evade individuality. The policeman cannot fix guilt on that which has the character of being 'untruth'.

In reaction to this crowded, collective, Christendom, there is also in *Repetition* (because the young man is a figure of Kierkegaard's autobiography) an implicit identification with Job, who is declared to be 'at the boundaries of faith',[54] and who is therefore an isolated, marginal and double figure. Job is both the object of the superiority of his Comforters (who stand in for Kierkegaard as the judgmental figure of surveillance) and the person who is nonetheless proved right. As the young man writes, 'Was Job proved to be in the wrong? Yes, eternally, for there is no higher court than the one that judged him. Was Job proved to be in the right? Yes, eternally, by being proved to be in the wrong *before God.*'[55] Unlike Blake's Job, memorialized in his illustrations as the image of self-satisfied religious worldliness and Utilitarianism, Kierkegaard's Job is the exceptional individual, which is a much more dangerous concept because of its tendential elitism. Job is caught, as it were, in 'Christendom' and its judgements, and yet not caught at the last, when, against all expectation, he is heard by God, and given an absolute judgement, outside the textual system which is Christendom. This victory is a kind of 'repetition', meaning the return of the different. But while pure repetition, if it ever took place, would be transcendence, I have already implied that such transcendence can never be established by the text. The example of Job suggests there is no getting out of Christendom into the category of the individual, or transcendence, let alone into a pure form of church. Modernity disallows such a distinction between the true and the false.

Concluding Melancholic Postscript

What helps in laying these contradictions side by side may be Kierkegaard's melancholia, on which, of course, much has been written[56] and which, he says, gripped him from the very beginning, even acknowledging that it was 'on the point of preventing my being a human being'.[57] Melancholia in Kierkegaard is inseparable from those other ambiguous states he tries to conceptualize: irony, anxiety, and the sickness unto death (despair). Its primacy emerges in *Either/Or*, where it is, effectively, part of the way of describing 'Christendom':

> People have now been talking long enough about the frivolity of this age; I believe that it is now high time to talk a little about its melancholy ... is not melancholy the defect of our age?[58]

These words are quoted by Adorno, who reads the concept of melancholy in Kierkegaard as double; initially as part of a cultivation of bourgeois inwardness, or 'interiority' which Adorno rejects on account of its lack of attention to external history.[59] In melancholy, the subject assumes a privileged position, as does, by implication, religion. Melancholy is the way in which the inadequacy of the 'aesthetic state' is brought home to the subject; once the young man in *Repetition* learns this he ceases to exist in a condition of immediacy and spontaneity, both characteristics of the 'aesthetic'. Adorno's point is that Kierkegaard disregards the aesthetic, having no inclination to take it as a non-immediate state, a condition from which cognition takes place.[60] There is a willed simplicity in Kierkegaard's analysis of the age (again the comparison with Carlyle is relevant), beginning with his construction of Christendom as a non-mediated condition. By doing so, he denies Christendom the potential of critique.

But melancholy can also be read, as Adorno takes it and finds it in Kierkegaard, through the lens of Benjamin's *The Origin of German Tragic Drama*. Here Benjamin pairs melancholy with allegory, as a way of breaking up appearances, for it is central to allegory to reject the appearance of things, to show that no state can be immediate. Allegory is paired with Kierkegaard's irony since both, according to Naomi Lebowitz, 'break up false unions of the self with ideal selves, with the world, and through literature preserve and reflect our fall from distant origins'.[61] For Benjamin, allegory and melancholy, both working with the fragmentary, the non-totalizable, are as antithetical to the idealities and totalities of thought, complete systems which they demonstrate to be constructions. Kierkegaard's allegorical forms are appropriate for a reality which is not divisible into the true and the false, and where the concept of a discrete and separate church is impossible.

Kierkegaard's melancholy, like anxiety, is the suspension of a definite emotion, since it does not refer to anything definite: anxiety 'is altogether different from fear and similar concepts that refer to something definite ... anxiety is freedom's actuality as to the possibility of possibility.'[62] What makes anxiety modern is that, in thinking about the 'possible', it is an undecidable state of meditation on 'the object riddled with error'. And here it is possible to formulate a distinction between Kierkegaard and Carlyle. In the latter, definite emotions do not, finally, mutate into melancholy, but it is the marker of Kierkegaard's modernity that he *is* able to read emotions as so mutating and melancholy as to suspend those emotions. The desire to work with the concept of Christendom can be seen as commitment to a hesitation *between* definite emotions, especially determinate truth and falsehood. If the concept of Christendom is insufficient in the way it frames Kierkegaard's area of interest, it nonetheless provides in its doubleness a paradigm of the ambiguity in which the present age exists.

Notes

1. Søren Kierkegaard, *The Point of View: On My Work as an Author; The Point of View for My Work as an Author; Armed Neutrality*, tr. Howard V. Hong and Edna H. Hong (Princeton: Princeton University Press, 1998), p. 23.
2. John W. Elrod, *Kierkegaard and Christendom* (Princeton: Princeton University Press, 1981), p. 274.
3. Søren Kierkegaard, *Concluding Unscientific Postscript*, tr. David F. Swenson and Walter Lowrie (Princeton: Princeton University Press, 1941), pp. 72–80.
4. Peter Fenves, *"Chatter": Language and History in Kierkegaard* (Stanford: Stanford University Press, 1993), pp. 145–51.
5. See Christopher Norris, *The Deconstructive Turn* (London: Methuen, 1983) and 'De Man Unfair to Kierkegaard? An Allegory of (Non)-Reading' in Birgit Bertung (ed.), *Kierkegaard: Poet of Existence* (Copenhagen: C.A. Reitzel, 1989); and Louis Mackey, *Points of View: Readings in Kierkegaard* (Tallahassee: The Florida State University Press, 1986).
6. Quoted in Mackay, *Points of View*, p.160.
7. Kierkegaard, *The Point of View*, p. 23.
8. Ibid., p. 29.
9. Ibid., p. 61.
10. Walter Benjamin, *Charles Baudelaire: A Lyric Poet in the Era of High Capitalism*, tr. Harry Zohn (London: New Left Books, 1973), p. 34.
11. Kierkegaard, *The Point of View*, p. 108.
12. Ibid., p. 24.
13. Ibid., pp. 87, 79–84.
14. See Eric J. Ziolkowski, 'The Laughter of Despair: Irony, Humour and Laughter in Kierkegaard and Carlyle' in Virgil Nemoianu and Robert Royal (eds), *Play, Literature, Religion: Essays in Cultural Intertextuality* (Albany: State University of New York Press, 1992), pp. 99–123.
15. *Poetry and Prose of William Blake*, edited by Geoffrey Keynes (London: Nonesuch Press, 1927), p. 398.
16. Bruce H. Kirmmse, *Kierkegaard in Golden Age Denmark* (Bloomington: Indiana University Press, 1990), p. 25.
17. Alastair Hannay (ed.), *Soren Kierkegaard: Papers and Journals, a Selection* (Harmondsworth: Penguin, 1996), p. 672.
18. Elrod, *Kierkegaard and Christendom*, pp. xviii, 193.
19. Kirmmse, *Kierkegaard in Golden Age Denmark*, p. 3.
20. Quoted in Elrod, *Kierkegaard and Christendom*, p. 276.
21. *William Blake*, p. 58.
22. Søren Kierkegaard, *Fear and Trembling and Repetition*, tr. Howard V. Hong and Edna H. Hong (Princeton: Princeton University Press, 1983), pp. 148–9. The editors annotate 'ethical' as 'pagan'. See also p. 366.
23. See Gilles Deleuze, *Difference and Repetition*, tr. Paul Patton (London: Athlone Press, 1994).
24. Kierkegaard, *Fear and Trembling*, p. 186.
25. Kierkegaard, *The Point of View*, p. 118.
26. Ibid., p. 43.
27. Ibid., p. 54.
28. Ibid., p. 56.

29 Benjamin, *Charles Baudelaire*, p. 103.
30 *William Blake*, p. 244. For Blake on 'contraries', see pp. 149, 210.
31 See Fenves, *"Chatter"*.
32 The same journal entry continues thus: 'But when in the course of time and in the steady advance of nonsense it transpired that being a Christian is synonymous with being a human, the Christian congregation became the human race ... The Christian congregation is now the general public, and in the eyes of every cultured clergyman, to say nothing of lay people, it is offensive to speak of 'the single individual' – *Papers and Journals*, p. 475.
33 Pat Bigelow, *Kierkegaard and the Problem of Writing* (Tallahassee: The Florida State University Press, 1987), p. 180.
34 Kierkegaard, *The Point of View*, p. 67.
35 Søren Kierkegaard, *The Sickness Unto Death: A Christian Psychological Exposition for Upbuilding and Awakening*, tr. Howard V. Hong and Edna H. Hong (Princeton: Princeton: University Press, 1980), p. 64.
36 Kierkegaard, *Fear and Trembling*, p. 200.
37 Hannay (ed.), *Papers and Journals*, p. 265.
38 Benjamin, *Charles Baudelaire*, p. 40.
39 Søren Kierkegaard, *Two Ages: The Age of Revolution and the Present Age*, tr. Howard V. Hong and Edna H. Hong (Princeton: Princeton University Press, 1978), pp. 81–2.
40 Kierkegaard, *Two Ages*, p. 107.
41 Kierkegaard, *The Point of View*, pp. 87, 122.
42 Theodor W. Adorno, *Kierkegaard: Construction of the Aesthetic*, tr. Robert Hullot-Kentor (Minneapolis: University of Minnesota Press, 1989), p. 42.
43 Kierkegaard, *The Point of View*, p. 78.
44 Ibid., pp. 87, 12.
45 See Elaine Showalter, *The Female Malady: Women, Madness and English Culture 1830–1980* (London: Virago, 1987); and Jeremy Tambling, 'Carlyle in Prison: Reading *Latter-Day Pamphlets*' in *Dickens Studies Annual*, 26 (1998), pp. 311–34.
46 Kierkegaard, *Fear and Trembling*, p. 135.
47 Ibid., p. 189.
48 Ibid., pp. 225–6.
49 Michel Foucault, 'The Order of Discourse,' in Robert Young (ed.), *Untying the Text: A Post-Structuralist Reader* (London: Routledge, 1981), p. 55.
50 Kierkegaard, *Sickness Unto Death*, p. 102.
51 Ibid., p. 104.
52 Benjamin, *Charles Baudelaire*, p. 38.
53 Kierkegaard, *Sickness Unto Death*, p. 119.
54 Kierkegaard, *Fear and Trembling*, p. 210.
55 Ibid., p. 212.
56 See Vincent A. McCarthy, *The Phenomenology of Moods in Kierkegaard* (The Hague: Martinus Nijhoff, 1978).
57 Hannay (ed.), *Papers and Journals*, p. 486.
58 Søren Kierkegaard, *Either/Or: Volume II*, tr. Walter Lowrie (Princeton: Princeton University Press, 1959), p. 24.
59 Adorno, *Kierkegaard: Construction of the Aesthetic*, pp. 59–60.
60 Ibid., pp. 14, 66.
61 Naomi Lebowitz, *Kierkegaard: A Life of Allegory* (Baton Rouge: Louisiana State University Press, 1985), p. 12.
62 Søren Kierkegaard, *The Concept of Anxiety*, tr. Reidar Thomte and Albert B. Anderson (Princeton: Princeton University Press, 1980), p. 42.

Chapter 9

Christ's Queer Wound, or Divine Humiliation Among the Unchurched

Kathryn Bond Stockton

Seriously, one is tempted to say, it is a question without irony. What can it mean to be martyred for clothes – to believe in clothes as one suffers from clothes, to bear the wounds that come with clothes, even to give up one's very self (but what would that mean?) for the cause of one's clothes? O vain shame ...

Forget for a moment that Christ's crucifixion is a drama set to cloth: the mocking of Jesus with a gorgeous purple robe, the rending of the temple veil at the point of death, the Romans dividing and gambling for Christ's clothes, along with the extrabiblical traditions of Veronica's handkerchief and the Turin shroud.[1] Forget, that is, that cloth seems required for the marking of Christ's wound or the textured capture of his act of sacrifice (markings and textures repeated in the Church's obsession with the robes and vestments of its priests, its 'men of the cloth'). Remember only Thomas, who, doubting and wishing for a sign, made a set of bodily wounds a synecdoche for Christ: 'Except I shall see in his hands the print of the nails ... and thrust my hand into his side, I will not believe' (John 20:25). Recall that Matthew and Luke contribute to this view of the wound-as-magic-window by having (their versions of) Christ return for display of his wounded parts as proof: 'Behold my hands and my feet' (Luke 24:39); 'And they came and held him by the feet, and worshipped him' (Matthew 28:9).

Here, evidently, was a claim to be embraced as readily as a lord. The bodily wounds inflicted on Jesus (the Roman marks of death and shame) signal a humiliation held to be divine. This was an axiom that influenced the teachings of the first Church theorist, the apostle Paul; especially as he oversaw the transformation of religious outcasts into the regulated Body of Christ. Giving testimony to a wound was *de rigueur*, however it might best be accomplished. Indeed, believers were asked by Paul to consider numerous ways that they might 'bear in [the] body', as Paul writes to the Galatians, 'the marks of ... Lord Jesus' (Galatians 6:17). Martyrdom was only the most spectacular display of Christ's wounds as one's own. There were still more surprising methods that could testify to 'the marks of ... Lord Jesus'. Consider Paul's tricky stand on circumcision, one of the watershed issues for those 'called out' of Judaism into Christ's fold, where *ecclesia*, 'church', means 'called out': 'As many as desire to make a fair shew in the flesh, they constrain you to be circumcised; only lest they should suffer persecution for the cross of Christ' (Galatians 6:12). The bodily mark of circumcision was so unrelated to testifying to the marks of Christ that Paul, in this case, could associate circumcision with a 'desire to make a fair shew in the flesh' – a show that could even signal one's unwillingness to 'suffer persecution for the cross of Christ'. By this logic, the *absence* of the mark of circumcision on a Jew was a new kind of wound and a new kind of witness. Seriously, the idea of the Church was founded on the rock of odd wounds.

But how was the larger body of people to be so marked? Would it embrace humiliation, for instance, by encompassing different kinds of outcasts, those 'called out' of society and religious institutions? Paul appeared to imply as much since he made extensive figural reference to the Church-as-the-Body-of-Christ, which Body was supposed to encompass 'those members ... which we think to be less honourable' (I Cor. 12:23). Paul explains: "If the foot shall say, Because I am not the hand, I am not of the body; is it therefore not of the body? ... For our comely parts have no need: but God hath tempered the body together, having given more abundant honour to that part which lacked' (I Cor. 12:24–5).

One wonders what was the literal referent, in terms of people, of those 'members ... less honorable'? How far could the Church extend its embrace to those 'uncomely' members – sexually different Christians, for instance – before it reached a moral or theological limit, a border beyond which the Church would not go, giving rise to an oxymoron: a body of believers 'called out' of the Body, a church outside the Church, the 'unchurched', for whom Christ's wounds might have a surprising life.

This queer life, among the unchurched, of the sign of Christ's wounds, forms the basis of this essay. This wound-life, among unchurched queers, who believe in their clothes, even returns us to Christ's gorgeous robe: 'And they stripped him and put on him a scarlet robe ... and [they] mocked him, saying "Hail, King of the Jews!" And they spit on him' (Matthew 27:28–30). Fittingly, this garment (scarlet in Matthew, purple in Mark, plain 'gorgeous' in Luke) eerily dresses up a body in the color of its blood or a bruise. More fitting still, Jesus is made to wear a sign of vanity (here, faux-royalty) as a sign of shame.

This vain shame is a trope for queer life. Indeed, it still surprises that shame can adhere to forms of beauty, especially to the contours of beautiful cloth. (Women wrapped in beautiful clothes may betray the vanity said to be their shame. Men who rush to their own cloth-beauty likely suffer a woman's vain shame.) It is more surprising to learn, from certain novels, that this debasement clinging to beauty can make the wearer of beautiful garments a martyr to clothes. As a foray into this logic, I will sample novels from three distinct histories, offering martyrs – all unchurched – as diverse as those of the mannish lesbian of Great Britain's 1920s, American butches and femmes of the 1960s, and even sailors from post-war France. These remarkably various fictions specify, remarkably, not entirely various logics, even as they range from fictional lesbian autobiographies, without any claim to aesthetic density, to the high modernist camp of Genet, aesthetic texts of such dense weave, such lyric sheen.

Taking up the cause of clothes, as if clothes are a dangerous rite which they would defend, all three novels imagine scenes of sacrifice. However, in ways we might not expect, sacrifice is joined to sexual fantasy. The throwing of oneself outward in sacrifice merges with the goal of being caught by other arms – a sexy Pieta.[2] This odd motion of throwing and being caught calls our attention to something odder still. Clothing itself is a throwing and a catching, a centrifugal force. In the act of clothing, one is thrown outward into cloth arms (the arms of one's clothes), caught and held as a public gesture, in the social field. Clothing is this act of public self-betrayal. But could clothing also be a social self-enclosure, a kind of Pieta, a strange cloth church inside which one believes? Could clothes offer a kind of social holding, a social self-hoarding, as odd as that may seem, of one's humiliation at the hands of something loved?

If so, we are likely to see a debasement freed from its command performance as either oppression or subversion, or, in the now familiar Butlerian sense, both-at-once.[3] This would not be debasement as subversion; clothing as performative; multiple selves as radical selves; or miming as undoing or the failure to undo. This would be (at least a partial) calling out (*ecclesia*) from the subversion/oppression calculations of recent theory. For the goal of this debasement is a turning, church-like, towards different forms of sociality that use humiliation for attraction and aesthetic delight. And though this debasement might sound familiar from Leo Bersani's smart formulations, its stress on *social* embrace makes a different kind of move from Bersani's strong stress on the anti-communal nature of sex as self-debasement. Recall that Bersani (through Freud and Bataille) defines the act of sexual pleasure as 'self-shattering', 'a kind of nonanecdotal self-debasement', in which 'the sexual itself [is] the risk of self-dismissal', and, therefore, 'ascesis'.[4] All of this leads Bersani, even in his readings of Genet, to celebrate 'solitude' as the proper goal of the 'anticommunal, antiegalitarian, antinurturing' nature of sex.[5] By contrast, I will argue for the social nature of sartorial sacrifice, stressing the role of clothing as a fabric that fosters group fantasy and sets a group apart. Does it take at least two members of a Body to shatter a self into social attitude?

According to our novels, from three different histories, that depends dramatically upon how one negotiates the wounds that come with cloth.

One: The Cloth of Woundedness

There are many ways to be hurt by one's clothes:

- a psychic wound may emerge from wearing certain clothes, as if one's thoughts show a certain cut of cloth;
- a woman's genital 'wound' (à la Freud) must be announced or dismissed by one's clothes, calling out on every woman's garment a vagina; on every man's garment, escape from this sorrow;
- some may hand out bodily wounds to those who wear 'unnatural' clothes, wounds which themselves may be worn as clothes: a bruise, for example, as a kind of purple cloth;
- finally, perhaps most intriguing of all: one may suffer the divine humiliation of devotion to ... fabric: a sailor, for example, may feel a coat of 'coal dust

on his body, as women feel, on their arms ... the folds of a material that transforms them into queens'.[6]

These are cloth wounds. Which makes both Freud and the dictionary wrong (or simply defensive) when it comes to cloth. The dictionary tells us clothes are designed to cover, protect, or adorn the body, slyly saying nothing of their darker intent to reveal, wound, or debase the body that they pretend to cover.[7] Moreover, we are told that 'cloth' is related to the Old English *clitha*, meaning 'a poultice': a soft moist mass, of flour or herbs, applied to a sore or inflamed body part.[8] By this rendering, cloth is seen as a solace for sufferings, not as an agent, as cloth also is, for a wounded appearance.

Freud, for his part, adheres to a covering. Recall that at the end of his essay 'Femininity', Freud imagines pubic hair as a natural model for human clothing, since it covers and conceals a woman's genitals. Here is the 'unconscious motive', Freud tells us, for women's contribution (their only contribution) to civilized development: plaiting and weaving, which, of course, only 'imitates' Nature's invention of the pubes.[9] 'The step that remained to be taken,' says Freud, in the passage from pubic hair to clothes, 'lay in making the threads adhere to one another, while on the body they stick into the skin and are only matted together.' In other words, as it solves the problem of sticking, cloth is a greater adherence to a covering.

What is being covered? Not a person's body in any simple sense. Not, even more particularly, the genitals. Freud is more specific still. What is being covered, in Freud's own phrase, is 'genital deficiency' – his essay is on 'Femininity', after all. Indeed, what has led Freud to pubic hair and cloth is his last, rushed, rag-bag discussion of 'a few more psychic peculiarities of mature femininity': vanity and shame. Peculiar, indeed, is the feminine adherence of one to the other, shame to vanity, vanity to shame, so that they would appear to wear each other's clothes. As it happens, one is a cover for the other. 'The vanity of women,' Freud famously informs us, is 'a late compensation for ... original sexual inferiority.' Vanity, in other words, is fancy-pants shame, which 'has as its purpose', says Freud, '... concealment of genital deficiency'. Yet, this is no real concealment at all. Vanity is calling out: 'look at my cover.' Clothing is not primarily concealment; it is not primarily a more attractive version of its model, pubic hair. Clothing, rather, is bold revelation, a splendid inversion, a cover turning inside out: it reveals the *category* of a person's genitals it purports to cover. On every woman's sweater, a vaginal wound.

You know this. If I have offered the fictions of Freud – lacking in all subtlety and cloaking historicity, when it comes to clothes – it has been to dramatize how Freud gets it right in this case when he is wrong, stressing concealment when he points to revelation. Even his lack of historical regard does not keep him, in 1933, just five years past Radclyffe Hall's *The Well of Loneliness*, from his own peculiar timeliness. I think it would even be fair to say that Freud and Hall were voicing something in much stronger terms than were their contemporaries: not just the sociopolitical disadvantage attached to women's clothes, but the bodily and psychic wounding that adheres to them.

Even the psychoanalyst J.C. Flugel did not put the matter of clothes so starkly in his famous treatise, *The Psychology of Clothes* (1930), launched from a series of talks he gave for the BBC in 1928, when *Well* was being censored.[10] Flugel had no theory of wounding. True, he himself theorized clothes (in a move Freud intensified) as satisfying two 'contradictory tendencies' (those of 'decoration' and 'modesty'). This makes clothes resemble, he said, the neurotic symptoms of people who suffer 'attacks of ... blushing' as they negotiate between the states of 'shame' and 'exhibitionism', so that 'clothes resemble a perpetual blush upon the surface of humanity.' Yet, in spite of this theory of blushing, Flugel had no theory of wounding.[11]

Nor exactly did the turn-of-the-century commentators in the debates on New Women have any such theory of clothes wounding women, though they were clearly grappling with what women's clothes mean and limit.[12] Rather, it was when these debates replayed themselves among historians in the 1980s that interpretations of cloth wounds emerged.[13] Feminist historians sought to understand the stakes attached to a woman's refusal of women's clothes. Some historians predictably championed those New Women (Woolf, for example) whom they imagined 'adopted male dress as a self-conscious political statement', believing that 'clothes are cultural artifacts, lightly donned or doffed.'[14] They explained with less ease the 'Mannish Lesbian', whose costume change was not so easy, and whose 'symbols [thus] acquired a second, darker message ... public condemnation, social ostracism, and legal censorship'.[15] It was left to those more sympathetic to this figure to explain the Mannish Lesbian's bold refusal of women's clothes as a brave move that embraced 'the stigma of lesbianism (just as the effeminate man is the stigma-bearer for gay men)'.[16]

What interests me is this mention of 'stigma'. Notice the assumption that a woman refusing women's clothes would find herself (still) bound up with a wound – more pointedly, a stigma ('stigma': 'a distinguishing mark burned or cut into the flesh, as of a slave or criminal'; 'marks resembling the crucifixion wounds of Jesus'; 'a mark, sign, etc. indicating that something is not considered normal or standard').[17] What is it about women's clothes that makes the woman crossing from them, as well as the man crossing to them, bear a greater burden (a stigma) than the woman who conventionally wears them (though, by Freud's logic, she is wounded, too)? Is the crossing of convention the only trespass here? Or is the act of revealing a wound (the wound that 'normal' women wear) itself a queer act? Is it queer to know a cloth wound when you see one? Is it even stronger to wear wounds in the act of refusing them?

This makes me think about queer aesthetics, in which a wounding due to clothes is often prominent. It also makes me think of the Church whose robed and vested men of the cloth not only dress, in a sense, as women but also wear the wound that is the sign of the cross. One may wonder about such scenes of sacrifice. The theorist of queer aesthetics may ask: what do the clothes that wound offer to queers beyond a symbol for their social stigma in the obvious sense? Here another novelist comes into view – Georges Bataille – one likely thoroughly read by Genet.[18] Bataille is heuristically interesting on sacrifice among the unchurched. His essays make us see what questions we could ask of a martyrdom to clothes, and further how this sacrifice goes hand-in-hand with fantasy. Briefly, Bataille, in *Theory of Religion*, deems 'religion's essence ... the search for lost intimacy',[19] which, we realize in no way necessitates the established Church. Lest this 'intimacy' sound too immediately relational or sexual, we should realize that this is a call to 'the intimacy of the divine world', whose chief feature is its 'unreality', its separation from 'real relations' and the 'world of things'.[20] In fact, it is the main function of sacrifice to destroy 'an object's real ties', by drawing 'the victim out of the world of utility', while restoring it to a world of 'unintelligible caprice', thus giving it 'an appearance of puerile gratuitousness'[21] – qualities not often claimed by Christian churches, despite Christ's injunction that 'whosoever shall not receive the kindgdom of God as a little child, he shall not enter therein' (Mark 10:15). **Question one**: could sacrifice surrounding clothes, whatever that might look like, destroy a person's 'real ties' to the 'world of utility'? And would this be a different 'calling out' than that of the established Church?

We have said the destruction that is sacrifice has a fanciful nature – taking one towards both caprice and unreality. Now we must see that sacrifice is also tied to a movement so often tied to fantasy. Here I mean a casting of one's self outside oneself (in fantasy, a mental leap out of real life), so as to break not just with one's reality, but also with one's 'individuality', according to Bataille[22] – a 'calling out' (that is, an *ecclesia*) from one's very self. With the act of sacrifice, such casting out turns physical, and, of course, violent. In fact, this break with one's individuality lies at the heart of the sacrificial urge, according to Bataille, and constitutes the intimacy of sacrificial violence. In his lurid essay 'Sacrificial Mutilation and the Severed Ear of Vincent Van Gogh', Bataille proclaims that automutilation (the chopping off of one's finger, for example) reveals what's at stake in religious sacrifice: the need to externalize the self, to throw oneself out of oneself, to disrupt the homogeneity of the self, whether by the sacrifice of animal proxies (a religious cop-out) or the madman's chopping off of his ear (67).[23] (Or, in a ritual Bataille fails to mention, by the Christian Eucharist, in which Christ offers his Body to the Church as something perpetually externalized and eaten.)

Question two: could clothing be both an act of fantasy *and* an act of sacrifice, allowing one to throw oneself, to feel oneself as a kind of thrown self, and so, in a rather odd way, to church oneself, to call oneself *out into* enclosure? Our selected fictions to be sure, are going to show that a martyrdom to clothes is a kind of self-betrayal. For when you give up loneliness to make yourself a character, by means of either fantasy or cloth, you give yourself away. But are you caught and held? Is there a 'church' (out) there to catch you? Are the (wo)men of the cloth there to hold you?

Two: The Cloth of Loneliness

Arguably the most famous lesbian novel, Hall's *The Well of Loneliness* (1928), answers no: one is not embraced in a martyrdom to clothes. As any reader of the novel will remember, *The Well* begins and ends with intense salvific scenes, using religion as a narrative wrap. The novel's heroine, Stephen Mary Gordon (who carried in her name a butch/femme cross between a famous church martyr and one who wraps a martyred son in arms), is born on Christmas Eve and bears, as one lesbian character puts it, the 'outward stigmata of the abnormal – verily the wounds of One nailed to a cross'.[24] Yet, in what seems a cross-dresser's joke, Stephen, the novel's most loyal cross-dresser, wears the martyr's cross on her clothes.

Realize, however, that for all of its pains, the novel is actually shockingly flat – at the level of the sentence (no sentence will transport you), and even at the larger level of its plot. This very flatness has clearly aided those who, since 1928, have wished to read the novel as fairly 'factual' – to find in *The Well* a historically accurate portrait of the second-generation New Woman (her lesbian lust announced by her clothes) or to find a fiction 'still true' to butch women, and thus one easily altered on spec.[25] Consider, for example, that, according to a recent oral history of a lesbian community (*Boots of Leather, Slippers of Gold*), Hall's French twist on 1920s British aristocracy was thought to speak to its readers' lives in the American 1950s factory town of Buffalo, New York.[26] Truly, *The Well* has proved a cross-over text of vast proportions, only rivalled now by *Stone Butch Blues* (from 1993) which allows its readers to universalize the life of 1950s Buffalo lesbians.

None of this intrigue surrounding historicity is beside the point. The wonder of *The Well*'s sentimental realism, its relentless portrait of a lachrymose Christ, is for me its tragicomical 'clothemes' (to coin a comic word), that is to say, its mythemes (as Roland Barthes would call them), its myths surrounding clothes. I believe these clothemes are somewhat detachable from the specific plot-lines that engage them; but, as they emerge in different plots and other histories, they are largely altered.

Here is what I mean. In *The Well of Loneliness*, strutting, deflating, tearing cloth and shedding tears (all involving clothes) are the central clothemes, the pillars of loneliness, one might say, all of which resurface in *Stone Butch Blues* (1993) to a similar logic but different effect. For here in *The Well*, at the dawning of these clothemes, sacrifice fails, fantasy fails – even as religion is always failing Stephen throughout the novel. As the narrator tells us: 'It was quite true that inverts were often religious, but churchgoing in them was a form of weakness; they must be a religion unto themselves' (407). Stephen struggles along this border, trying to be a church – a public self-enclosure for belief and worship – outside the Church. And yet, her clothes are not enough to 'church' her; they do not catch and hold her. Especially at the novel's start, there are no arms of a public sort, or of a sort that hoard humiliation *for* the self and its private beauties, to catch a humiliated Stephen in embrace. Further in the novel, there are no social holdings (no public structures), at least of the sort that Stephen can trust, to make her self-humiliation into solitude. Later, we learn: 'As long as she lived Stephen never forgot her first impression of the [queer] bar known as Alec's – that meeting-place of the most miserable of all those who comprised the miserable army ... who, despised of the world, must despise themselves beyond all hope, it seemed, of salvation' (387). Bereft of a church any larger than herself, Stephen Mary Gordon forges a martyrdom that goes awry. She succeeds only in sacrificing clothes.

I refer, of course, to the tragicomic scenes at the start of the novel in which first love, first clothes, and first wounds all stick together in a first plot block. Stephen has fallen for the housemaid Collins, as nursery stories have 'stirred her ambition'.

> She, Stephen, now longed to be William Tell, or [Lord] Nelson, or the whole charge of Balaclava; and this led to much foraging in the nursery rag-bag, much blurting up of garments once used for charades, much swagger and noise, much strutting and posing ... Once dressed, she would walk away grandly ... going, as always, in search of Collins, who might have to be stalked to the basement. (19)

Stephen courts Collins dressed as a boy – Lord Nelson, in particular, that famous martyr from the Battle of Trafalgar. Collins, for her part, laughs at Stephen and appears distracted, since she is suffering from housemaid's knee. Seeing, perhaps, that masculine clothes cannot bear any comedy, that they shrink from laughter and suggestions of vanity, Stephen finds herself 'thoroughly deflated', having dressed up 'as Nelson in vain', ' – she now feels she must tear off the clothes she dearly loved donning, to replace them by the garments she hated' (20). Dressed once again as a girl, in the garments that make her feel truly shamed, the girlboy turns her efforts into martyrdom (a clever ploy for working *with* her wounding due to clothes). Nightly she cries in 'an orgy of prayer':

> Please, Jesus, give me a housemaid's knee instead of Collins ... Please, Jesus, I would like to bear all Collins' pain the way you did ... I would like to wash Collins in my blood ... This petition she repeated until she fell asleep, to dream that in some queer way she was Jesus, and that Collins was kneeling and kissing her hand, because she, Stephen, had managed to cure her by cutting off her knee, with a bone paper-knife and grafting it onto her own. The dream was a mixture of rapture and discomfort, and it stayed quite a long time with Stephen. (21–2)

For all of these elaborate dreams of sacrifice, Stephen's fantasy of Collins' mutilation (a grafting of Collins' knee onto her own), is not yet self-sacrificial enough. Just as sadly, this fantasy collapses into Stephen's loneliness instead of solving it. And so, since she cannot come to wear Collins' knee in this direct way, Stephen, yet again, changes her strategy. Getting mad at Jesus ('"You don't love Collins, Jesus, but I do"' (22), Stephen cries: '"I've got to get housemaid's knee my own way – I can't wait any longer for Jesus!"' (23). However, this bid for attaching her heart to a wounded knee makes a cloth wound more than anything else:

> The nursery floor was covered with carpet, which was obviously rather unfortunate for Stephen ... All the same it was hard if she knelt long enough ... Nelson helped her a little ... She would think: 'Now I'm Nelson. I'm in the middle of the Battle of Trafalgar – I've got shots in my knees!' But then she would remember that Nelson had been spared such torment ... [Still] there were endless spots on the ... carpet, and these spots Stephen could pretend to be cleaning ... Enormous new holes appeared in her stockings, through which she could examine her aching knees ... [T]his led to rebuke: 'Stop your nonsense, Miss Stephen! It's scandalous the way you're tearing your stockings!' (22–3)

Just as the earlier failure to extract the needed power from Nelson's clothes led to Stephen's tearing them, now her failure to elicit any wound from him leads to different tears as she comically copies the movements of her servant, making her the figure of a carpet-cleaning Christ. As this saviour, Stephen only succeeds in revealing, metaphorically and literally, the wound that sits on her women's clothes ('enormous new holes appeared in her stockings'). Moreover, because the invert child has scandalously torn her feminine garments, wounding a woman's proper cover, the head-servant orders Collins to lie, to tell the child her knee is getting better from these efforts. This fabrication, which even Stephen questions, is emblematic for the book as a whole. The heroine's faithful martyrdom to clothes is productive of nothing more than exile and tears:

> She sobbed as she ran ... tearing her clothes on the shrubs in passing, tearing her stockings and the skin of her legs ... But suddenly the child was caught in strong arms, and her face was pressing against her father ... [S]he crouched here like a dumb creature that had somehow got itself wounded ... 'I'm going to send Collins away tomorrow; do you understand, Stephen?' ... Bending down, [her father] kissed her in absolute silence – it was like the sealing of a sorrowful pact. (28–9)

Gone is the purpose behind her wounding: to be held by Collins *and* her own boy's clothes, really to be held in her masculine clothes. Even this final wrapping by her father is no solution. (Her father later dies; her lover, Mary, leaves, when she sends her away.) It only closes off this first plot block, which repeats in different fashions throughout Hall's *The Well*, recycling unmistakable clothemes of loneliness.[27]

Three: The Cloth of Communal Adherence

Out of the 1990s comes a solace for loneliness. In Leslie Feinberg's *Stone Butch Blues* (1993), loneliness seems taken up and transformed in the space that Stephen could never seen to trust: the lesbian bar. Shot through with its nostalgia for community – 1950s and 1960s bar life in Buffalo, along with labour struggles in a string of city factories – *Stone Butch Blues* begins, even so, with a lonely letter. It has been written at the story's end, to a lover lost at the story's middle (though it is placed at the story's start): 'Dear Theresa, I'm lying on my bed tonight missing you ... hot tears running down my face ... as I have each night of this lonely exile'.[28] It could appear that *Stone* is picking up where *The Well* left off; as if, years after sending her away, Stephen is writing to her great love, Mary, to reminisce about a lost community.

And yet, what has changed between these novels' settings, between the loneliness of *The Well*'s late 1920s and the bracing sociality of *Stone*'s 1960s, is something very 1993 (the novel's date of publication). Call it 'feminist butch nostalgia'. I refer to the phenomenon, still underway, of a feminist affirmation of butch-femme relations – the once dirty secret of a lesbian history. This embrace, sometimes with a dose of nostalgia, takes many forms; among them, as one could readily imagine, is a reading of these couples as deconstructing pairs.[29] But I am more struck by Feinberg's sense of sacrifice; the way in which her butch, who is physically wounded due to her clothes, as we will see, wears her resultant gashes and burns for the sake of her femme, who wears women's clothes. This is a social working out of women's wounds, and one in which the presence of the femme (even as the letter's worshipped ghost) makes all the difference.[30] True, gone is Hall's Catholic discourse, but not its sense of martyrdom – the very word 'stone' maintains a cryptic link to the church's first martyr. Now, though, unlike the setting in *The Well*, there are communal structures – an erotic system, even – to suggest how debasement offers social self-enclosure. This is even a happy self-betrayal: a feminist fantasy of *in*equality, a fantastic embrace of differential roles. Indeed, as if to underscore its fantasy structure, the novel's lonely letter is a form of pillow talk to a lost great love, but pillow-talk remembrance of the (good old) raids of the 1960s when butches were beaten up by the cops. Here is a memory of a raid on a bar:

> That's when I remember your hand on my belt, up under my suit jacket ... where you hand stayed the whole time the cops were there ... 'Stay with me baby, cool off,' you'd be cooing ... like a special lover's song sung to warriors. The law said we had to be wearing three pieces of women's clothing ...[31] I never told you what they did to us down there ... but you knew ... We never cried in front of the cops ... Did I survive? ... only because I knew I might get home to you ... You bailed me out ... You gently rubbed the bloody places on my shirt and said, 'I'll never get these stains out.' ... You laid out a fresh pair of white BVD's [a brand of men's underwear] and a T-shirt for me and left me alone to wash off the first layer of shame. I remember it was always the same ... you would find some reason to come into the bathroom ... In a glance you would memorize the wounds on my body like a road map – the gashes, bruises, cigarette burns. Later, in bed, you held me gently ... You didn't flirt with me right away, knowing I wasn't confident enough to feel sexy. But slowly you coaxed my pride back out ... You knew it would take you weeks again to melt the stone ... You treated my stone self as a wound that needed loving healing. (8–9)

Here is *Well*'s recognizable sentiment, mixed with reportage. Again, we are held by an intricate chain of interlocking clothemes. We are asked to see how the members of this couple – a Body of larger sense – wear their deviance as a witness shared between them, a deviance that neither can sustain on her own. In unequal ways, as members of a Body performing different functions, they are marked by the discipline and punishments of gender.

The femme's deviance is strangely unmarked when she's on her own. She can't be seen for the deviant she is, since she blends, passes, and wears the expected wound of her gender, as is expected, on her clothes. The butch, by contrast, looks to be refusing the women's clothes that would signal her wound. Yet, it is by this act of refusal that she melts the stone so the butch can go back, again and again, to encounter the law ('it was always the same'). Together, what they advocate is a repetition of wounding and refusal at the hands of their clothes (the femme wears the wound, the butch fights the wound, the cops intervene, the butch wears the wound ...). All of this puts them about the business of holding, as a couple, a psychic wound they never would have made each other wear. One might even say, reading back to Hall's *The Well*, that on this stone they found what for Stephen would have been the invert's church.[32]

Four: The Cloth of Curve

Stone Butch Blues may be a rather unimaginable lesson in how to have a feminist fantasy – how to imagine two women addressing the shame of their clothes by returning, in sacrificial cycles, to a beating. Genet's *Querelle* (1953) is more circular still, proposing the queer's devotion to fabric (his wish to be held, as it were, by his clothes) as an elegant, self-embracing shame. This is shame, not just because it resembles a woman's vanity, but because it points towards other men's arms. The wish to be held by one's own clothes is a wish to be held by arms that both are and are not one's own. Wrap-around shame that comes from the thrill of men's tightly wrapped clothes is tightly tied, moreover, to sacrificial scenes. Sacrifice is a kind of wrapping in *Querelle*. It mimes the act of clothing by being a casting outward of self that allows the subject to touch back upon himself as if he were a different set of arms from his own.

Tellingly, the fighting in *Querelle* is as oddly self-reflexive as the clothing. In this novel about sea and sailors, sailors in port, workmen and sailors, and the dark circuitry between cops and criminals, who are sailors – set in the seaside city of Brest (destroyed by bombs in the Second World War) – fighting is a way of calling arms upon oneself. Even the act of murder in the novel, performed by a sailor in glamorous clothes, is revealed to be self-sacrifice – as is any crusade whose flourishing of its sword (as the Church or Body Militant) is closely tied to martyrdom. This is hinted at by the title *Querelle*, taken from the self-reflexive French verb, *se quereller*, 'to pick a fight', as if one's fight is with oneself. Any soldier knows this. Killing is self-reflexive in war. A soldier's state-sanctioned murder of other soldiers like himself may, at any time, turn back upon himself as his state-ordered death (the command that he sacrifice himself for his brothers). In Genet's novel, the link between this turn-around and clothing's wrap-around is forged by fantasy. In *Querelle*, fantasy is central to narration, as is always the case in Genet. Here, however, it is even fabrication of the most communal and literal sort: actually the filling of an outfit by the narrators. They fantasize a fighting man in clothes they wish to wear. They launch him as a character in what they start to tell. They sacrifice their insides (their thoughts, their desires) in order to throw themselves outside themselves in this act of clothing.

If this seems an unforeseen devotion to fabric, let's admit it is. The novel is narrated by a 'we', who address themselves to 'inverts'.[33] Indeed, we begin on the edge of their fantasy: the sailor's uniform 'cradles the criminal, it enfolds him', 'envelops him in clouds', 'in the tight fit of his sweater, in the amplitude of his bell-bottoms' (4). This is an outfit the narrating 'we' would like to fill out – ideally, with themselves. And so they do. They fabricate a sailor from themselves:

> Little by little, we saw how Querelle – already contained in our flesh – was beginning to grow in our soul, to feed on what is best in us, above all on our despair at not being in any way inside him, while having him inside ourselves ... (We are still referring to that ideal and heroic personage, the fruit of our secret loves.) ... [T]o become visible to you, to become a character in a novel, Querelle must be shown apart from ourselves. (17–18)

Querelle is not just sweater and trousers. He is a state of mind that gets externalized. Indeed, by making narration fabrication, the filling of a sailor's suit, the narrators ostentatiously betray themselves. They sacrifice hidden desires inside themselves, in order to throw themselves outside themselves, making Querelle a desire they can cling to – and now a concept to 'get inside'. That they imagine their fantasy man to be a murderer seems only right, for this lets him take a more virile route to their own self-sacrificial position, as if virility bends to their fantasy. For when Querelle's murders turn into sacrifice, he can be seen to put his virility at the service of their wish for passivity, to share with the narrators a longing to be caught in glamorous arms: those of a body or a dangerous weapon or a beautiful cape.

It is this very concept of the wrap-around that grounds the narrators' devotion to fabric, their interest in tightly fitting sweaters as a social self-enclosure. The novel's only invert, Lieutenant Seblon, even wears their fantasies gayly on his sleeve, for the cops to see:

> [B]efore the two police officers had left [his] cabin, the Lieutenant wanted to put on his cloak of navy blue, and then did so with such coquetry – which he at once, and clumsily, corrected – that the total effect was not of just 'putting it on,' – that would have been far too manly, but rather that of 'wrapping himself in it' – which, indeed, was the way he thought of it himself. Again, he expected embarassment, and he made up his mind (once more) never to touch a piece of material again in public. (92)

But, of course, he does. In fact, he becomes the novel's poster-boy for divine humiliation, betraying (in the sense of revealing) that the fantasy filling up Querelle is a man's secret wish to be surrounded. Here is the Lieutenant on the subject of protection, blowing vanity's cool cover to uncover sacred shame:

> When I became an officer, it wasn't so much in order to be a warrior, but rather to be a precious object, guarded by soldiers. Which they would protect with their lives until they died for me, or I offered up my life in the same manner to save them. It is thanks to Jesus that we can praise humility, for he made it into the very characteristic of divinity ... Humility can only be born out of humiliation. Any other kind is a vain simulacrum. (265)

The Lieutenant knows that just as he and his soldiers wrap around to meet each other, playing, interchangeably, savior and saved, the soldier's protection is a social embrace, now making weaponry, like his cloak of navy blue, a sign of erotic self-revelation: a dead give-away. So we read, the Lieutenant, who 'took care never to be caught counting the stitches of any imaginary needlework ... [n]evertheless ... betrayed himself in the eyes of all men whenever he gave the order to pick up arms, for he pronounced the word 'arms' with such grace that his whole person seemed to be kneeling at the grave of some beautiful lover' (24). Here, in the graceful lining of the sentence, lies the Lieutenant's wish for embrace, betraying both his loneliness (as a grieving lover) and his longing for a lover-at-arms. Earlier he mused:

> After having been so overwhelmed by the loneliness to which my inversion condemns me, is it really possible that I may some day hold naked in my arms ... those young men whose courage and hardness place them so high in my esteem? ... My tears make me feel soft. I melt. (8–9).

No wonder the narrators' fantasy man, Querelle, feels depressed when he contemplates faggots. For he must be seen to shun such softness so he can be hard for the narrators' fantasy. Yet, he is made to wear his shunning as a shawl:

[This] quite depressing thought [about faggots] generated up his spine an immediate and rapid series of vibrations which quickly spread out over the entire surface of his black shoulders and covered them with a shawl woven out of shivers (88).

For the narrators who have crafted it, Querelle's depressing thought about faggots is a social self-debasement, as if they are wrapping themselves in a shawl of delicious shame, going both fabric soft and orgasmic in a feminine spread of shivers.

Their self-envelopment, via Querelle, is even more fluid after his homicides. Here is Querelle flowing out of himself, then flowing in to fill himself, after killing a sailor like himself:

Querelle grabbed [Vic] by the throat ... As Vic had the collar of his peacoat turned up, the blood ... ran down the inside of his coat and over his jersey ... The murderer straightened his back. He was a thing, in a world where danger does not exist ... Beautiful, immobile, dark thing, within whose cavities, the void becoming vocal, Querelle could hear it [himself as a thing] surge forth to escape with the sound, to surround him and to protect him. (61)

Here, of course, is that all-important wrapping: a kind of surround sound. Then, Querelle, after a pause, 'snorted twice ... moved his lips so that Querelle might enter, flow into the mouth, rise to the eyes, seep down to the fingers, fill the thing [himself] again' (62). Querelle is doing what the narrators do, both in fantasy and clothing: flowing out of themselves to surround themselves. He is how they hear themselves. He is even how the narrators see themselves – see themselves sacrificed.

In fact, unexpectedly, Querelle seeks to sacrifice himself sexually after the killing. To 'wash him[self] clean', he seeks to be buggered by the owner of a brothel (a man named Nono). "This would be capital punishment', we read, a 'sacrificial rite' (68). 'It came ... from an imperative that had issued from within himself'; 'his own strength and vitality were ordering him to bend over' (72). Odder still, this sacrifice commences with a curious act of clothing. At the moment of Querelle's 'self-execution', the men surprise each other by performing 'a perfectly synchronized' gesture which indicates their mutual experience of wearing sailors' belts that buckle at the back – a sign of 'their submission', say the narrators, 'to the glamor of the naval uniform' (73). Submitting to this 'glamor' in the sacrificial act, Querelle receives a genital wound. He is opened, like a sailor's belt, at the back. But notice the fanciful terms of this sacrifice. Nono, penetrating, 'was holding Querelle with seemingly the same passion a female animal shows when holding the dead body of her young offspring – the attitude by which we comprehend what love is: consciousness of the division of what previously was one ... while you yourself are watching yourself' (75). Here in the strangeness of the animal metaphor are those breaks from real relations and from individuality that Bataille predicts. Nono, as a mother in an animal Pieta, is showing how, in sacrifice, even an animal proxy gets to watch itself being thrown from itself in happy division. Then, as if the figure of the cop is required for this fantasy, too, making Nono's holding a more public display, we read: 'Querelle felt floored by the full weight of the French Police

Force: ... [a cop's] face was attempting to substitute itself for that of the man who was screwing him. Querelle ejaculated onto the velvet; (76). In *Querelle*, sacrifice passes through the martyr's body onto cloth. It is a gorgeous giving up of the ghost, for even the law to see, as if, at the height of his crucifixion, Christ had climaxed on a lush altar cloth (and lived to tell the tale).

Realize, now, that the novel ends by returning to a Pieta, one in which Querelle, then the Lieutenant, plays the role of Christ. Actually, by a set of intricate ploys, Querelle bequeaths martyrdom to the Lieutenant. With Querelle's help, the Lieutenant accuses himself of a crime in order to aid a young man in jail.[34] This self-betrayal allows the Lieutenant to wrap himself in the humility that he believes defines not only Christ's physical person, but also the symbolic, or ecclesial, Body of Christ. Cloth is required to mark this shame, largely because any wound to the cloth (even a stain) makes one aware of a uniform's glamour, thus showing outwardly how humility can mark divinity. So the Lieutenant, on a tryst, in a thicket, happens to lie, belly down, on some waste, staining his coat:

> Shame went right to work on him ... In the mist ... he still glimpsed the gold of the braids on his cuffs. As pride is humiliation's child, the officer now felt prouder than ever ... From this particular spot in Brest ... a light breeze, gentler and lovelier than the petals of Saadi's roses, spread the humility of Lieutenant Seblon over the ... world. (265–6)

Fittingly, this is the prelude to an ending, joining the Lieutenant to the fantasy, Querelle. Their farewell is a scene of embrace, such as the Lieutenant and the narrators have longed for. In fact, Querelle, almost playing the faggot, is sending the Lieutenant off to sacrifice himself:

> [T]he officer pulled the sailor's head toward him, and Querelle rested his cheek on Seblon's thigh ... Then he got up, throwing his arms round the officer's neck, and ... riding the crest of a wave of femininity from god knows where, this gesture became a masterpiece of manly grace ... Querelle smiled at the thought of drawing so close to that shame from which there is no return, and in which one might well discover peace ... [T]his phrase formed in his mind, saddening in all that it evoked of autumn, of stains, of delicate and mortal wounds: 'Here's the one [Lieutenant Seblon] who will follow in my footsteps.' (274)

Then the Lieutenant, as if he is answering, though he is in custody: 'I shall not know peace until he makes love to me, but only when he enters me and then lets me stretch out on my side across his thighs, holding me the way the dead Jesus is held in a Pieta' (275). This imagined wrapping in arms forms the climax of the narrators' erotic fabrication of Querelle, their making for themselves an animated garment. It forms as well Genet's fantastic fusion of the novel's divine humiliation with the humiliation of devotion to fabric. By this juncture, fantasy has turned the invert reader away from persecution towards a Pieta that insulates, as does a cloak, or would a church, the strangely self-embracing queer. This is a betrayal that reveals a secret grace:

> Thus [Lieutenant Seblon] dreamt of wearing a wide black cape, in which he could wrap himself ... Such a garment would set him apart, give him a hieratic and mysterious

appearance ... To wear a pelerine, a cape ... In such a garment I would feel rolled up inside a wave, carried by it, curled up in its curve. The world and its incidents would cease at my door. (191-2)

As you will have guessed, the character and the novel *Querelle* are such a cape: something any invert, to assuage her loneliness, can crawl inside and read like a book.

Five: Conclusion

These are things that novels know about the curve of cloth. As witness to Christ's wounds and the life they may lead outside the Church, clothes, as their own kind of social self-enclosure, may function like a church: a structure or fabric that sets a group apart, a site of devotion productive of belief (or, more fittingly, fantasy), a group of believers, taken for a Body, who practice sacrifice, much like the clergy (men and women of the cloth).

By these novel portraits we can ask ourselves why sacrifice – Christ's wounds as cloth wounds – appears in queer aesthetics among the unchurched? One reason must be obvious: a queer aesthetic that uncovers the shame that is so attached to beauty is likely to seem theological if it wishes to hold onto beauty. The effort to value the value of shame (always a curve) is central to the legacy of a martyred god (as Hall knows and Genet lampoons, in his serious way). Shame, theologically, but so, too, aesthetically, is a kind of blush in the face of beauty. Shame is a way of pointing at the glamour (by definition, 'a seemingly mysterious and elusive fascination') that must in part escape us; even, by definition, must amaze us (as it amazes the butch who can only embrace it for femmes).

More intriguing, at least for this essay, clothing mimics the action of sacrifice; it is the site of a social sacrifice. The subject-in-clothes is cast to a realm outside itself – to a kind of 'unreality', according to Bataille. Clothing, of course, would seem to contradict this, and, in some respects, it does. The subject of clothing seems, if anything, thrown to a public all too real, caught and held by a social world devoid of caprice. Here, however, is the insight of our novels: if the act of clothing is this public self-betrayal, in a known social field, it can also be a Pieta: a certain social holding of one's humiliation at the hands of something loved. When clothes seem inappropriate to wearers – for example, butch women adopting men's clothes – they discernibly signal a body broken from established versions of 'real relations'. As a result, the social field must hold, and behold, this wearer as one humiliated, cast beyond its reach. The question then arises of how the subject bears humiliation and its seeming break from sociality, even as it's held, on public display.

This is where the contexts of our novels are so telling. *The Well*'s negativity over social shame seems to stem from its Catholic groundings – ironically, the very source of Stephen's martyrdom – and its sense that the lesbian establishments of the 1920s (particularly perhaps for the British aristocracy) were sad places of humiliated loneliness. Consequently, there can be no holding of humiliation that is anything but loneliness. There is no Pieta for Stephen or her clothes. By contrast, of course, *Stone Butch Blues*, which upholds the labour union and the lesbian bar as sites of productive failure and shame, shows a Pieta of a striking sort. The couple, sartorially split from itself, is a fascinating figure for the holding *by* one's clothes. Each reads her shame from the other one's arms, so that their holding becomes humiliation at the hands of something loved – and, indeed, loving. Beyond the enclosure of something like Feinberg's fantasy of barlife, Genet concocts the dreamscape of a military fog. Here, as we have seen, in the narrators' fantasy of beautiful Querelle, or in something simpler like an officer's cape, public self-betrayal of a murderous sort is what the martyr risks. But this is a gamble for very large stakes, as I have been arguing all along. This is a wager for a kind of a social holding that begs no pity: an unchurched church: the social solitude of a beautiful shame.

Notes

1. According to legend, the image of Jesus' face is said to have appeared on the handkerchief used by Veronica, a woman of Jerusalem, to wipe the bleeding face of Jesus as he made his way to Calvary. The shroud of Turin, which bears the imprinted image of a crucified man, is thought by the faithful to be the burial shroud of Jesus.
2. The Pieta (in Italian, 'the Piety') is a representation in painting or sculpture of Mary, the mother of Jesus, cradling, in her grief, the body of her Son after the Crufixion.
3. See, for example, Judith Butler's 'Gender is Burning: Questions of Appropriation and Subversion' in her book *Bodies That Matter: On the Discursive Limits of 'Sex'* (New York: Routledge, 1993); see also *Gender Trouble: Feminism and the Subversion of Identity* (New York: Routledge, 1990).
4. Leo Bersani, 'Is the Rectum a Grave?', in *AIDS: Cultural Analysis/Cultural Activism*, Douglas Crimp, ed. (Cambridge, Massachusetts: The MIT Press, 1988), pp. 217, 222.
5. Ibid., p. 215. See also Bersani's *Homos* (Cambridge, Massachusetts: Harvard University Press, 1995), p. 168.
6. Jean Genet, *Querelle*, tr. Anselm Hollo (New York: Grove Press, 1974), p. 88; hereafter referred to as *Q*.
7. The modesty/protection/decoration trinity (with varying emphases placed on each) is the single greatest theme in the voluminous history of commenting on clothes. Nearly all studies relate themselves to these three 'fundamental motives' (as J.C. Flugel deems them) for human clothing; see J.C. Flugel, *The Psychology of Clothes* (New York: International Universities Press, 1930). Studies of clothing in the context of consumption, most obviously Thorstein Veblen, *The Theory of the Leisure Class* (New York: Penguin, 1987), and even of fashion as a system – for example, Ruth P. Rubinstein, *Dress Codes: Meanings and Messages in American Culture* (Boulder: Westview Press, 1995); Juliet Ash and Elizabeth Wilson, eds, *Chic Thrills: A Fashion Reader* (Berkeley: University of California Press, 1993); Jane Gaines and Charlotte Herzog, *Fabrications: Costume and the Female Body* (New York: Routledge, 1990) – also route themselves along this axis, though 'decoration' is the category they expand in any number of social, political and semiotic ways. As one would expect, commentary on the fashion system comes the closest to claiming that we are damaged by clothes.
8. These definitions are taken from Webster's New World Dictionary, Third College Edition.
9. Sigmund Freud, 'Femininity', tr. and ed. James Strachey, *New Introductory Lectures on Psychoanalysis*, Lecture XXXIII (London: The Hogarth Press, 1974), p. 132. All further references to Freud are from the same page.
10. For the atmosphere and events surrounding the banning of *The Well of Loneliness*, see

Vera Brittain, *Radclyffe Hall: A Case of Obscenity?* (New York: A.S. Barnes, 1969).
11 Flugel, *Psychology of Clothes*, pp. 20–21. From reading Flugel, one is reminded that, apart from Freud, the vast majority of clothes commentators address themselves to 'shame' generally. That is to say, though they all recognize sex and gender differences as critical to the meaning of clothes and to the development of fashion systems, they do not assign differential shame to the fact of men or women wearing clothes. Flugel, for example, discusses 'modesty' and 'decoration' (in Freud 'shame' and 'vanity') as a compromise made by both sexes: 'Clothes serve to cover the body, and thus gratify the impulse to modesty. But, at the same time, they may enhance the beauty of the body, and, indeed, as we have seen, this was probably their most primitive function. When the exhibitionistic tendency to display is thus lured away from the naked to the clothed body, it can gratify itself with far less opposition from the tendencies connected with modesty than it could when it was concentrated on the body in the state of Nature' (pp. 21, 22).
12 For starters, one could consult writings by Jane Addams, Charlotte Perkins Gilman, Mary Wooley, Gertrude Stein, Virginia Woolf, Djuna Barnes and Natalie Barney.
13 A famous pair of articles may be taken as an index to these debates. See Carroll Smith-Rosenberg, 'Discourses of Sexuality and Subjectivity: The New Woman, 1870–1936' in Martin Duberman, Martha Vicinus and George Chauncey, Jr, eds, *Hidden from History: Reclaiming the Gay and Lesbian Past* (New York: Meridian, 1989), a revision of her final chapter to *Disorderly Conduct*, 1985, and Esther Newton, 'The Mythic Mannish Lesbian: Radclyffe Hall and the New Woman' in the same volume (a revision of her essay in *Signs* from 1984).
14 Smith-Rosenberg, 'Discourses of Sexuality and Subjectivity', pp. 276, 279.
15 Ibid., p. 279.
16 Newton, 'The Mythic Mannish Lesbian', p. 283.
17 These definitions are from Webster's New World Dictionary, Third College Edition.
18 For commentary on the largely antagonistic relationship between Bataille and Genet (in spite of their mutual 'love of Sade, Gilles de Rais, Nietzsche, a taste for violence, steely eroticism and Catholic pomp'), see Edmund White, *Genet: A Biography* Anselm Hollo (New York: Vintage, 1994), pp. 360, 397–8, 565.
19 Georges Bataille, *Theory of Religion*, tr. Robert Hurley (New York: Zone, 1992), p. 57.
20 Ibid., p. 44.
21 Ibid., pp. 43, 45.
22 Ibid., p. 51.
23 Georges Bataille, 'Sacrificial Mutilation and the Severed Ear of Vincent Van Gogh', in *Visions of Excess: Selected Writings, 1927–1939*, tr. and ed., Allan Stoekl (Minneapolis: University of Minnesota Press, 1985), p. 67. The madman's automutilation illustrates the elements of sacrifice previously mentioned, especially those that link to fantasy: the destruction of real ties, the link to unreality, the withdrawal from utility, and the restoration to unintelligible caprice.
24 Radclyffe Hall, *The Well of Loneliness* (New York: Anchor Books, 1990), p. 246; hereafter referred to as *WL*.
25 Of course, these portraits can be overlapping categories. Esther Newton, in her essay on Hall (cited in note 8 above), may be bridging both views.
26 See Elizabeth Lopovsky Kennedy and Madeline D. Davis, *Boots of Leather, Slippers of Gold: The History of a Lesbian Community* (New York: Penguin, 1993), pp. 9, 34, 328–31.
27 The novel ends, of course, with Stephen's grandest sacrifice. Concerned to preserve Mary's future as a potentially normal woman, Stephen fakes unfaithfulness to Mary, thus sending Mary off to the arms of Martin. (As another character puts it: 'Aren't you

being absurdly self-sacrificing?', *WL*, p. 433.) To be sure, Hall's novel draws to a close not with the assurance of salvation but with an odd kind of demon possession: 'Oh, but there were many, these unbidden guests ... The quick, the dead, and the yet unborn – all calling her ... Aye, and those lost and terrible brothers from Alec's, they were here, and they also were calling: "Stephen, Stephen, speak with your God and ask Him why He has left us forsaken!" She could see their marred and reproachful faces with the haunted, melancholy eyes of the invert' (*WL*, p. 436). The novel concludes with Stephen's unanswered plea to God: 'We believe ... We have not denied you ... Acknowledge us, oh God ... Give us also the right to our existence!'

28 Leslie Feinberg, *Stone Butch Blues* (Ithaca, New York: Firebrand Books, 1993), p. 5; hereafter referred to as *SBB*.

29 On femme/butch as an erotic system, see the essays in Sally R. Munt and Cherry Smith, eds, *Butch/Femme: Inside Lesbian Gender* (London: Cassell, 1998), especially the essay by Ann Cvetkovich, 'Untouchability and Vulnerability: Stone Butchness as Emotional Style'. See also Sue-Ellen Case, 'Toward a butch-femme aesthetic', *Discourse* 11 (1) (Fall 1988/Winter 1989), pp. 55–73; Joan Nestle, ed., *The Persistent Desire: A Femme-Butch Reader* (Boston: Alyson Publications, 1992) and Judith Halberstam, 'Lesbian masculinity or even stone butches get the blues', *Women and Performance* 8:2 (1996), pp. 61–73.

30 The acknowledgments to the novel are quite telling on this score. From how the femmes in her life are thanked, we are asked to recognize the femme as demanding, critical, political, protecting and even seminal in wisdom. This voice of gratitude and admiration for femme strengths is clearly the voice of a feminist butch.

31 As it happens, it is not at all clear there was any such rule: 'According to Professor Nan Hunter of the Brooklyn College Law School, no such law exists (personal communcation, January 1992). It is her guess that a judge in a particular case made a ruling that two or three pieces of clothing of the "correct" sex negated male or female impersonation and that set a precedent used by law enforcement agencies' (Kennedy and Davis, *Boots of Leather*, p. 411).

32 From a cross-comparison with the Kennedy and Davis oral history of this same community (*Boots of Leather, Slippers of Gold*, 1993), the possible fantasy work of *Stone Butch Blues* becomes apparent: particularly its investment in wounds as communal refusal of the cops. Though I don't want to ride this point too strongly by appearing to correct Feinberg's novel with a history, and though it may be that the 1960s showed a strikingly different picture than the 1950s, it appears, if *Boots* is accurate, that there were very few raids in the 1950s (not the stream of altercations Feinberg depicts); police harrassment was largely directed at black lesbians and cross-dressing men. White lesbians, according to these sources, mostly took their beatings from each other or from their attempts to 'expand their territory' into other bars.

33 One could regard this narratorial 'we' as the royal 'we' of a singular narrator; I am purposely deciding to take the 'we' more literally – as a plurality.

34 We read in the novel: 'The fact that the cop had recognized his generosity spurred the Lieutenant on to further sacrifices. It elated him ... He [the Lieutenant] became more and more attached to the young mason, in a mystical and specific way', (*Q*, pp. 209, 210).

Chapter 10

Histoires de l'Église: The Body of Christ in the Thought of Julia Kristeva

Luke Ferretter

> Analysis is not less than religion but more – more, especially, than Christianity, which hews so closely to its fundamental fantasies.
> Julia Kristeva, *In the Beginning was Love*

For Julia Kristeva, the postmodern age is a post-religious age. Whilst she finds traces of their historical monotheism still in evidence in the structure of Western societies, and whilst she sees the religious tendencies of humankind still at work in the construction of various substitute religions, for Kristeva a living religious faith is no longer a real intellectual possibility.[1] She describes St Bernard's spiritual texts as meaningful only for 'those few who have chosen to live outside of time'.[2] Nevertheless, it is not without a certain nostalgia that she recognizes religious illusions as such. According to Kristeva, the Christian church was a community founded upon a series of acute psychological insights, which provided its members with a corresponding series of psychological satisfactions and benefits. She goes as far as to say that faithful membership of the church can amount to a therapy for various traumatic disorders. The church, argues Kristeva, could still constitute such a community today if it were not that its doctrines had been shown to be illusory. Its loss as a space of imaginary and symbolic satisfaction has left the modern Western subject with many unrepresented mental conflicts, whose resolution, in Kristeva's view, must now be found in aesthetic or psychoanalytic experience. Put simply, psychoanalysis offers a negotiation of unconscious traumas that recognizes its imaginary quality, whereas the church offers such a negotiation in the deluded belief that its content is true.[3] In *Histoires d'amour* (1983), Kristeva describes her work as 'a contribution ... to the history of subjectivity', a project she develops in several similarly structured volumes.[4] In each of these historical surveys she includes analyses of the church, as a fundamental institution in the expression and development of Western subjectivity. In this essay, I will examine these analyses, and assess their consequences for the role of the church in postmodern culture.

The first of the histories in which Kristeva discusses the psychological economy of the church is *Powers of Horror* (1980). As is well known, this work contributes to psychoanalytic theory the concept of the pre-Oedipal mechanism of 'abjection'. According to Kristeva, abjection is a psychic process of expulsion that the pre-

Oedipal infant performs on the way to becoming a subject in the linguistic and social symbolic order. Before it conceives of itself as an individual subject opposed to individual objects, not having fully distinguished itself from its mother, the infant rejects that in this dyadic relationship which it loosely perceives as threatening to its nascent sense of being a self. The pre-Oedipal infant's world consists of its own and its mother's bodies, not yet perceived as two, and abjection is the first stage in the process by which the position of individuality begins. The 'abject', that which is psychically rejected in the process, is that in this duality of bodies which seems to disturb the boundaries of individuality. It remains in adult life in feelings of disgust, horror and abhorrence, and it is above all experienced in relation to that which makes the borders of individual corporeal existence imprecise, such as food, excrement, skin disease, or the corpse. Kristeva analyzes Western religions as a series of expressions at the social level of the mechanism of abjection. 'Abjection,' she writes, 'accompanies all religious structurings and reappears ... at the time of their collapse.'[5] She argues that it takes the form of a system of exclusion or taboo in Judaism, and that it becomes fully internalized as sin with Christianity. In each case, she argues, membership of the religious community is a means by which the archaic sense of horror at the possibility of being engulfed by the other, which remains with each individual subject, can be effectively defused in adult social life. She writes, 'The various means of *purifying* the abject – the various catharses – make up the history of religions' (17).

She begins with an analysis of the economy of the community of Israel, the people of God which the Catholic Church describes as the 'preparation and ... figure' of the church.[6] She argues that the system of Levitical rules concerning ceremonial purity, which determines Israel's identity as the community of Yahweh, has the same structure as the process of abjection. Like the abject, Levitical impurity threatens the individual subject of the social order, except insofar as it can be clearly demarcated within the signifying codes of that order. Again like the abject, it is associated with food, changes in the body, death, the feminine body and incest. Kristeva analyzes the purity laws in Lev. 11–18, and argues that they constitute a 'strategy of identity', according to which the one God and the community of his individual subjects are posited by means of a 'series of separations ... generally material, and in the last analysis relating to fusion with the mother' (94). As anthropology has already recognized, the Levitical prohibitions designate the whole and proper as pure, and that which disturbs the boundaries of such identity as impure. Kristeva presses this distinction further. Since menstruation and childbirth make a woman impure, doubly so if she bears a daughter, she argues, 'The terms, impurity and defilement ... are now attributed to the mother and to women in general' (100). She notes that the cut of circumcision, the mark of the Israelite's membership of God's covenant community, is that which separates the male child from this impurity of the maternal body. Hence she writes:

> Judaism seems to insist in symbolic fashion ... that the identity of the speaking being (with his God) is based on the separation of the son from the mother. (100)

Kristeva hypothesizes that the entire structure of the Levitical abomination of the improper and the non-identical is founded upon the 'attempt to keep a being who speaks to his God separated from the fecund mother' (100). She finds this corroborated by the prohibitions concerning a mother animal and its young, like the thrice-repeated command, 'You shall not boil a kid in its mother's milk' (Ex. 23:19; 34:26; Deut. 14:21). She takes this as a metaphor for the prohibition of incest, and concludes:

> Biblical abjection thus translates a crucial semantics in which the dietary ... blends with the maternal as unclean and improper coalescence, as ... a defilement to be cut off. (106)

The rituals of purification which mark Israel as God's community are, in Kristeva's view, expressions at the social level of the process of the abjection of the maternal pre-object at the individual level. She writes that the economy of these rituals

> carries into the private lives of everyone the brunt of the struggle each subject must wage during the entire length of his personal history in order to become separate. (94)

The identity of Israel as the community of God is constituted by reinforcing the dissociation each of its members has already undergone from his or her mother, whose body threatened precisely such identity.[7]

For Kristeva, with the teaching of Christ and the establishment of the church as the new Israel, a new economy of abjection is set up, which leads to a 'wholly different speaking subject' (113). The novelty of Christ's teaching in this respect is that abjection is no longer exterior. Kristeva writes, 'Threatening, it is not cut off, but is reabsorbed into speech' (113). Christ taught, 'It is not what goes into the mouth that defiles a person, but it is what comes out of the mouth that defiles' (Matt. 15:11), and repeatedly emphasized that purity concerns the inside rather than the outside of the person. The Christian, therefore, is led to 'introject the drive quality attached to archaic objects', that is, to locate the abject within his own psyche (116). Whilst the abject ceases to threaten him from without, it continues to torment him from within, 'as the ineradicable repulsion of his henceforth divided and contradictory being' (116). The horrifying non-thing which threatens one's identity as an individual subject of the community, that is, becomes for the Christian something within his own psyche. Its theological name is sin. It splits the Christian subject within, who, no longer able physically to distance himself from the abject, must do so within the logical order of speech. Kristeva writes that the Christian subject, to whom all external things are clean, '[seeks] no longer his defilement but the error within his own thoughts and speech' (117). She sees the church as an institution in which the abject, thus interiorized, is subsequently defused.

It is above all in its sacraments that, for Kristeva, the church provides for this process. She takes a high view of the psychological value of the Eucharist, and argues that it is instrumental in the Christian's negotiation of the abject. She writes that the aggressive fantasy of devouring is a part of the process of abjection, and argues that 'the Eucharist is the catharsis' of this fantasy (118).[8] It removes the guilt from the fantasy of devouring the mother's body which remains with each adult subject. As Kristeva writes, 'Because it identified abjection as a fantasy of devouring, Christianity effects its abreaction' (119). The participant in the Eucharist, that is, eats a body as he had once imagined doing, but instead of the act being a response of fear at the possibility of ceasing to be a subject, as in his pre-history, it identifies him with the ideal subject, Christ, and as an individual member of his community. Reconciled in this way with the body of the other, 'the Christian subject, completely absorbed into the symbolic, is no longer a being of abjection but a lapsing subject' (119). He no longer abhors the body of the other, as the Israelite did, but logically differentiates and names the abject as his own sin. It is the identification of the Eucharistic bread with the body of Christ that founds this negotiation of the abject, for Kristeva. On the one hand, eating his body in the Eucharist reconciles the communicant to the maternal body, and on the other, the divinity of this body raises corporeality in general into the spiritual order.[9] It is Christ's 'heterogeneity', as both man and God, fully body and fully spirit, that, for Kristeva, 'saves [the sinner] from the abject', by raising bodily relations into the symbolic, into the signifying codes of the Christian community (122). This abreaction works most effectively of all, she argues, in the sacrament of penance, or confession. She writes that the verbal confession of sin constitutes

> the ultimate interiorisation of sin within discourses, by the final postulate that does away with an offence because of its enunciation before the One (130).

In confession, the abject is named as sin in the speech of the penitent and thereby '[toppled] ... into the Other' (130). It is absolved in the speech of the confessor, in the name of the Other, and it is by this dialogue, argues Kristeva, that the sin is remitted and the abject abreacted. In the sacramental dialogue, she writes, the abject is 'not suppressed, but subsumed into a speech that gathers and restrains' it (131).[10]

In *Powers of Horror*, Kristeva is concerned primarily with analysis of the psychological economy of membership in God's community, whether Israel or the church. The object of her analysis is the kind of subject formed by the religious community and the ways in which it allows him or her to negotiate the traumas of becoming such a subject. Ultimately, she concludes that abjection is 'the other facet of religious, moral and ideological codes', which are 'abjection's purification and repression' (209). The church, in this perspective, is an institution in which the abject is successfully repressed, which Kristeva portrays as a kind of second best to psychoanalysis' honest though painful recognition of it as such. In *In the Beginning Was Love* (1985) and *Black Sun* (1987), the emphasis of her analyses of Christian faith and practice shifts to a more positive appreciation of the psychological value of the church.

In the latter book, in which Kristeva traces the theme of melancholy in Western culture, she argues that the church offers a potential remedy for some of the traumas of subjectivity, in particular those which can lead to depression. Again, she argues that the Eucharist in particular, the sacrament of Christ's body, is a source of psychological benefit. Kristeva writes that Christ's crucifixion alters the meaning of sacrifice, from that of violent death into that of an acceptable gift. For the Christian believer, she argues, the sacrifice of Christ is 'closer to nutrition than to the simple destruction of value', insofar as he gives his life for that of others.[11] She finds this corroborated by the oral rite of the Eucharist which Christ instituted in memory of his death. Through Eucharistic participation in Christ's crucified body, 'sacrifice (and concomitantly death and melancholia) is *aufgehoben* – destroyed and superseded' (131). Melancholy is determined, in the Freudian view, by aggression towards a lost object, which has become identified with the ego.[12] Since this aggressivity is not part of the sacrifice in which Christ offers himself to the Father, Kristeva argues that to participate in this sacrifice through the Eucharist is to annul and transcend the roots of depression.

Kristeva does not suggest by this that Christ's Passion is merely a secondary aspect of his sacrifice. On the contrary, she also finds psychological value in the Passion. She describes Christ's dereliction on the cross as a 'psychically necessary discontinuity', insofar as it 'provides an image ... for many separations that build up the psychic life of individuals' (132). As we have already seen with the theory of abjection, Kristeva sees the process of becoming a speaking subject of society as a series of corporeal separations – she cites 'birth, weaning, separation, frustration, castration' – culminating in the dissolution of the Oedipus complex. In the psychoanalytic view, mental health depends on a successful execution of each of these separations. Insofar as the Christian subject identifies with Christ, whose resurrection and ascension into heaven depend upon the crucifixion and death of his body, he or she has a model according to which the archaic bodily separations necessary for mental health can be maintained in adult life. Kristeva writes:

> Because Christianity set that rupture at the very heart of the absolute subject – Christ ... , it brought to consciousness the essential dramas that are internal to the becoming of each and every subject. (132)

This ideal representation of the individual's struggle to become a speaking subject has, for Kristeva, 'a tremendous cathartic power' (132). Whilst not making these archaic struggles conscious, in the manner of psychoanalysis, it has the same effect, of preventing regression in adult life into neurosis and symbolic collapse. It offers, in particular, a representation of the condition Kristeva calls 'narcissistic depression', which is a response not to a lost object but to a sense of loss within the ego itself (12). In healthy development, this sense of loss is negotiated by a series of identifications with a third party, the first of which is the pre-Oedipal father (23). The lack of such identifications results in inadequate entry into the symbolic order and later in depression and its sense of meaninglessness. Since membership of the church requires that the Christian subject identify with Christ, Kristeva argues, it offers the space for precisely such an identification. Since he or she identifies both with Christ's experience of meaninglessness and lack of paternal relationship, and also with the consequent restoration of this relationship at the resurrection, church membership 'appears ... as an antidote to hiatus and depression' (134).[13]

In *In the Beginning Was Love*, Kristeva's essay on 'psychoanalysis and faith', she also emphasizes the psychological value of the church. Here she makes clear her adhesion to the Freudian position that religious beliefs and practices are 'illusions', that is, wish-fulfilments whose truth-content cannot be verified.[14] Whereas Freud regarded such illusions as personally and socially damaging, however, Kristeva, who does not share his empiricism, ascribes a higher value to them. She writes that the function of psychoanalysis itself is in part 'to reawaken the imagination and to permit illusions to exist'.[15] In allowing the analysand to develop an imaginary relationship through the transference, the analyst leads him to bring these desires and traumas to speech and thereby to abreact them. The object of psychoanalysis, the analysand's discourse and the analyst's interpretations of this discourse, is 'fundamentally an object of the imagination', through which the inaccessible reality of the unconscious can appear (19). As Kristeva writes, 'What today's analyst must do ... is restore to illusion its full therapeutic and epistemological value' (21). Since illusion and the imaginary play such a significant part in the psychoanalytic diagnosis and cure, Kristeva also sees the church, a community founded on a common set of illusions, as a psychologically acute and beneficial institution.

She discusses the bond of faith which is the condition of adult membership in the church. As we have seen, Kristeva holds that the process of identification with a series of third parties is essential to the healthy development of subjectivity. For Freud, the first of these identifications, which has a lasting effect on the character of the ego, is that with the 'father in ... personal pre-history'.[16] Kristeva sees Christian faith in God as a repetition of precisely this kind of identification 'with a loving and protective agency', all of which reinforces the stability of the subject's constantly threatened identity (24). She writes, 'Because it is a gift of the self, it both encourages and hinders the disintegrative and aggressive agitation of the instincts' (25). It encourages the process of abjection and hinders the dissolution of the ego's composite identity, maintaining the fragile borders of subjectivity in adult life. Christian faith in God, Kristeva writes, 'repairs the wounds of Narcissus', by which she means that the direct identification which constitutes it reinforces the ego as a psychic entity and thus as a potential object of love (25). In personal pre-history, this love was narcissistic – it came from the store of libido in the id; in being a Christian, the narcissistic need is satisfied by a God who loves first and without requiring merit.

Kristeva also finds value in the church's veneration of the Virgin Mary, who in Catholic theology is the 'mother of the church'.[17] She deplores the historical 'proscription of female sexuality' to which the doctrine of the virgin birth has contributed, but argues that it nevertheless offers a psychological benefit to the church's subjects. 'We want,' she writes, 'our mothers to be virgins, so that we can love them better or allow ourselves to be loved by them without fear of a rival' (42). The belief in a virgin mother gratifies the subject's longing for the pre-Oedipal relationship with the mother, who immediately fulfilled its desires, before the prohibition of this relationship by the paternal third party. The doctrine of the virgin mother removes, at the imaginary level, both the father and the mother from a sexual relationship which would interrupt that of the subject and its mother. As Kristeva writes,

> By eliminating the mother as well as the father from the primal scene, the believer's imagination protects itself from a fantasy that is too much for any child to bear: that of being supernumerary, excluded from the act of pleasure, that is the origin of its existence (42).

The primal scene, the image that the infant forms of its parents in sexual intercourse, is, for the subject of the church, defused of its pathogenic potential by the virginity of Mary, the mother of the absolute subject with which he or she identifies. According to Kristeva, the doctrine of the virgin birth prevents this scene from becoming, for the Christian, one of exclusion from parental love for the Christian, which is at the root of neurotic symptoms.[18] In 'Stabat Mater' (1977), she adds that the cult of the Virgin Mary also provides psychological benefits for women. Specifically, Kristeva argues, 'the virginal maternal is a way (not among the less effective ones) of dealing with feminine paranoia.'[19] Mary satisfies the paranoiac's desire for power, as Queen of Heaven and Mother of the Church, but impedes this desire by her own subjection to her son. She fulfils the paranoid woman's fantasy of being unique, which, for Kristeva, amounts to a denial of her mother, but checks this desire by the bodily renunciations necessary to achieve this uniqueness.[20] Kristeva calls the church's belief in the Virgin Mary 'a skilful balance of concessions and constraints involving feminine paranoia'.[21] She argues that it satisfies the desires of the church's female subjects for identification, and that this identification contributes to their maintaining a healthy adult subjectivity.[22]

In *Strangers to Ourselves* (1988), the emphasis of Kristeva's analyses of the church shifts again – this time to a consideration of the ethical value of the church as a community. In this book, Kristeva traces the history of Western attitudes to the foreigner. She argues that this history culminates in Freud's discovery of the unconscious, whose primary role in mental life means that foreignness is ultimately within us. She writes:

> Freud introduced the fascinated rejection of the other at the heart of that "our self" ... which precisely no longer exists since Freud and shows itself to be a strange land of borders and othernesses.[23]

For Kristeva, psychoanalysis provides the basis for an ethical attitude towards the foreigner. In showing me that I am a foreigner to myself, and in offering me the possibility of reconciliation with this internal otherness, it allows me to recognize the foreigner as one like myself. Kristeva writes, 'If I am a foreigner, there are no foreigners', and hence no forms of discrimination against them (192). This is the basis of psychoanalytic ethics, for Kristeva, and she writes that it 'implies a politics', a society in which the internal otherness of each individual is the basis of his or her solidarity with all the others (192). It is precisely this kind of community of others that Kristeva sees in the church.

She writes that, despite the exclusion of other peoples implied by the Old Testament's understanding of Israel as the people of God, there is also a counter-current of 'Biblical universalism', which stresses the ultimate inclusion of all mankind into God's community (66). She points out the repeated emphasis in the Torah on Israel's duty towards foreigners, having themselves been 'strangers in the land of Egypt' (Ex. 22:21; Lev. 19:34; Deut. 10:19). She points out that Abraham, the founder of Israel, himself became a foreigner in order to enter the land to which God called him (Gen. 12:1). Furthermore, Kristeva argues, the story of Ruth the Moabite indicates with particular clarity that the identity of Israel as the people of God depends on the presence of the foreigner at the heart of the community. The immigrant Ruth, herself the widow of an exile, marries the Israelite Boaz, and gives birth to Obed, grandfather of David, who unites Israel, begins the building of the Temple in Jerusalem, and to whose line Yahweh promises perpetual kingship over his chosen people (2 Sam. 7:12–16). Kristeva calls this an 'insertion of foreignness at the very root of Jewish royalty' (74). She adds that Moab, Ruth's ancestor, was himself the fruit of the incestuous relation between Lot and his daughters (Gen. 19:37), and writes, 'Foreignness and incest were thus at the foundation of David's sovereignty' (75). Kristeva calls this dependence of the Davidic line – the chosen rulers of Israel, from which Christ descends – on Ruth, a foreigner of improper ancestry, 'an invitation to consider the fertility of the other' (75). She writes:

> David's sovereignty ... opens up – through the foreignness that founds it – to the dynamics of a constant ... questioning, eager for the other and for the self as other (75)

The community of Israel, for Kristeva, depends for its identity as the people of God upon the place of the other at the heart of the community.

Kristeva argues that this is also the structure of the early church. The church, in the teaching of St Paul, she argues, was constituted as 'a community of those who were different, of foreigners who transcended nationalities by means of a faith in the Body of the risen Christ' (77). She points out that many of Paul's early converts were socially marginal figures – women, slaves, itinerant merchants, diaspora Jews, and so on. They became a community of others, therefore, 'mutually welcoming each other in holy places where, precisely, the foreigner was safe from any affront' (79). As Kristeva observes, St Paul tells the Ephesian church, 'You are no longer strangers and aliens [*xenoi kai paroikoi*], but you are citizens with the saints and also members of the household of God' (Eph. 2.19). The term 'alien' denotes the status of the foreigner in Israel, which, for Kristeva, indicates that it was by precisely those foreigners on the edge of the community that the church was initially constituted. She writes:

> This new dimension where the former foreigners found their cohesion at last became the foundation of the Pauline *Ecclesia*. (80)

Kristeva argues that it was St Paul's psychological intuition that enabled him to gather these heterogeneous groups of outsiders into a new community. It was not merely to the material difficulties of being a foreigner that Paul spoke, she writes, but also 'to their *psychic* distress' (81). It was Paul's message of the crucified and risen body of Christ, and of the corresponding death of the old physical self and resurrection of the Christian's new spiritual self, that answered to the divided condition of the foreigner. The foreigner, for Kristeva, is a person in flight, someone who has lost his or her maternal home and endlessly seeks its substitute.[24] In positing a life constituted precisely by a flight from one world to another, 'the Pauline church assumed the foreigner's passion-inspired division' (81). Kristeva applauds Paul's insight in portraying that division as 'a split less between *two countries* than between two *psychic domains* within [the foreigner's] own impossible unity' (82). In positing the identity of the body of Christ, the church, and the Eucharist, Paul was able to weld his internally divided audiences into a community:

> There will be a possible *we* thanks only to that splitting that all wanderers are urged to discover within themselves after they first recognized themselves in Christ. (82)

In the crucifixion and resurrection of the body of Christ, she argues, the outsider finds a powerful model for his own internal division. Since this body is identified with the church itself (Eph. 1:23, 5:30; Col. 1:24), the latter becomes a community in which such subjects can identify with one another. These bonds are reinforced weekly in the church's incorporation of the body of Christ in the Eucharist. This is what Kristeva means when she writes, 'In order to understand the power of the ecclesiastical community, one must ponder the unity made up of church, risen Christ, and Eucharist' (81). She finds this logic completed in St Augustine's concept of charity, in which the neighbour whom Christ commands the church to love is any other human being: 'The alienation of the foreigner ceases within the universality of the love for the other' (84). In the church, as Paul and Augustine conceived of it, Kristeva finds the model of a community based on an ethics of respect for the other. It therefore anticipates psychoanalysis, she argues, and was in its time genuinely valuable as such.[25]

For Kristeva, however, this community was rarely realized in historical practice. As Christianity became integrated into the Roman empire after the conversion of Constantine, 'Christian cosmopolitanism bore in its womb the ostracism that excluded the other belief and ended up with the Inquisition' (87). From the time that Christianity was established as the official religion of the empire, the church began to expel the foreigner from within in the form of the heretic. As Kristeva points out, the anti-heretical legislation that began in the fourth century effectively returned heretics to the status of foreigners. She writes:

> Whereas faith was initially a means of transcending the political differences that afflicted foreigners, it eventually turned out that dissidence within the faith was perceived as a political threat. (90)

She recognizes the ethical value of the theory of the church, but argues that this theory was 'from the start' subject to partisan political interests (90). In *Powers of Horror*, she takes a similar view with respect to the church's practice of confession. Although in essence a psychologically beneficial act, confession was not in practice limited to the sacrament of reconciliation, in which the sin is remitted shortly after it is enunciated. In fact, she writes,

> The whole black history of the Church shows that condemnation, the fiercest censorship, and punishment are ... the common reality of this practice (131).

In the anti-heretical activities of the church, spoken sins are not sublimated and dissipated by the response of a confessor, but used by the authorities for the condemnation and punishment of the sinner. As the church becomes identified with the empire, so, for Kristeva, its psychological insights become subordinated to the political need to defend its identity against internal threats.

Although *Strangers to Ourselves* is the last of the broad historical surveys that Kristeva has written to date, she has continued to be interested in the psychology of the church. In recent years, she has begun to write on the economy specific to the Orthodox Church of her native Bulgaria. In 'Bulgarie, ma souffrance' (1995), she derives this specificity from the Trinitarian formula of the Orthodox Church, according to which the Holy Spirit proceeds from the Father *through* the Son (*per filium*), rather than from the Father and the Son (*filioque*), as in the Western text of the Nicene creed. According to Kristeva, this different account of the relations among the persons of the Trinity results in a different structure of subjectivity for the Orthodox church member. In 'L'Europe divisée' (1998), she writes that the Catholic *filioque* allows the Christian who identifies with the Son to identify with an autonomous figure, with an individual role in the Trinitarian economy. The Orthodox per *filium*, however, 'suggests a delicious but pernicious annihilation of [both] the Son and of the believer' who identifies with him.[26] The Orthodox Son, although as divine as the Father, nevertheless plays a subordinate role in the procession of the Holy Spirit, and it is this subordinate position that the Orthodox subject consequently occupies, for Kristeva. This has significant psychological consequences with respect to his or her negotiation of the Oedipus complex:

> The son of the *Per Filium* is invited not to Oedipal rebellion, but to occupy the place of the daughter: to be the woman who admires the Father that he/she will never be. (52)

This subjective structure, she writes, 'corresponds to an incomplete Oedipus complex', in which the son remains in the 'fusional dyad' characteristic of the pre-Oedipal relation to the mother, without fully negotiating the intervention into this relationship of the paternal third party (53). In the normal resolution of the Oedipus complex, the son identifies with the father, introjecting his prohibitions and setting them up as his superego. Since, in the Orthodox Church, this relationship with the father is not offered to the subject as a model with which to identify, the individuality and autonomy to which it leads are not, for Kristeva, characteristic of the Orthodox subject. On the contrary, such a subject tends to remain passive and sensual in orientation:

> Without an explicit insistence on the Oedipal triangulation which leads to the autonomous "oneself" ... , the Orthodox subject tends to remain in a logic of communion based on the dual relationship. (53)

This subject position leads, for Kristeva, to the characteristic mysticism of the Orthodox Church. Orthodox spirituality emphasizes that God cannot be represented in the symbolic order of words and images, but only experienced in a more holistic 'pre-verbal register' (55). For Kristeva, the Orthodox subject relates to God in the 'semiotic', or pre-symbolic, modes characteristic of the pre-Oedipal stages of infantile life.[27]

This subjective structure has both negative and positive consequences, in Kristeva's view. On the one hand, the dissociation of God from the symbolic order of logical knowledge runs the risk of removing the values grounded by the concept of God from adult social life. 'God is elsewhere,' she writes, 'he is not here where we live, speak, represent' (55). Orthodox mysticism can thus be said to lead to nihilism. As Kristeva observes, 'It is because God cannot be represented or questioned that everything is permitted in the order of representation' (56). This lack of a representable ground of value leads, for Kristeva, to the introverted psychological characteristics which cause the Orthodox states to play a minor part in modern European politics. The Orthodox subject, she writes, 'lacks the ascetic autonomy, the professional sobriety, the intellectual integrity of the Protestant seeking salvation in the text...and in the city'.[28] Despite these negative consequences, however, Kristeva also sees value in the mysticism of the Orthodox Church. She argues that to the 'new maladies of the soul', that is, to the disorders caused by our inability to represent psychic life, 'Orthodox anthropology opposes the excess [*trop-plein*] of the soul' (57).[29] Although the predominantly passive and affective position of the Orthodox subject hinders his economic success, this same position 'can also be a source and foundation for regaining an authentic and complex psychic life' (57). For Kristeva, the subject of modern technological capitalism is a solitary ego, engaged in competition with other individuals, and thereby alienated from them. She argues that this leads to a psychological need for dependence on, or relation with, another. The Orthodox Church, Kristeva argues, 'removes the guilt from this need for dependence'. She writes:

> The person inspired by [Orthodox mysticism] is not a performing subject, nor even a self, but an avowed adherence, a *sobornost*, a communion. (58)

The Orthodox subject, for Kristeva, is constituted by a passive, sensory, interpersonal communion which the modern Western individual lacks. She argues that the Orthodox Church amounts to a new model of freedom, the freedom for sensual relation with the other that the subject of Western capitalism is denied in his constant drive for 'better causes producing better effects' (57).

Although she has been widely criticized for doing so, Kristeva has elaborated a series of largely positive psychological descriptions of the church. In the body of Christ, she sees a representation, a therapy and an ethics for the split 'subjects in process' that we are. The divided subjectivity of Christ, whose body was crucified, raised and assumed into heaven, allows those who identify with him successfully to negotiate and maintain the series of divisions necessary for healthy maturity. The church provides for this identification in many ways. It offers Christ as an object of faith, and it offers the individual a ritual experience of his crucifixion and resurrection in its sacraments. For Kristeva, both this faith and the sacraments help prevent regression and stabilize the split subjectivity of the church's members. Furthermore, in positing Christian life as a journey from an old self to a new, the church opens itself precisely to such split subjects, and in particular to those marginal figures who experience this split socially as well as psychologically. The identification of the entire church with the body of Christ is, for Kristeva, the ethical *tour de force* by which it becomes a community of equal rights for all. Whilst she sees this ethics to have been altogether subordinated in the historical practice of the church as a politically significant institution, Kristeva nevertheless argues that a return to the experience provided by the church as a faith community is essential if we are to remain free subjects in a technological capitalist society. Kristeva never considers the church as a theological entity, and so makes no contribution to ecclesiology as such. Nevertheless, her psychological analyses clearly issue a challenge to the contemporary church to become the healing and welcoming community it was founded to be.

Notes

The author thanks the British Academy and Susan Sellers for their assistance in the production of this chapter.

1. See Julia Kristeva, *About Chinese Women*, tr. Anita Barrows (New York and London: Marion Boyars, 1977), pp. 22–3; 'Women's Time', *The Kristeva Reader*, ed. Toril Moi (Oxford: Blackwell, 1986) p. 208; *Pouvoirs et limites de la psychanalyse I: Sens et non-sens de la révolte (discours direct)* (Paris: Fayard, 1996), pp. 51–7.
2. Julia Kristeva, *Tales of Love*, tr. Leon S. Roudiez (New York: Columbia University Press, 1987), p. 169.
3. See Julia Kristeva, *In the Beginning was Love: Psychoanalysis and Faith*, tr. Arthur Goldhammer (New York: Columbia University Press, 1987): 'Analysis is not less than religion but more – more, especially, than Christianity, which hews so closely to its fundamental fantasies' (p. 52).
4. Kristeva, *Tales of Love*, p. 16.
5. Julia Kristeva, *Powers of Horror: An Essay on Abjection*, tr. Leon S. Roudiez (New York: Columbia University Press, 1982), p. 17. Subsequent references to this work appear in parentheses in the text.
6. 'Lumen Gentium' no. 9, *The Documents of Vatican II*, tr. and ed. Walter M. Abbott and Joseph Gallagher (London: Geoffrey Chapman, 1966), p. 25. Cf. Gal. 6:16.
7. The Prophets associate Israel itself with the female body, as they describe the community as an adulterous wife (Jer. 3:1–10; Hos. 2:2–13). Kristeva argues that such imagery is 'predicated on the very position of the logic of separation' (*Powers of Horror*, p. 107). The language of the abject becomes a meaningful denunciation of Israel, that is, only in the context of the process of abjection by which the latter constitutes itself as the community of God.
8. See *Powers of Horror*, p. 39.
9. The same process can be discerned in St Paul's identification of the church with the body of Christ in Eph. 5:25–32. On the one hand, he compares it to the feminine body, and on the other asserts that Christ has purified this body, presenting it to himself 'without a spot or wrinkle or anything of the kind' (v. 27).
10. In 'Feminist Theology', David Power argues that Kristeva offers a view of the sacraments which does not derive from a patriarchal ideology. Insofar as the sacraments embrace and reconcile both the drives and the symbolic, he argues, their institutional celebration is misunderstood as an exclusively male prerogative. See *Theological Studies*, 55 (1994), pp. 693–702. Several critics have pointed out that Kristeva's work restores a central place in religious life to women. See Diane Jonte-Pace, 'Situating Kristeva Differently: Psychoanalytic Readings of Woman and Religion', *Body/Text in Julia Kristeva: Religion, Women and Psychoanalysis*, ed. David R. Crownfield (Albany: State University of New York Press, 1992), pp. 1–22, and Marilyn Edelstein, 'Metaphor, Meta-Narrative and Mater-Narrative in Kristeva's "Stabat Mater"', ibid., pp. 27–52.
11. Julia Kristeva, *Black Sun: Depression and Melancholia*, tr. Leon S. Roudiez (New York: Columbia University Press, 1989), p. 130. Subsequent references to this work appear in parentheses in the text.
12. Sigmund Freud, 'Mourning and Melancholia', *The Penguin Freud Library*, ed. Angela Richards and Albert Dickson (London: Penguin, 1973–86), vol. 11, pp. 256–9. Subsequent references to this edition will be abbreviated to *PFL*.
13. In 'Kristeva and Feminist Theology', Cleo McNelly Kearns underestimates the value Kristeva ascribes to the doctrinal content of the church's faith. She is right to point out Kristeva's high view of the sacraments, composed as they are of both material and

verbal elements, but wrong to contrast this with Kristeva's view of credal formulae as such. For Kristeva, the church's articles of faith in Christ and in Mary, in particular, offer the split subject satisfactions at both the semiotic and symbolic levels, and are effective for precisely this reason. See *Transfigurations: Theology and the French Feminists*, C.W. Maggie Kim, Susan M. St. Ville and Susan M. Simionatis, eds (Minneapolis: Fortress, 1993), pp. 63–77.

14   Freud, 'The Future of an Illusion', *PFL*, vol. 13, p. 212.
15   Kristeva, *In the Beginning was Love*, p. 18. Subsequent references to this work appear in parentheses in the text.
16   Freud, 'The Ego and the Id', *PFL*, vol. 11, p. 370.
17   See *The Documents of Vatican II*, p. 86.
18   See Kristeva, *In the Beginning was Love*, p. 3. It might be added that the doctrine of church as the bride of Christ allows the Christian subject to experience, at the imaginary level, the satisfaction of an uninterrupted dyadic relationship.
19   Kristeva, *Tales of Love*, p. 257.
20   Ibid., pp. 257–8.
21   Ibid., p. 259.
22   The church's requirement that its members 'receive the kingdom of God as a little child' (Mark 10:15) does not contradict Kristeva's view that its doctrines can help prevent neurotic regression to infantile states. For Kristeva, this text would contribute to the healthy subjectivity of the church member, insofar as it provides an imaginary satisfaction of desire for the maternal body on the one hand, and a spiritual discourse into which this desire can be displaced on the other.
23   Julia Kristeva, *Strangers to Ourselves*, tr. Leon S. Roudiez (New York: Columbia University Press, 1991), p. 191. Subsequent references to this work appear in parentheses in the text.
24   See ibid., p. 3.
25   See ibid., p. 195.
26   Julia Kristeva, 'L'Europe divisée: politique, éthique, religion', *Infini* 63 (1998), p. 51. Subsequent references to this work appear in parentheses in the text. Citations are in my translation.
27   See Julia Kristeva, *Revolution in Poetic Language*, tr. Margaret Waller (New York: Columbia University Press, 1984), pp. 25–30.
28   Julia Kristeva, 'Bulgarie, ma souffrance', *Infini* 51 (1995), p. 51. My translation.
29   See Julia Kristeva, *New Maladies of the Soul*, tr. Ross Gubermann (New York: Columbia University Press, 1995), pp. 3–26.

Chapter 11

The Private Parts of Jesus Christ

Nicholas Royle

private: *adj.* independent, own, relating to personal affairs, not public, not open to the public, not made generally known, retired from observation, alone.
part: *noun* something less than the whole, a portion, a member or organ, share, region, participation, concern, interest, a role or duty, a side or party, a character taken by an actor in a play, the words or actions of a character in a play or in real life, a voice or instrument in concerted music, a section of a work in literature or in music.

Excerpts from *Chambers Dictionary*

) **The private parts of Jesus Christ**, how will you read that, subvocalizing in silence, that is my question, I have no interest in getting beyond it, only in trying to think what might be going on in it, how to hear this phrase, if it is a phrase, in other words at once a small group of words expressing a single idea or constituting a single element in a sentence and also an idiomatic expression, a pithy saying or catchword, in short a kind of shibboleth. (

)

Already plural, irreducibly, despite the appearances of the single and unitary, for example in the 'the' or in the phrase 'phrase'. (

)

At issue are the writings of Jacques Derrida in relation to Christianity and the question of how to think, after Derrida, about writing and messianicity, in one's own manner, with a view to the solitude of an unidentifiable church, to inventing one's own religion or rather (as Derrida says) doing or making a truth that perhaps does not come 'under any religion, for reason of literature, nor under any literature, for reason of religion'.[1] (

)

The private parts of Jesus Christ: does this phrase, if it is a phrase, sound blasphemous, idolatrous, perverse? If so, to whom will one have been listening, to what voice or tone within oneself that would not be one's own, perhaps, but the voice or tone of another within oneself one who speaks ill (as the etymology of the word 'blasphemy' suggests), one to whom blame might be assigned? Is the voice or tone of blasphemy within oneself or outside oneself, and who can bear witness to this? It is a matter of trying to think the question of religion, and specifically here Christianity, in terms of performative utterance. As Hent de Vries puts it:

> Religion is to be conceived of as the problem of performative utterance 'as such', but of an utterance that does not – not yet or no longer – attain the determinability *qua* content and structure that remains presupposed (without further justification, metaphysically, and in the guise of some 'presentism') by the modern theories of the performative (Austin) and of the speech act (Searle).[2]

In other words, it is a question of acknowledging and elaborating on the fact that, as de Vries goes on to say:

> ... the possible success of the religious performative – the very performativity of *religion*, the word no less than its effects, but also the religiosity of every performative – is never guaranteed by preestablished or simply given contextual requirements ... Any religious utterance, act, or gesture, stands in the shadow of – more or less, but never totally avoidable – perversion, parody, and kitsch, of blasphemy and idolatry.[3] (

)

The private parts of Jesus Christ: can this phrase not also sound perfectly dignified, solemn and respectful? In other words, might it not be heard as belonging to the category of what may provisionally be called successful religious utterance? But if it were successful, it would only be thanks to the necessary possibility of failure, of perversion, parody, blasphemy. And more (and less) than that, its success might be identified with what Derrida describes as 'a promise that cannot be *sure of succeeding* except by succeeding in failing'.[4] Everything comes down or comes back to tone, to how one would fail in succeeding to hear, a tone one cannot trace. This is, at least on one occasion, how Derrida defines God. *Tone* [*Ton*], he writes in *The Post Card*, 'is the name of God, my God, the one that I do not find'.[5] (

)

'A title is always a promise', Derrida says.[6] If this is true it should be possible to demonstrate it in the case of 'the private parts of Jesus Christ'. The being-promise of this title will entail a sense of excess. As Derrida remarks in *Mémoires*:

> A promise is always excessive. Without this essential excess, it would return to a description or knowledge of the future. Its act would have a constative structure and not a performative one. But this 'too much' of the promise does not belong to a (promised) content of a promise which I would be incapable of keeping. It is within the very *act* of promising that this excess comes to inscribe a kind of irremediable disturbance or perversion. This perversion, which is also a trap, no doubt unsettles the language of the promise, the performative as promise; but it also renders it possible – and indestructible. Whence the *unbelievable*, and comical, aspect of every promise, and this passionate attempt to come to terms with the law, the contract, the oath, the declared affirmation of fidelity. (94)

Let me emphasize two words, adjectives designating a certain privacy, in that final sentence. The first of these Derrida himself stresses: it is the 'unbelievable'. There is something unbelievable about every promise. Nothing happens without an experience of the unbelievable; as he has said elsewhere, the essence of belief or faith can only ever be a matter of 'believ[ing] in the unbelievable'.⁷ The unbelievable is happening as soon as we open our mouths. What Derrida calls 'the declared affirmation of fidelity' entails a notion of faith as 'Not religion, to be sure, nor theology, but that which in faith acquiesces before or beyond all questioning, in the already common experience of a language and of a "we".'⁸ It is a matter of what he refers to as 'faith in language': 'even perjury, lying and infidelity would still presuppose *faith in language*; I cannot lie without believing and making believe in language, without giving credence to the idiom.'⁹ The second word is 'comical': there is something comical about every promise. To say this is not to suggest that we start taking Derrida less seriously, but rather that what is in some ways perhaps most serious about his work is its insistence on the necessary possibility of comedy even in the most solemn of performative utterances. There is here, as elsewhere in his work, a resonance between the minimal 'yes' of the promise and what he calls 'the question ... of a laughter which *remains*, as a fundamental, quasi-transcendental tonality'.¹⁰ (

)

No private parts of Jesus Christ without deconstruction, no deconstruction without the private parts of Jesus Christ. (

)

It has become increasingly clear – and this is in part the burden and force of Hent de Vries's *Philosophy and the Turn to Religion* (1999) – that the question of religion is at stake in the treatment of philosophy, psychoanalysis, literature, phenomenology, science and knowledge in Derrida's work from the very start, and at the same time that this is a question that is inseparable from the most everyday reality of the world, in particular in the form of what Derrida has called 'mondialatinization' (translated by Samuel Weber as 'globalatinization'), taking the form of a 'strange alliance of Christianity ... and tele-technoscientific capitalism' (FK 13), or as de Vries glosses it, 'the becoming Christian of the modern world (or, for that matter, the becoming worldly and, in a sense, abstract, of Christianity)', a process that 'is linked to the faith (and fate) of a certain Europe'.¹¹ How does Derrida talk about religion, and Christianity in particular? He has said that he is not an enemy of religion (FK 7). At the same time he has said that his thinking is guided by a desire 'for what, in politics, is called republican democracy as a universalizable model, binding philosophy to the public "cause"', and that this entails a preference for 'the enlightened virtue of public space, emancipating it from all external power (non-lay, non-secular), for example from religious dogmatism, orthodoxy or authority (that is, from a certain rule of *doxa* or of belief, which, however, does not mean from all faith)' (FK 8). The logic of this 'at the same time' is quietly spoken, even subvocal, but still perhaps cataclysmic. (

)

It might help to juxtapose Derrida's work here with that of Nietzsche. The latter

observes: 'From the start Christianity was, essentially and fundamentally, the embodiment of disgust and antipathy for life, merely disguised, concealed, got up as the belief in an "other" or a "better" life ... .' Christianity, for Nietzsche, is the embodiment of 'Hatred of the "world", the condemnation of the emotions, the fear of beauty and sensuality, a transcendental world invented the better to slander this one, basically a yearning for non-existence, for repose until the "sabbath of Sabbaths"'.[12] Derrida is in some sense perhaps more explicit than Nietzsche in foregrounding that strangely *unheard-of* force of affirmation which is the basis of hatred and love alike. His focus is less on the 'hatred of the "world"' *per se* that Nietzsche here identifies with Christianity, than on the *yes* of affirmation that is the condition of every 'I hate you' and every 'I love you'. It is this allergic condition of affirmation that Derrida refers to with the deconstructive notion of a new enlightenment and with what he says in *Politics of Friendship* about 'a friendship prior to friendships, an ineffaceable friendship, fundamental and groundless, one that breathes in a shared language (past or to come) and in the being-together that all allocution supposes, up to and including the declaration of war'.[13] Derrida's way of proceeding is crucially different from Nietzsche's. He has never spoken out, and it is difficult to imagine him ever speaking out, in this Nietzschean fashion against Christianity or any other religion. His style is rather that of the subvocal survey, ghost-writing, eerie elucidation of what (as will be seen) he calls 'internal critique'.
(

)
Specters of Marx (1993) has rightly attracted considerable attention among Marxists and others concerned with the future of world politics. It has been less noticed as a book about Christianity, about the continuing importance of Christ as 'the most spectral of spectres' (144). The book is concerned with what might be termed a de-Christification of experience, that is to say with a thinking of messianicity that would not involve any 'identifiable messiah' (28), with 'a messianism without religion' (59), a non-messianic messianicity. Derrida stresses the notion of 'the *messianic* rather than *messianism*, so as to designate a structure of experience rather than a religion' (167–8). His messianic is concerned with a 'formal structure of promise' that at once 'exceeds' and 'precedes' both Marxism and the religions it criticizes (59). Marxism's error and Christianity's error would entail what Derrida calls 'the animist incorporation of an emancipatory eschatology which ought to have respected the promise, the being-promise of a promise' (105). This messianic is itself 'irreducible to any deconstruction', he suggests. It involves a 'suspension'(*epokhē*), trembling or hesitation that is 'essential to the messianic in general' (59), for the messianic, he holds, 'would no longer be messianic if it stopped hesitating' (169). *Specters of Marx* is war literature, engaged with and in 'the world war' that is gathered around the figure of Jerusalem but is 'happening everywhere' (58). It is a work of war literature, calling for another thinking of war and literature alike. The question is how to think, how to be open, how to welcome the future without 'killing [it] in the name of old frontiers':

> Like those of the blood, nationalisms of native soil not only sow hatred, not only commit crimes, they have no future, they promise nothing even if, like stupidity or the

unconscious, they hold fast to life. [The] messianic hesitation does not paralyse any decision, any affirmation, any responsibility. On the contrary, it grants them their elementary condition. It is their very experience. (169) (

)

Subvocal frontiers. (

)

What is Jesus thinking, I ask myself, has this question ever been asked, feeling it provoked in a singular, even unprecedented fashion by a painting by Leonardo da Vinci known as the *Madonna Litta* (Hermitage Museum, St Petersburg – Plate 2), a picture that is an art historian's nightmare, they all seem to want to condemn it, damn it, write it off as 'ruined' (Kenneth Clark)[14] or as what Robert Payne calls 'a mockery'.[15] It's not the Madonna herself that's the problem: her face, says Payne, 'remains to remind us of Leonardo's extraordinary accomplishment',[16] even if that face raises a host of questions in turn, starting from the characteristic 'touch of something sinister' that Walter Pater identifies with the 'unfathomable smile' of Leonardo's women.[17] No, it's the baby that is the problem, as Cecil Gould notes, between dashes – 'a very big baby'[18] – an infant Jesus that is, in the words of Martin Kemp, 'so awkward that it can hardly have been executed by Leonardo himself – even allowing for the oddness of his early works'.[19] It's as if art historians cannot quite bear to look at this picture, don't know how to countenance it, it's so odd it cannot be authentic, even granting in the first place that the picture has been (as Clark points out) 'totally repainted at least twice'.[20] Payne sums it up when he writes:

> The overall effect is static, overdecorative, intellectual; the wonder and the tenderness are absent; there is no flow of feeling between the Virgin and Child. Many things have gone wrong since Leonardo painted it, and what has chiefly gone wrong is the Child's face, which is almost a caricature, with an enormous disembodied eye demanding attention, and there are two fingers like fungi pressing against a breast that looks like a loaf of bread. It is as though two separate paintings have somehow become fused together and they cry out to be separated.[21] (

)

It's a hybrid, a chimera, postmodern Leonardo, but everyone sees something different, each time a different witnessing, Robert Payne sees two fungi and a loaf of bread, I see no fungi or loaf of bread, what makes it so monstrous to these art historians I find stunning, of all the pictorial figurations of all the bodies of Christ I know, this is perhaps the strangest and most haunting. What is it that doesn't get said in the condemnation of this painting of the Child Jesus? Where does the sense of horror, if that is what it is, come from? Doesn't this picture stage the hesitation of the unbelievable as such? What is it that makes it so difficult for the art historians to attribute it to Leonardo? The figure of Jesus has been added on, so the argument would go, a supplement that can be confidently condemned as not Leonardo's, too 'awkward', too 'odd', it's a vicarious or substitute Jesus, substituting for the

Plate 2   Leonardo da Vinci, *Madonna Litta*

irreplaceable, like every substitution. Isn't there a strange leap, the art historians' leap of faith, in the decision of classifying this Jesus as a mockery, as if it were simply not possible to suppose that the repainting of this figure were in fact a mockery in another sense, in other words a faithful mimicry, faithful to Leonardo's supposedly non-existent original? It's as if they were fearful of a ghost, a certain kind of spectrality, as in Macbeth's exclamation: 'Hence horrible shadow! / Unreal mockery, hence!' [*Exit ghost*] (III.iv.105–6). Why not spell it out, the necessary failure of the performative of such an exorcism, what is really happening if one looks, what truth to make of this picture of the infant Jesus too large, a little old or at least precocious, 'too old' or 'precocious' being already perhaps a kind of impossible formulation, for how can one speak of a precocious Jesus, irresolvable questions concerning private parts of Christ's life, the aporias generated by considering Jesus as an 'early developer' or becoming 'old before his time'. (

)

'Cry out to be separated.' (

)

Parts of life as private as dreaming. As Leo Steinberg has put it: 'Jesus dreaming is inconceivable.'[22] It goes along with the state of childhood as characterized by what St Augustine calls 'irrational affections'.[23] Both dreaming and that 'strange intoxication' which Augustine attributes to children are states of human experience which 'Jesus does not assume', says Steinberg, 'evidently because they involve deprivation or suspension of consciousness'.[24] What truth to make, I ask, of this picture of an infant Jesus with a look not quite directed at the viewer, neither at the Virgin Mary nor at the viewer of Leonardo's painting, in short an uncanny look, as of what perhaps 'ought to have remained secret and hidden but has come to light',[25] a look reserved and apparently knowing, undecidably of satisfaction ('I am the breast', as a Freudian baby would have it) and indifference, absorbed and absorbing endlessly. (

)

Is this infant Jesus dreaming? How could one know? How can a painting depict the state of dreaming, or rather give assurance of a distinction between dreaming and vigilance, especially if the subject in question is at the mother's breast, 'strange intoxication' to recall Augustine's phrase, a speaking look that says nothing, an infantilism of secrecy, one need look no further for the private parts of Jesus Christ. It recalls what Derrida says of the Matthew Paris picture of Socrates and Plato: 'A pictorial performative which never ends' (PC 98). (

)

Above all what all these art historians seem to miss, or seem unwilling to remark upon, is the fact that the eye of the child in this Leonardo painting calls us in, even as it screens or rebuffs, it provokes the question, what is Jesus thinking, it draws us into an interiority, a private part or parts of what can be named, as equivocally as possible, the thinking of Jesus. In the head: even the windows in this picture give the appearance of eyes, as if we are lodged within the head of another, looking out, inside out of someone else's mind. What is he thinking? Divine. (

)

Already cut. At the heart of Derrida's essay published in English as *The Gift of Death* (1995, originally given as a lecture in 1990) is a question about the nature of the self and trembling, trembling in private, a trembling of the private. He writes: 'The question of the self [*moi*]: "who am I?" no longer in the sense of "who am I" but "who is 'I'"? who can say "who"? what is the "I", and what does responsibility become when, *in secret*, the identity of the "I" trembles?'[26] Derrida presents a reading of Christ's teaching in the Gospel of Matthew and in particular focuses on the conception of God as 'thy father which seeth in secret' (Matt. 6:4, 6, 18), noting that Jesus uses the phrase three times and that, repeated 'like some obsessive reminder to be learnt by heart' (97), it takes on the force of a kind of shibboleth. *The Gift of Death* traces what Derrida describes as 'a mutation ... in the history of secrecy' (100). This mutation has to do with how Christ's saying 'Ye are the light of the world (*lux mundi / phos tou kosmou*)' (Matt. 5:14) is understood as the specification of a light 'in us, within the interiority of the spirit'. Derrida asserts: 'The interiorization of the photological source marks the end of secrecy but it is also the beginning of the paradox of the secret as irreducible in its interiority' (100). This leads him to formulate a 'new' definition of God. He proposes that 'We should stop thinking about God as someone, over there, way up there, transcendent, and ... capable ... of seeing into the most secret of the most interior places' (108). Instead, he suggests:

> God is the name of the possibility I have of keeping a secret that is visible from the interior but not from the exterior. Once such a structure of conscience [*conscience*, also 'consciousness'] exists, of being-with-oneself, of speaking, that is, of producing invisible sense, once I have within me, *thanks to the invisible word as such*, a witness that others cannot see, and who is therefore *at the same time other than me and more intimate with me than myself*, once I can have a secret relationship with myself and not tell everything, once there is secrecy and secret witnessing within me, then what I call God exists, (there is) what I call God in me, (it happens that) I call myself God [*je m'appelle Dieu*] – a phrase that is difficult to distinguish from 'God calls me' [*'Dieu m'appelle'*], for it is on that condition that I can call myself or that I am called in secret. God is in me, he is the absolute 'me' or 'self' [*moi*], he is that structure of invisible interiority that is called, in Kierkegaard's sense, *subjectivity*. (108–109/101–102)

This reformulation of how to think of God (thanks to the teaching of Christ) is said to be 'at the same time evangelical and heretical' and is part of an '*internal* critique of Christianity' (109, emphasis added). It affirms, following Christ, the presence or testimony of an other (here named 'God') that is '*at the same time other than me and more intimate with me than myself*'. It brings into play a spectrality, a sort of ghost-writing within and across the experience of belief, a trembling which at once belongs and does not belong to Christianity. This double movement is implicit in the phrase 'internal critique of Christianity' – the adjective 'internal' being at once supplementary and essential to what is going on in Derrida's account. (

)

Elaborated through readings of Baudelaire ('The Pagan School') and Nietzsche (*The Genealogy of Morals*), *The Gift of Death* expounds another thinking of God and, in particular, another understanding of Jesus Christ's words, 'and thy father which seeth in secret ... shall reward thee'. This exposition follows 'the traditional Judeo-Christiano-Islamic injunction' (108) but does so explicitly at the risk of turning this tradition against itself. Derrida writes:

> It is a matter of unfolding the mystagogical hypocrisy of a secret, putting on trial a fabricated mystery, a contract that has a secret clause, namely, that, seeing in secret, God will pay back infinitely more ['thy father ... shall reward thee']; a secret that we accept all the more easily since God remains the witness of every secret. He shares and *he knows*. We have to *believe* that he knows. This knowledge at the same time founds and destroys the Christian concepts of responsibility and justice and their 'object'. (112)

The focus is thus on 'the reversal and infinitization that confers on God, on the Other or on the name of God, the responsibility for that which remains more secret than ever, the irreducible experience of belief' (115, translation modified). Derrida has more recently articulated this irreducible experience in terms of the trembling of the undecidable: 'To say "I made a decision" is a necessary lie, a presumption. That is the meaning of God, as the only one who can know if someone has made a decision.'[27] In *The Gift of Death* he stages this trembling in the first person plural, a royal 'we': 'We have to believe that he knows.' Only 'faith in language' secures this 'we' with the minimal coherence of an identity; it is the royal 'we' of a ghost-writing. For Derrida is not speaking for himself here, he is not a Christian, it is and is not 'his' *we* that is being testified to here.[28] *Specters of Marx* suggests a further intertextual turn to this ghost-writing. For Derrida's description of God in *The Gift of Death* as '*at the same time other than me and more intimate with me than myself* [*à la fois autre que moi et plus intime à moi que moi-même*]' will uncannily come back in *Specters of Marx*, when he talks about that '... stranger who is already found within (*das Heimliche-Unheimliche*), more intimate with one than one is oneself [*plus intime à soi que soi-même*], the absolute proximity of a stranger whose power is singular and anonymous (*es spukt*), an unnameable and neutral power, that is, undecidable, neither active nor passive, an an-identity that, *without doing anything*, invisibly occupies places belonging finally neither to us nor to it' (172, 273). The uncanny: God, for example. (

)

In *The Gift of Death*, Derrida may appear to take on the position of Christ – in other words the position of postman, representative of the postal principle, the PP, the private parts.[29] He notes that one doesn't see God looking, but one 'can, and must, only hear him', and this 'most often' happens 'through the voice of another, another other, a messenger, an angel, a prophet, a messiah or postman [*facteur*]' (91). Derrida does not, however, elaborate on this specifically in terms of Jesus. The entire account of how Christ's words about 'thy father who seeth in secret' produce a mutation in the nature of secrecy and therefore of privacy, alter the very history and thinking of private parts, alter the nature of the self in private, this entire account is mediated through the private parts of Jesus Christ himself, in other words through the role of Christ as messenger, as the one who knows what in effect God has communicated to him in private – we have to believe that Christ knows, we have to believe this the most spectral of postmen, at the same time as or even *before* believing that God knows, and without questioning, it would seem, whether or how far Christ himself might be thought to 'see in secret'. (

)

'The private parts of Jesus Christ': difficult to think about without engaging with the question of what we might call, in the wake of a kind of deconstructive anachrony, the telepathic. There are numerous occasions in the Bible when Jesus appears telepathic, apparently seeing in secret, knowing the thoughts of others. For example, in Matthew, Chapter 9:

> And, behold, they brought to him a man sick of the palsy, lying on a bed: and Jesus seeing their faith said unto the sick of the palsy; Son, be of good cheer; thy sins be forgiven thee. And, behold, certain of the scribes said within themselves, This man blasphemeth. And Jesus *knowing their thoughts* said, Wherefore think ye evil in your hearts? (Matt. 9:2–4, my italics)[30]

What Derrida has elsewhere talked about as the angelic structure of all discourse[31] means here of course that Christ's apparently telepathic powers are indissociably linked with the telepathic narration: Jesus may know the thoughts of the scribes, but the narrator already has to know not only this but also what the scribes 'said within themselves'. The stakes of such a telepathic performativity perhaps remain to be thought.[32] (

)

Uncanny vicar. Not I. (

)

When Derrida says that 'We should stop thinking about God as someone, over there, way up there, transcendent, and, what is more – into the bargain, precisely – capable, more than any satellite orbiting in space, of seeing into the most secret of the most interior places' (108), he invokes a 'we' that is only made possible by that which exceeds it, by a solitude that can be identified with the secret: it is, as he describes it in *The Gift of Death*, a secrecy that is 'incommensurable with knowing', concerned with the innermost possibility of having private parts, that is to say with the notion of having a secret self. This secret self, 'which can be revealed only to the other, to the wholly other, to God if you wish, is a secret that I will never reflect on, that I will never know or experience or possess as my own' (92). Consequently, asks Derrida,

> ... what sense is there in saying it is 'my' secret, or in saying more generally that a secret *belongs*, that it is proper to or belongs to some 'one', or to some *other* who remains some*one*? It is perhaps there that we find the secret of secrecy, namely, that it is not a matter of knowing and that it is there for no-one. A secret doesn't belong, it can never be said to be at home or in its place [*chez soi*].

It is uncanny, as he goes on to say: 'Such is the *Unheimlichkeit* of the *Geheimnis*' (92). Rather than the Christian hypocrisy or 'the disavowal of a secret that is always *for me alone*' and that is therefore only ever a secret '*for the other*' (92), Derrida foregrounds the experience of a secrecy 'incommensurable with knowing' (93) or what he elsewhere refers to as 'the absolute solitude of a passion without martyrdom', a solitude that (he suggests) one might call 'life' or 'trace' as much as 'death'.[33] Against 'knowledge' he stresses the experience of bearing witness, an experience of solitude, in which 'one precisely cannot here trust any definite witness, nor even any guaranteed value to bearing witness' (P 31). There is, he says, 'a solitude without any measure common to that of an isolated subject'. It is solitude as 'the other name of the secret', a solitude which is 'neither of consciousness, nor of the subject, nor of *Dasein*'. It is a solitude that 'does not answer', it is not 'captured or covered over by the relation to the other, by being-with or by any form of "social bond"' (P 30–31). (

)

It may appear that I have been talking about 'the private parts of Jesus Christ' in a circumspect, even circumlocutory or periphrastic manner. 'Private parts' will perhaps have been understood to refer to the genitalia, the penis and prepuce of Jesus Christ. Why would this so-called 'sexual' reading be privileged over other readings of the phrase? As Leo Steinberg remarks, the sexuality of Jesus Christ is 'widely recognized as Christianity's greatest taboo'.[34] But as he makes clear at the start of the book that he wrote with a view to breaking it, the taboo needs to be seen from the outset in historical terms. *The Sexuality of Christ in Renaissance Art and Modern Oblivion* (1983) begins by noting that

> The first necessity is to admit a long-suppressed matter of fact ... In many hundreds of pious, religious works, from before 1400 to past the mid-16th century, the ostensive unveiling of the [Christ] Child's sex, or the touching, protecting or presentation of it, is the main action ... All of which has been tactfully overlooked for half a millennium.[35]

Close inspection of Leonardo's 'Madonna Litta' will suggest that there is nothing unconventional at least in the picture's depiction of Christ's penis as uncircumcised. Assuming we know what a penis is, and where circumcision begins and ends.[36] Leo

Steinberg's monumental tome on the sexuality of Christ offers only brief discussion of Jesus and circumcision, in a section entitled 'Resisting the physical evidence of circumcision'. He concludes that 'the refusal of Renaissance art to acknowledge [the] visual effect [of Christ's circumcision] remains an unexplained puzzle'.[37] (

)

Concerned with 'founding another religion' or 'refounding all of them ... playfully' (222), Derrida's autobiothanatoheterographical 'Circumfession' is one of his most bizarre texts. Running along the lower part of the pages of a book called *Jacques Derrida*, the upper part of each page of which comprises Geoffrey Bennington's 'Derridabase', Derrida's contribution is subtitled 'Fifty-nine periods and periphrases [*périodes et périphrases*] *written in a sort of internal margin, between Geoffrey Bennington's book and work in preparation (January 1989–April 1990)*'. '*Période*' in French suggests both 'period' and 'intermission'; 'periphrasis', in English as in French, means 'circumlocution' or 'round-about expression' (from the Greek *peri* around, *phrasis* speech). The title 'Circumfession' is itself at once period and periphrasis, a strange kind of intermission in itself, announcing the text without being part of it, anticipating the text to come. It is a promise. The title-word is a sort of portmanteau that combines 'circumcision' with 'confession' ('confession' in the Augustinian sense of 'praise' as well as 'acknowledgement of faults'). In a text internal to the internal margin, a notebook-entry dated 20 December 1976, quoted in 'Circumfession', Derrida declares: 'Circumcision, that's all I've ever talked about' (70).[38] What is the relationship between 'circumcision' and 'confession' or, perhaps more generally, between circumcision and writing? How are the stakes of such a question made to reverberate in the singular case of Jesus' penis? (

)

Let me cut away, as carefully as I can, a few little pieces of 'Circumfession' together with one or two other excerpts from Derrida's writings, by way of conclusion, grafting them, without interposing any punctuation besides commas, the word 'comma' I note parenthetically from the Greek verb *koptein* to cut, to comma, write a church, without identifiable messiah, an almost secret sect, a new party, 'without party', 'untimely', 'barely public' (SM, p.85), but also barely private, doing the truth of a new international, no more Derrida's than mine, I snip from section 22 as follows,

> one cannot *do* without truth but it's not the one they think they're confessing, they still haven't understood anything about it, especially those I see queuing up, *too late*, to get themselves circumcised and authorise themselves to speak for the 'Jews', this 'for' which makes you burst out laughing, obscene though it remains, either *in favour* or *in place* of the 'Jews', Jews 'themselves' knowing that they must not speak 'for' them, do I do that, (C, 114)

cut it there, do I do that, question without interrogation mark, trembling as does the I, circumcision and confession always *too late*, never on time, hatred here in

Derrida's words, hatred for what is obscene, for a mystical or religious purity of ethnic or national identity, but this is also funny, it makes you burst out laughing at the same time, what is hateful and what is risible being themselves founded on a yes that would be the condition of every identity, every authority, every 'for', that's the truth, it is in the same sentence, (

)

the same lifedeath sentence, a little later on, Derrida grafts another passage, internal section, this time dated Christmas Eve, as one may care to call it, 24 December 1976, again extracted from one of the notebooks envisaged as 'The Book of Elijah' (89), addressing his 'dear reader' and 'himself' by his 'secret name' (87), Elie, he invokes, and I quote,

> the only philosopher to my knowledge who, accepted – more or less – into the academic institution, author of more or less legitimate writings on Plato, Augustine, Descartes, Rousseau, Kant, Hegel, Husserl, Heidegger, Benjamin, Austin, will have dared describe his penis, as promised, in concise and detailed fashion, and as no one dared, in the Renaissance, paint the circumcised penis of Christ on the incredible pretext that there was no model for it, come off it, now if I do not invent a new language (through simplicity rediscovered), another fluid, a new *sentence* [*une nouvelle phrase*], I will have failed in this book, which does not mean that that's the place to begin, on the contrary, you have to drag on in the old syntax, train oneself with you, dear reader, toward an idiom which in the end would be untranslatable in return into the language of the beginnings, learn an unknown language, (115–16/110–11, trans. slightly modified)

how to read this sentence which is not a sentence, more the period (duration/intermission) and periphrasis of a sentence that will have launched itself towards the experience of a new language, a new *sentence* that would link this injunction 'learn an unknown language' to the injunction with which *Specters of Marx* in some respects could be said to appear and vanish, namely 'learn to live' and this isn't separable, in the original French text, from 'teach to live', all recognizable models of pedagogy, mastery and discipleship dissolving in this injunction, but read this graft from 'Circumfession' to begin with perhaps in the light, as always in Derrida, of a double-motif, the first motif being that this passage just cited performs as well as states, performs stating, states performing, altering both, failing both, to paint in words Christ's circumcised penis, to paint what 'no one dared, in the Renaissance, paint', it implies in doing so or does so by implying that there is indeed a model for it, like any model, founded and structured on a logic of repetition and alterity, what Derrida platitudinously calls *différance*,[39] every circumcision is unique but this uniqueness is nevertheless *cut*, spiked, spooked, a resistance to what can be thought, as he observes at the start of the text entitled 'Shibboleth', I quote,

> One time alone: circumcision takes place but once.
> Such, at least, is the appearance we receive, and the tradition of the appearance, we do not say of the semblance [again then, as ever, a matter of ghosts, of the apprehension of an appearance or apparition].
> We will have to circle around this appearance. Not so much in order to circumscribe

or circumvent some *truth* of circumcision – that must be given up for essential reasons. But rather to let ourselves be approached by the resistance which 'once' may offer to thought,[40]

once, one time, once upon a time, circumcision as 'what comes to mark itself as the one-and-only time: what one sometimes calls a *date*',[41] that is to say the spectrality of dates and of every story, concerning Derrida's proposition that 'circumcision takes place but once' Robert Smith notes that 'the uniqueness of its moment, never to be repeated, nevertheless gives onto further moments, generating a genre, a series of cases or a genus and race – the Jews, for example',[42] the exposure of Christ's circumcised penis would be a sort of phantomological revelation of the familiar-unfamiliar, an uncanny memento of the inscription of Christ's body within the logic of repetition and alterity that itself renders possible something like an ethnic or religious identity (Jew, Christian, Muslim or other), the second motif being that this passage from 'Circumfession' that I cited a few moments ago is a writing about other writings (for instance those of Augustine), a writing about itself and its so-called author (the 'philosopher' Jacques Derrida) and a writing about its incipient fault or failure as writing, a writing about the other as the untranslatable, as what precisely cannot be invented, even if it is just what calls to be affirmed, even if it is affirmation itself, the condition of every invention and every translation in the so-called traditional sense, (

)

interposing, posthuming, two 'memories of my childhood', for the love of Leonardo, first, once upon a time, being circumcised, I was three, my first night alone in a hospital, given a small tin toy-train and train-track, consigned to the general, and afterwards the bandaging, the pungent yellow ointment, the pain, the anguish and love of my mother and her sister, will I have been Jewish, who am I in secret, second, being expelled from my first school, a Church of England primary school, I was five, for 'refusing to pray', publicly reprimanded during the Lord's prayer by a teacher who declared 'you're just moving your lips, you're not really praying', subvocally, will I ever have done anything else, (

)

cut back to it once more, 'now if I do not invent a new language (through simplicity rediscovered), another fluid, a new *sentence*, I will have failed in this book', there is only period and periphrasis, there is no pure expression or idiom, there is no pure presentation, for example as the phrase 'stream of consciousness' might suggest, there perhaps being a naive temptation to describe Derrida's 'Circumfession' as 'stream of consciousness', as if nothing had happened (call it twentieth-century thought) to trouble or complicate the conception of language and consciousness, consciousness and the unconscious, better perhaps to think of the drift of a gift, yes, confession, adrift, as Derrida says 'like a gift confession must be from the unconscious, I know no other definition of the unconscious' (233), 'Circumfession' apparently adrift, then, in a miming of the apparitions of spontaneity of Augustine's

Confessions, and driven at the same time by an urgency without ground, an urgency whose force seems to come from a language of the future, 'pass[ing] over much because I am hurrying on to those things which especially urge me to make confession to you, and there is much that I do not remember',[43] failed phrase, the private parts of Jesus Christ carrying the secret of the promise as of a still unheard-of language, an absolute idiom,[44] circumcision alone, to be painted, Derrida's or mine, last of the Jews and last of the Christians.[45]

(*Good Friday 2000*)

Notes

1 Jacques Derrida, 'Circumfession', in Geoffrey Bennington and Jacques Derrida, *Jacques Derrida*, tr. Geoffrey Bennington (Chicago: Chicago University Press, 1993), p.48. Originally published in French as 'Circonfession' in *Jacques Derrida* (Paris: Seuil, 1991). Further page references to the English translation are given in the text, in parentheses, abbreviated 'C', followed by a slash and page reference to the original French text where appropriate.
2 Hent de Vries, *Philosophy and the Turn to Religion* (Baltimore: Johns Hopkins University Press, 1999), p. 11.
3 Ibid.
4 Jacques Derrida, 'Back from Moscow, in the USSR', tr. Mary Quaintance, in *Politics, Theory, and Contemporary Culture*, ed. Mark Poster (New York: Columbia University Press, 1993), pp.197–235: here, p. 234.
5 Jacques Derrida, *The Post Card: From Socrates to Freud and Beyond*, tr. Alan Bass (Chicago: Chicago University Press, 1987), p.114. Further page references are given in the text, in parentheses, abbreviated 'PC'.
6 Jacques Derrida, *Mémoires: for Paul de Man*, tr. Cecile Lindsay, Jonathan Culler and Eduardo Cadava (New York: Columbia University Press, 1986), p.115. Further page references are given in the text, in parentheses.
7 Jacques Derrida, *Specters of Marx: The State of the Debt, the Work of Mourning, and the New International*, tr. Peggy Kamuf (London: Routledge, 1994), p. 143. Originally published in French as *Spectres de Marx: L'État de la dette, le travail du deuil et la nouvelle Internationale* (Paris: Galilée, 1993). Further page references to the English translation are given in the text, in parentheses, abbreviated 'SM', followed by a slash and page reference to the original French text where appropriate.
8 Jacques Derrida, 'Faith and Knowledge: the Two Sources of "Religion" at the Limits of Reason Alone', tr. Samuel Weber, in *Religion*, eds Jacques Derrida and Gianni Vattimo (Cambridge: Polity Press, 1998), pp. 1–78: here, p. 61. Further page references are given in the text, in parentheses, abbreviated 'FK'.
9 Jacques Derrida, *Monolingualism of the Other; or, The Prosthesis of Origin*, tr. Patrick Mensah (Stanford: Stanford University Press, 1998), p. 85. Further page references are given in the text, in parentheses.
10 Jacques Derrida, 'Ulysses Gramophone: Hear Say Yes in Joyce', tr. Tina Kendall and Shari Benstock in *Acts of Literature*, ed. Derek Attridge (London and New York: Routledge, 1992), pp. 256–309: here, p. 295.
11 de Vries, *Philosophy and the Turn to Religion*, p.161.
12 Friedrich Nietzsche, 'Attempt at a Self-Criticism' [1886], in *The Birth of Tragedy* (London: Penguin, 1993), pp. 8–9.

13　Jacques Derrida, *Politics of Friendship*, tr. George Collins (London: Verso, 1997), p. 236.
14　Kenneth Clark, *Leonardo da Vinci: An Account of His Development as an Artist* (London: Penguin, 1958), p. 48.
15　Robert Payne, *Leonardo* (London: Robert Hale, 1979), p. 35.
16　Ibid.
17　See Walter Pater, *The Renaissance* (New York: Modern Library, [1873] 1919), p. 102.
18　Cecil Gould, *The Artist and the Non-Artist* (London: Weidenfeld and Nicholson, 1975), p. 65.
19　Martin Kemp, *Leonardo da Vinci: The Marvellous Works of Nature and Man* (London: Dent, 1981), p. 54.
20　Clark, *Leonardo da Vinci*, p. 48.
21　Payne, *Leonardo*, p. 35.
22　Leo Steinberg, *The Sexuality of Christ in Renaissance Art and in Modern Oblivion*, 2nd edition (Chicago: Chicago University Press, 1996), p. 293.
23　St Augustine observes that the human infant, 'although he is ignorant of where he is, what he is, by whom created, of what parents born, is already guilty of offense, incapable as yet of receiving a commandment ... He cannot be aroused out of his sleep, so as to recognize even these facts; but a time must be patiently awaited, until he can shake off this strange intoxication ... Infants are disturbed with irrational affections, and are restrained [only] by pains and penalties, or the terror of such.' See *On the Merits and Remission of Sins and on the Baptism of Infants*, in *Saint Augustine: Anti-Pelagian Writings*, Select Library of the Nicene and Post-Nicene Fathers, 5 (New York, 1908), I, 68, p. 42. (Quoted by Steinberg, *Sexuality of Christ*, p. 292.)
24　Steinberg, *Sexuality of Christ*, p. 293.
25　See Sigmund Freud, 'The "Uncanny"', tr. James Strachey, in *Art and Literature, Pelican Freud Library*, vol. 14 (London: Penguin, 1985), p. 345. In his essay on Leonardo, Freud characterizes the artist in terms of precisely such uncanny childish play: 'Indeed, the great Leonardo remained like a child for the whole of his life in more than one way; it is said that all great men are bound to retain some infantile part. Even as an adult he continued to play, and this was another reason why he often appeared uncanny and incomprehensible to his contemporaries.' See Freud, 'Leonardo da Vinci and a Memory of His Childhood', in *Art and Literature*, p. 220.
26　Jacques Derrida, *The Gift of Death*, tr. David Wills (Chicago: Chicago University Press, 1995), p. 92, translation modified. The original French version was first given as a lecture in 1990 and published in *L'éthique du don: Jacques Derrida et la pensée du don*, eds Jean-Michel Rabaté et Michael Wetzel (Paris: Métailié-Transition, 1992), pp. 11–108: here, p. 88. A somewhat revised version has more recently appeared as *Donner la mort* (Paris: Galilée, 1999). Further references to Wills' translation are given in the text, in parentheses, followed by a slash and page reference to the original 1992 French version where appropriate.
27　Jacques Derrida, seminar ('Derrida's Arguments') at Queen Mary and Westfield College, University of London, 10 March 2000.
28　Cf. Hent de Vries's summary of this strange duplicity: 'Derrida adopts or, rather, lets himself be adopted by a *doubly heretical* tradition marked by a certain secrecy: one that is heterodox with respect to Judaism as well as with respect to Christianity, one that challenges, without ever blurring, the distinction between the Judaic and the Christian. In short, one that peregrinates between the inner conviction and the outer appearance or vice versa, partaking of both while belonging to no one strictly speaking. It is as if one carried a certain tradition along with oneself, as that which can be neither excluded nor included, that is neither totally alien nor intimately familiar, neither distant nor nearby,

or both' (*Philosophy and the Turn to Religion*, p. 351). It is, we may say, uncanny: experience of the uncanny, experience as uncanny.
29 Or, as Derrida calls it on one occasion in *The Post Card*, the 'PrePuce' (*le PréPuce*): see *The Post Card*, p. 221, 237.
30 We might also consider here, for example, Matthew 12:25; Luke 5:22, 6:8, 9:47; and John 4:29, 39.
31 See Jacques Derrida, 'Of an Apocalyptic Tone Newly Adopted in Philosophy', tr. John P. Leavey, Jr, in *Derrida and Negative Theology*, eds Harold Coward and Toby Foshay (Albany, NY: SUNY Press, 1992), p. 57.
32 The convention, of course, has been to talk about the Bible in terms of omniscient narration. For a detailed account, see Meir Sternberg, *The Poetics of Biblical Narrative: Ideological Literature and the Drama of Reading* (Bloomington: Indiana University Press, 1985), especially Ch. 3 ('Ideology of Narration and Narration of Ideology'), pp. 84–128. In a forthcoming essay ('The "Telepathy Effect": Notes toward a Reconsideration of Narrative Fiction'), I argue for a shift away from thinking in terms of omniscience towards a thinking of telepathic narration.
33 See Jacques Derrida, 'Passions: "An Oblique Offering"', tr. David Wood, in *On the Name*, ed. Thomas Dutoit (Stanford: Stanford University Press, 1995), pp. 3–31: here, p. 31. Further references are given in parentheses in the text, abbreviated 'P'.
34 Steinberg, *Sexuality of Christ*, p. 219.
35 Ibid., p. 3.
36 On issues concerning the identity, divinity, humanity and, in a range of respects, the supplementarity of Christ's foreskin, including the theological problem of 'whether, in the interval between the Resurrection and the Ascension, Jesus' foreskin was resurrected along with his penis' (p. 349), see Marc Shell, 'The Holy Foreskin; or, Money, Relics, and Judeo-Christianity', in *Jews and Other Differences: The New Jewish Cultural Studies*, eds Jonathan Boyarin and Daniel Boyarin (Minneapolis: University of Minnesota Press, 1997), pp. 345–59: here, p. 349. Besides the inexhaustibly provoking infant Jesus in this Leonardo painting, the eerie serenity of the mother (if she is the mother), the maternity gown with laces loosened, the translucent veil, the numerous penile (circumcised?) fingers (especially the thumb of Jesus' left hand, holding the bird that symbolizes transience or the Passion) and the mountainous, even apocalyptic scene beyond the windows, we may ask ourselves a double question: What would Freud have made of this painting? (His essay, 'Leonardo da Vinci and a Memory of His Childhood', makes no mention of the 'Madonna Litta'.) And what would this painting make of Freud? (To be continued.)
37 Steinberg, *Sexuality of Christ*, pp. 165–7: here, p. 165.
38 If, as Jeffrey Mehlman has suggested, Derrida with *Glas* (1974) 'turned his work into a protracted meditation on the institution of circumcision' (*Legacies of Anti-Semitism in France*, Minneapolis: University of Minnesota Press, 1983, p. 82), 'Circumfession' (1990) constitutes a crucial supplementary turn in the meditation. On the crucially related but different question of 'female circumcision', see Chantal Zabus, 'Bouches cousues: L'autobiographie de l'excisée', in *L'animal autobiographique: Autour de Jacques Derrida*, ed. Marie-Louise Mallet (Paris: Galilée, 1999), pp. 331–52.
39 As Derrida observes regarding '*différance*' in the essay of that title: '"There is no name for it": a proposition to be read in its *platitude*. This unnameable [*différance*] is not an ineffable Being which no name could approach: God, for example. This unnameable is the play which makes possible nominal effects.' See Jacques Derrida, *Margins of Philosophy*, tr. Alan Bass (Chicago: Chicago University Press, 1981), p. 26.
40 Jacques Derrida, 'Shibboleth', tr. Joshua Wilner, in *Acts of Literature*, ed. Derek Attridge (London: Routledge, 1992), pp. 373–413: here, p. 373.

41 Ibid., p. 474.
42 See Robert Smith, *Derrida and Autobiography* (Cambridge: Cambridge University Press, 1995), p. 41.
43 Saint Augustine, *Confessions*, tr. Henry Chadwick (Oxford: Oxford University Press, 1991), p. 50.
44 Cf. Derrida, *Monolingualism of the Other*, p. 67.
45 On the undecidable force of Derrida as 'the last of the Jews' (C, p.190), see Hent de Vries, *Philosophy and the Turn to Religion*, p. 30.

Church After Church: In Conclusion

John Schad

In *Brewer's Dictionary of Phrase and Fable*, the definition of 'Church Visible' ends with the impossible direction 'See CHURCH INVISIBLE.' These essays, I suggest, help us to do precisely that; they help us to see in modern writing what is normally invisible – namely, a church outside the church, a church after or beyond 'the age of the church'. The overall effect of the essays is to make us see the church in the most unfamiliar places and unlikely incarnations – we have seen, for example, the church as an hippopotamus, a panopticon, a telephone exchange, a pharmacy, a fold in the mist, a secret, a crowd, and even cloth. The lesson is that on the page, in the mind of the writer, the church can become almost anything. In one sense this is nothing new – in traditional Christian rhetoric the church is all sorts of things: body, bride, mother, army, house, fold, city, ship, kingdom. In another sense, though, this *is* new – Carlyle was right, books really are the church of the modern country, and so for us the play of the text endlessly reconfigures the cultural space that once was church. At times, this may well lead the reader of this volume toward an anxious, disquieting sense that nothing is sacred, that the church has vanished into textuality. At other times, though, it may also lead us to an uncanny, haunting sense that in the very act of reading and writing we are somehow 'in church', somehow being churchy; it is akin to Tambling's sense that 'there is no outside of the church.'

Another way of thinking about this is to say that the church does not stop; for another lesson of this volume is that the church is no museum piece, not something belonging to an age that is wholly finished. Several essays clearly demonstrate that the church still evokes strong passions – recall Wright on the church's post-Holocaust guilt, Schad on its Jubilee rage against third-world debt, and Stockton on its almost queer sense of humiliation. If these passions appear in some way negative they are checked or countered by the volume's simultaneous witness to the ecclesial passions of Faith, Hope and Charity – recall Wolfreys on the faith of *In Memoriam*, Royle on the hope of the Derridean promise, and Zizek on the love that animates the body of Christ.

'Faith, hope, charity ... but the greatest of these is charity' (1 Cor. 13:13), and it is charity that we most need; we who read the writing of the church need charity to cope with our differences. And that is precisely what the contributors to this volume have accomplished, they have agreed to write side by side even though there are, as is obvious, enormous differences in religious conviction, theoretical assumptions and critical style. Insofar as charity has made this possible, the volume might just suggest that 'English Literature', the discipline founded on the ruins of the Victorian church, is itself a kind of church, a community held together by a common passion.

That passion, a passion for words, is never far from Christ's Passion, the Passion *of the Word* – note that the final essay, Royle's essay on Derrida's 'Circumfession', is dated 'Good Friday, 2000'. Good Friday is, of course, an awful long way from Easter Sunday, but to get there we could always quote 'Circumfession' itself:

> ... today [is] April 15th, 1990, rainy Easter Sunday ...[1]

Note

1   Jacques Derrida, 'Circumfession', in Jacques Derrida and Geoffrey Bennington, *Jacques Derrida* (Chicago: Chicago University Press, 1993 [1991], p. 282.

Index

Aarsleff, Hans 81
abjection 146–50
Ackroyd, Peter 28
Adorno, Theodor W. 120, 124
Africa 47, 48–9
Algeria 48
America 51
anti-Semitism 26–30, 49
Armstrong, Isobel 59–60, 64–5,
Augustine, Saint 32, 52, 91, 95, 165

Bacon, Francis 13
Barrett Browning, Elizabeth 9
Barth, Karl 106
Barthes, Roland 50, 133
Bataille, Georges 129, 131–2, 139, 141
Bauckham, Richard 83
Beer, Gillian 77, 79–81, 84
Benjamin, Walter 114, 117, 120, 124
Bennington, Geoffrey 22, 170
Benz, Ernst 79
Bergsten, Staffan 32
Bersani, Leo 129
Bicknell, H.J. 95
Blake, William 115–18
blasphemy 159–60
Blitz, the 32, 99
Bloom, Harold 26
Bohr, Niels 45
Brashear, William 60
Buddhism 109
Butler, Judith 129

Carlyle 3, 76, 115, 121–2
Chardin, Teilhard de 79
Chartism 22
city, the 76, 84
Cocteau, Jean 47
Coleridge, Samuel Taylor 59, 63
comedy 44
computer 51
Critchley, Simon 55

cummings, e e 5

da Vinci, Leonardo 163–6, 169, 172
Dante, Alighieri 25, 30
Darwin, Charles 75–88
de Vries, Hent 160
Derrida, Jacques 3, 9, 11, 15–16, 20, 26,
    41–56, 57, 68, 87, 159–76
Dickens, Charles 53, 57, 111, 121
Dietzgen, Joseph 15
Drummond, Henry 79, 84–5

Eagleton, Terry 1, 9, 11, 21
Eckhart, Meister 33
Eliot, George 57, 81
Eliot, T.S. 1, 25–39, 62, 89–103, 111
Ellmann, Maud 26
Ellmann, Richard 53
Elrod, John 115
Engels, Friedrich 11–23, 76
excommunication 42
eye, the 82–3, 85–6

Fairhall, James 44
Feinberg, Leslie 135–6
Fenves, Peter 118
Feuerbach, Ludwig 49
fire 49
fission 46
flâneur, the 120
Flugel, J.C. 131
Foucault, Michel 1, 111, 114, 118, 122
Frank, Lawrence 81
Freud, Sigmund 48, 129–31, 149
Frye, Northrop 32

Gardner, Helen 28, 32
Gaskell, Elizabeth 76
Genet, Jean 41–56, 137–41
Gordon, Lyndall 25, 28, 32
Groys, Boris 108

Hair, Donald 60–61, 71
Hall, Radclyffe 130–135
Hamacher, Werner 65
Hannay, Alistair 115
Hart, Kevin 65
Hartman, Geoffrey 49
Hegel, G.W.F. 33, 41–56, 108
Heisenberg, Werner 45
Herbert, George 26
Hiroshima 45
Holocaust 28, 30, 49–50, 55
Hooker, Richard 95, 98
Houghton, Walter 76
Huxley, T.H. 75

James, Henry 3, 29
Jameson, Frederic 11
Jardine, Alice 9
Jordan, Elaine 60, 64
Joyce, James 28, 41–56, 57, 111
Jubilee 42–3
Julius, Anthony 28–9, 36

Kallen, Horace 27
Kant, Emmanuel 66
Kemp, Martin 163
Kierkegaard, Søren 33, 113–26
Kincaid, James R. 68
Kingsley, Charles 76, 77, 79, 83
Kirmmse, Bruce 115
Kristeva, Julia 122, 145–57

Lebowitz, Naomi 124
Lee, Hermoine 28
Levinas, Emmanuel 72

Marx, Karl 11–13, 49, 76
Mattes, Eleanor Bustin 67
Maurice, F.D. 79, 89
Maurras, Charles 30
Miller, J.Hillis 81
Milward, Peter 33
Minear, Paul 93
Montmartre 48
Moody, David 32, 36, 90
Moore, A.L. 75
Moore, James, R. 78
Moore, Marianne 9
Morrison, Toni 20

NATO 20

Newton, Isaac 13
Nietzsche, Friedrich 1, 45, 57, 161–2

Oizerman, Teodor 12
Ospovat, Dov 80
Orwell, George 28

Panopticon 120–22
Pater, Walter 163
Payne, Robert 163
pharmacy 44
photography 50
physics 45
police 52, 120–23
Pound, Ezra 2
Preston, Raymond 32
psychoanalysis 111, 145–57

Rabaté, Jean-Michel 50
Ramsey, Michael 96
Robinson, John 94

sea 50–53
Scofield, Martin 89
Sinfield, Alan 65
Smith, Robert 172
Spencer, Herbert 85
Spivak, Gayatri Chakravorty 55
Steinberg, Leo 165, 169–70

Taylor, Mark C. 45–6, 55–6
telepathy 168
telephone 41
Tennyson, Alfred 59–74, 76
translation 51
Trevelyan, Mary 31

Ward, Graham 72
Weber, Samuel 161
Weil, Simone 27
West, Cornell 15
Wheeler, Michael 69, 71
Whitman, Walt 111
Williams, Charles 91, 96
Wood, James 27
Woolf, Leonard 28
Woolf, Virginia 28

Young, Robert 54

Zizek, Slavoj 9

For Product Safety Concerns and Information please contact our EU
representative GPSR@taylorandfrancis.com
Taylor & Francis Verlag GmbH, Kaufingerstraße 24, 80331 München, Germany

www.ingramcontent.com/pod-product-compliance
Lightning Source LLC
Chambersburg PA
CBHW052121300426
44116CB00010B/1756